WHAT EVERY REAL ESTATE
INVESTOR NEEDS TO KNOW ABOUT
CASH FLOW

WHAT EVERY REAL ESTATE INVESTOR NEEDS TO KNOW ABOUT CASH FLOW

... And 36 Other Key Financial Measures

Updated Edition

FRANK GALLINELLI

New York   Chicago   San Francisco   Athens   London   Madrid
Mexico City   Milan   New Delhi   Singapore   Sydney   Toronto

2 3 4 5 6 7 8 9 10   DOC   21 20 19 18 17 16

ISBN   978-1-259-58618-7
MHID   1-259-58618-9

e-ISBN   978-1-259-58619-4
e-MHID   1-259-58619-7

This publication is designed to provide accurate and authoritative information in regard to the subject matter covered. It is sold with the understanding that neither the author nor the publisher is engaged in rendering legal, accounting, securities trading, or other professional services. If legal advice or other expert assistance is required, the services of a competent professional person should be sought.

—From a Declaration of Principles Jointly Adopted
by a Committee of the American Bar Association
and a Committee of Publishers and Associations

Library of Congress Cataloging-in-Publication Data
Gallinelli, Frank, author.
  What every real estate investor needs to know about cash flow... and 36 other key financial measures / Frank Gallinelli. — Updated edition.
      pages cm
  Includes index.
  ISBN 978-1-259-58618-7 (alk. paper) — ISBN 1-259-58618-9 (alk. paper)
1. Real estate investment. 2. Real estate investment—Finance. 3. Cash flow.
I. Title.
  HD1382.5.G35   2016
  332.63'24—dc23
                                                        2015028857

For Jean, whose patience made this book possible.

Contents

PART II

THIRTY-SEVEN CALCULATIONS EVERY REAL ESTATE INVESTOR NEEDS TO KNOW

Preface

Before you make your next investment—that is, before you decide whether to use that $20 bill in your wallet to buy this book or to order a pizza—it would be a good idea to ask yourself if you're at all serious about wanting to make money investing in real estate.

You can make a lot of money investing in income-producing property. You can also make a little money when, with some better preparation, you could have made a lot. You can even *lose* money in real estate when, in fact, you could have made, both literally and figuratively, a great deal.

Well-worn clichés assure you, "Hey, real estate's a no-brainer. After all, they're not making any more of it. You can't go wrong, right?" Wrong.

In real estate, as in life, there is a right way and a wrong way to do most things. If you want to succeed, if you want to make money, then learn to do it the right way. If you'd rather depend on luck, buy this book anyway; I'll put a map to a casino in the Appendix.

Real estate investing is a numbers game, and the purpose of this book is to show you how to "do the numbers." This task is not difficult, but it is absolutely essential to your success. This book is not about how to make millions while starting off with no money, no credit, and no time. Instead, you'll learn here about cash flow, rates of return, property value, financing guidelines, and a few dozen other key measures. With a bit of practice, you'll be able to read a property's vital signs and judge its health as an investment.

I have been involved with income-property investments for more than 40 years. In the early 1980s, I founded a software company, RealData®, to produce programs that could help investors and developers evaluate prospective real estate deals. During these four decades, I have talked to a great number of investors and would-be investors, and, amazingly, I've encountered some who have been completely unburdened by any knowledge whatsoever of how an income-property investment really works. A handful of those people appear somehow to have survived with their net worth intact. Most, however, have turned into material for case studies on how to lose a lot of money.

When you learn how to crunch the numbers—a task that you'll discover is easier than you imagined—your chances of success will be vastly improved, and you'll have a substantial degree of control over the results of your investments. Try that with the stock market. If you own property already, you'll understand it better, and that understanding can translate into real dollars. I once received a reassessment notice for a commercial building I own. Like everyone who receives a new tax bill, I thought it was too high. I prepared a concise, one-page presentation of the property's net operating income and capitalization rate—topics covered in this book—and showed them to the assessor. He looked at my figures and replied, "Someone obviously plugged the wrong cap rate into the formula when they assessed this property. We'll correct it." I didn't need to make any emotional appeal for justice, and I didn't get an argument. The numbers told the whole story. Knowing how the numbers work has saved me thousands of dollars per year in taxes on this one property.

Let me say a bit about how this book is organized. The Introduction will lay out the four ways that you make money with real estate. You'll see these four elements manifest themselves throughout the rest of the text. Part I follows a narrative format, building from some basic ideas about money and investing, and working its way through examples of how you should look at income properties. Part II presents a reference for what I believe are the most important calculations you should know, again with plentiful examples. Most of the calculations in this section relate to topics discussed in Part I, and many of them are necessarily interwoven with each other. The knee bone is indeed connected to the shin bone. You may find it worthwhile to read through Part II in its entirety, but if you use it strictly as a reference, then take note of cross-reference topics that you'll find helpful.

Downloadable Forms and Excel Templates in This Book

You'll find in both Parts I and II a number of useful forms, as well as spreadsheet templates that you can download from my company's website.

These will simplify many of the calculations in this book. They're not fancy, but they get the job done if you need to make a mortgage calculation, figure a property's appreciation, or fill out an Annual Property Operating Data form.

You can download any of the Excel files shown at http://www .realdata.com/book. Click on the link for the file you want. If you have Excel on your computer and your browser is configured to recognize such spreadsheet files, the template will open and you can use it. You can also save it onto your computer; use Excel's File Save menu and save it to your desktop or to "My Documents." If your browser didn't recognize the file, you'll see a message asking if you want to save the file or to open it. Choose "Save," and save it to your desktop or to "My Documents."

Notice that the web page also includes a link to a Free Real Estate Calculator, which allows you to download the RealData Real Estate Calculator. This is a Windows-based application that will perform many functions that you, as a real estate investor, need to make good decisions.

This book is also loaded with examples, sample problems, and even full-blown case studies. It's not a traditional textbook, but there is no better way to learn how to work with this material than to run some numbers yourself. It's also a lot safer to practice in the margins of this book than to risk real money on real properties. Wherever possible, I use later examples to revisit topics that were covered earlier, so as to maximize the amount of review you can get with key concepts and calculations. However, you don't need to read the whole book to get a lot out of it. The key concepts underlying most real estate calculations are explained in depth in Part I, but Part II is designed as a reference guide and frequently repeats capsule summaries of the ideas elaborated in detail in Part I.

You'll also find Rules of Thumb throughout the book. I have taken the liberty of using these sections to offer my personal comments, insights, and opinions—and to separate clearly my opinions from facts. It may be a fact when I tell you how to calculate a gross rent multiplier, but it's an opinion when I tell you what values would seem unreasonable to me. Some of these "rules" may not fit a particular place and time, so I encourage you to test them against the realities of your market. I offer them as a guide, not as laws of nature.

You may be saying to yourself, "Math was not my best subject. I doubt that I can really do this." In fact, you can. Many of the most important calculations in this book require nothing more than finding the +, −, ×, /, and = buttons on your calculator. Yes, there are some really ugly formulas that underlie several of the topics we'll discuss. No, you don't really have to work those formulas out. I'll show you a few, just to make you glad there are easier ways. Then I'll show you those easier ways.

Of course, you could always try what some people do: scratch a few figures on the back of an envelope, make an offer, and hope for the best. In any game, when someone wins, someone else usually loses. In real estate investing, the profits and gains that are lost by the envelope scratchers accrue to those who take the time to do the math. The choice is yours.

Introduction

The Four Ways to Make Money in Real Estate

Whether you're an experienced income-property investor or a beginner just testing the waters for the first time, this book will tell you how to "run the numbers" on any real estate investment. It is designed to serve as an indispensable guide and reference.

Like all types of investing, real estate requires that you develop a proficiency with some basic measurements—rates of return, cash flows, and estimates of value, to name a few. The goal of this book is to explain how to make these calculations for virtually any income property and to explain the basic concept behind each calculation so as to make you a smarter investor. Without knowing these key formulas, you're really just guessing when you try to figure out whether a given property is a good investment. You may think you have a profitable property because it generates excellent rental income, but when you examine it more carefully using some of the rules of thumb in this book, you realize that what you have is a loser.

This handbook covers topics such as:

- How to estimate the current and future value of a property
- How to read between the lines of what a seller is telling about his or her property
- How to forecast your revenue streams, expenses, net operating income, and cash flows from a property—before you buy
- How to use the "time-value-of-money" concept to help you make good long-term investment decisions

- How to compare investment opportunities
- How to calculate financing, rates of return, potential tax liability, and more

What Do Successful Investors Really Buy?

Do successful investors prefer properties in perfect condition or those that need work? Do they favor residential or commercial, city or suburban, brick or frame, or blue or gray?

While any of these choices (except perhaps the color) may fit better into a particular individual's comfort zone, the true investor treats the physical property as a secondary issue. He or she is not so much interested in buying the property but in buying the property's anticipated economic benefits—what is called the income stream.

> **Rule of Thumb:** Don't make a decision to buy, hold, or sell based on emotional factors. In particular, don't buy a building because you've fallen in love with it; and don't hold because of a sentimental attachment when you really ought to sell. If you need that warm and fuzzy feeling, get a puppy.

To the extent that some attribute of the physical property or its surroundings will affect that income stream, then that attribute becomes meaningful. Will the arrival of a major new employer create an increase in the demand for apartments? If so, this may be the time to look at apartment buildings. Would the opportunity for increased rents more than offset the cost of rehabilitating a particular property? Perhaps you should look for a fixer-upper.

The prudent investor seeks a return on investment. To achieve that return, he or she has to look at the numbers carefully—at the current financial data and at reasonable projections of how the investment will perform in the future. As the preceding Rule of Thumb makes clear, no successful real estate investor buys a property—or worse yet, holds one too long—because of a sentimental attachment to that property. Decisions to buy and sell are based on financial measures, on the income stream, and on the return on investment that the income stream represents.

Begin your study of the concepts and calculations just as you would if you were constructing a new building. Start with the foundation: the four basic investment returns.

How You Make Money in Real Estate: The Four Basic Investment Returns

Virtually all the measures and concepts that we will discuss in this book connect to four critical elements that, to a greater or lesser degree, inhabit every income-property investment. They are the ways you make money with income property. You can call these elements the four basic returns:

1. Cash flow
2. Appreciation
3. Loan amortization
4. Tax shelter

Not every income-property investment will provide these returns in equal measure. Each property is unique and will blend the four benefits differently; some investments may even lack one or more. One property may give you a good annual cash flow; another may yield little or no cash from year to year, but offer the promise of a big payday when you sell. Nonetheless, these four returns compose the complete pool of potential benefits. The investment decisions you make will depend on your personal goals and on the strength of these various returns. If you understand where they come from and how to calculate them, then you're well on your way to success.

From this point on, almost every calculation and concept we discuss will relate in some way to these four basic returns. Let's look at them in greater detail now.

Cash Flow

Do you have a checkbook? If so, then you already understand cash flow. Money comes in; money goes out. When you want to know the balance in your checkbook, it doesn't really matter where the money came from or where it went. All that really matters is *how much* came in and *how much* went out.

You're interested solely in the flow of funds, hence the name "cash flow." If you look at a particular period of time (12 months is usually a convenient choice), you'll want to know if more cash comes in than goes out. If at the end of that time you can say that you took in more money than you spent, then you had a "positive cash flow" for the year. Another term you will sometimes see for positive cash flow is "net spendable cash," which refers to the cash flow that is left over after you pay your income taxes on the property's earnings. If a real estate investment has a positive cash flow (i.e., if there is money left over after all the bills are paid), that's money you can take off the table.

On the other hand, if you have spent more than you took in, you had a "negative cash flow." Nature abhors a vacuum (and banks aren't too fond of overdrawn accounts, either), so a negative cash flow implies a deficiency that you have to do something about. If you have a negative cash flow in your personal checkbook, then you know you have to put money in from some other source, perhaps savings. If it's your real estate investment that experiences the negative cash flow, then you have to make up the shortfall from funds outside the property account—in this case, your own pocket. A property with a negative cash flow doesn't provide you with any spendable cash. On the contrary, it requires that you put more of your personal funds into the property to make up the difference.

> **Rule of Thumb:** If there was any doubt before, there should be none now. It is absolutely vital to make the kinds of financial projections that this book is all about. For a small investor, a negative cash flow is not just an accounting entry. It means that, at a particular point in time, the property will not have enough cash to pay its bills. That in turn means that you, as the investor, will have to ante up your own personal money to make up the deficiency. However, the presence of an occasional negative cash flow doesn't mean that this is a fatally flawed investment; you may make up the loss in other years or through other of the "four returns." The potential for a negative cash flow, however, does bring an important point front and center: If you make your projections and judge the overall investment to be worthwhile, you can anticipate the negative cash flow and take it in stride. If you don't make your projections, you can get blindsided.

The math is simple enough:

Cash In
less Cash Out
= Cash Flow

Example. Let's look at a basic and fairly typical example of cash flow from an income property. You own a six-unit apartment building. Two units rent for $800 per month, two for $900, and two for $1,000. All units are occupied, and everyone pays on time. Each month you make a mortgage payment of $2,800. For the year just ended, you paid $14,100 in real estate taxes, $3,800 for property insurance, $4,200 for maintenance and repairs, $800 for water, and $75 for miscellaneous supplies. Do the math:

Cash In

(2 × 800) + (2 × 900) + (2 × 1,000) = $5,400 per month
5,400 × 12 months = $64,800 per year
Total Cash Inflows $64,800

Cash Out

Mortgage (2,800 × 12 months)	33,600
Real Estate Taxes	14,100
Property Insurance	3,800
Maintenance and Repairs	4,200
Water	800
Miscellaneous Supplies	75
Total Cash Outflows	56,575
Cash Flow	8,225

You have taken in more than you spent, so you have a positive cash flow.

You should note again that the source of the cash inflows and outflows doesn't concern you when calculating cash flow. Inflows may come from rent, loan proceeds, vending machine revenue, or any property-related source. The same is true of outflows. Payments for operating expenses, debt reduction, or even construction of additional rental units all represent outflows that reduce your overall cash flow.

Appreciation

Every investor hopes to see a good cash flow from his or her property because that means the investment is providing some spendable cash each year. Not all properties generate a meaningful cash flow, however, and for those that don't, the next most important of the four basic returns is appreciation. Not to be confused with what you wish you could get from your teenage children, appreciation is defined as the growth in value of a property over time.

The formula here is just as direct as that for cash flow:

Future Resale Price
less Original Purchase Price
= Appreciation

With cash flow, we asked if you had a checking account. Now we'll ask if you have a savings account. If you do, you've seen appreciation at work. You put $1 into the account today. Interest, an engine of appreciation, causes it to grow over time.

The questions that should come to mind immediately in regard to real estate appreciation are, "How much growth?" and "How much time?" To answer these questions, you need to consider a more fundamental issue, "What causes a property to appreciate in value?" Several parts of this book will address that very question, so we won't try to deal with it in depth here. In general, however, revenue—particularly net revenue (after operating expenses)—drives the value of income property. We're returning to one of our basic principles here, that real estate investors really buy the property's income stream. If you have more income stream to sell, you can expect to get more for it. Hence, the faster and the greater your revenue increases, the more likely it is that the value of the property will increase.

So, what makes revenue increase? Changing market conditions may make the property more attractive. An area that was once marginal may become fashionable, and consequently the balance of supply and demand shifts. General economic inflation may cause the cost of new construction to rise, putting upward pressure on rents.

External forces are not the only factors that can influence appreciation. You may make physical improvements to the property so that it can command greater rents. You may simply improve the management of the property, attracting and keeping better tenants, reducing vacancy losses, and minimizing wasteful expenditures.

You may not enjoy the benefit of appreciation until you sell, but when you do sell, the value of this benefit can be substantial. If this were a get-rich-quick book, we would probably talk about nothing else.

Example. You purchase a property for $1,000,000 and sell it at some future date for $1,450,000. What is the amount of appreciation?

The amount of appreciation is the difference between the selling price and your original purchase price, $1,450,000 less $1,000,000, or $450,000.

Future Resale Price	1,450,000
less Purchase Price	1,000,000
= Appreciation	450,000

Loan Amortization

It's really nice when someone else pays your bills. In effect, that's what happens when you use a mortgage loan to help you purchase an income property. Consider a $1 million office building. You could write a check for the full amount, but, sadly, that would almost clean out your bank account. On the other hand, you could write a check for just $300,000 and get a loan for $700,000. That would leave you with enough money to buy two more similar buildings and still have change left over.

Of course, a loan requires payments, usually monthly. Where will the money come from to make these payments? Recall our earlier cash flow example. The mortgage payment was one of the cash outflows, and it was paid with the cash that came in. With most properties, rental revenue makes up all or nearly all of the cash inflow, so essentially it is your tenants who pay your mortgage.

Each mortgage payment you make includes both interest and principal. In a later section (Part I, Chapter 3), you'll see more details about how to calculate the specific amount of each, but for now, you're more interested in the concept. You use a mortgage loan to purchase the property. Each month your tenants give you the cash needed to pay down that debt. They are helping you buy the property.

Amortization is the liquidation of this debt by the application of installment payments over time (for the Latin scholars, think of "ad" [toward] and "mort-" [death]—killing off the loan).*

Debt Service (i.e., total mortgage payment)
less Interest Paid
= Amortization

You will usually look at income-property data on an annualized basis, so you can expect to see the term "annual debt service" (ADS). The ADS on a mortgage is the total of all payments you make in a year.

Example.　You make monthly mortgage payments of $1,500. At the end of the year, your bank reports that you have paid $15,000 in interest for the year. What is your loan amortization for the year?

If you pay $1,500 per month, then your ADS is $1,500 times 12, or $18,000. You apply the formula:

Annual Debt Service ($1,500 × 12)　　18,000
less Interest paid for the year　　　　15,000
= Amortization for the year　　　　　　3,000

Tax Shelter

The last of the four basic returns is tax shelter. An income-property investment can shelter some of its own income from taxation and occasionally shelter income received from other investment sources as well. How does it do that? As owner of an investment property, you take in taxable rental income and pay out tax-deductible operating expenses like insurance and repairs (see Part I, Chapter 2, and Part II, Calculation 9, for a more detailed discussion), leaving you with a "net operating income" (NOI) on which you would expect to pay taxes. However, to promote the general economic benefits that tend to flow from real estate development (e.g., the creation of office and retail space, multifamily housing, etc.), the tax code permits further deductions.

---

*Note that there is also a tax-related concept called *amortization*, which we will discuss in a later chapter.

The first of these deductions is for mortgage interest. Interest is really a cost associated with acquiring the property rather than operating it, and even though your tenants appear to be paying the interest along with the rest of your mortgage, the IRS allows you to deduct that interest.

The second source of tax shelter is through the depreciation deduction, which is now called cost recovery in the tax code as of this writing, but is still usually called depreciation by real flesh-and-blood investors. Even though the market value of the property is probably increasing over time, you can make the assumption that the buildings (but not the land) are, in fact, wearing out over time and becoming less valuable—and you can take a deduction for that presumed decline in the value of your asset. (In case you're tempted to stop reading right now and run out to buy up the whole neighborhood, it's only fair to warn you that what the IRS giveth, it at least partially taketh away later when you sell. Read more about how to calculate the depreciation deduction in Part II, Calculation 34.)

The exhilarating part about depreciation, if any part of the tax code can be so described, is that it is a noncash deduction. In other words, you get a deduction without writing a check. It does not affect your cash flow, and it is not an operating expense. It is a deduction that can shield some or all of your property's year-to-year income from taxation. If the depreciation deduction is large enough, it can even exceed the amount needed to shelter the property's own income and provide shelter for other investment income as well. In that case, the deduction creates what is effectively a cash yield of its own by reducing your other tax liabilities.

To anyone who has ever attempted to fill out a tax form, it should come as no surprise that you cannot find a nice simple formula for the tax shelter component of a real estate investment. Nonetheless, you can at least get a feel for the concept by following this path:

Income
less Operating Expenses
= Net Operating Income

Then,

Net Operating Income
less Mortgage Interest
less Depreciation (Cost Recovery)
= Taxable Income

Example. Let's revisit the property you looked at in the preceding cash flow example. You can use the same rental income and operating expenses. You have rental income of $64,800 and operating expenses of $22,975. (Neither the entire mortgage payment nor just the interest portion is an operating expense, a concept you'll learn more about in Part I, Chapter 4.)

Income	64,800
less Operating Expenses	22,975
= Net Operating Income	41,825

You need to know your mortgage interest and allowable depreciation in order to complete the calculation. Say that your mortgage interest for the year is $32,000 and your deduction for depreciation is $8,000.

Net Operating Income	41,825
less Mortgage Interest	32,000
less Depreciation	8,000
= Taxable Income	1,825

Recall from the cash flow example that this property has a positive cash flow of $8,225. You can put $8,225 (less income tax payable) in your pocket, but you now see that you have to pay taxes on only $1,825. This is good. It's a tax shelter at work.

Summary

The foundation is now in place. You understand that every income property has the potential to provide you with as many as four different returns: cash flow, appreciation, loan amortization, and tax shelter. Cash flow is the money you have left after paying all your bills; appreciation is the growth in equity caused by an increase in the property's value; amortization represents the growth in equity caused by the gradual paydown of your mortgage; and tax shelter signifies the property's ability to shield from taxation some of its own income and perhaps even income from other investments. From this point on, almost every concept and calculation we discuss will bear some relationship to one or more of these four basic returns.

You're ready to get serious about real estate investing.

WHAT EVERY REAL ESTATE INVESTOR NEEDS TO KNOW ABOUT CASH FLOW

PART I

HOW TO ANALYZE A POTENTIAL REAL ESTATE DEAL

1

Do Your Homework: How to Gather the Data Needed to Make an Investment Decision

Before you delve into the basic calculations that underlie all real estate investments, you need to address a very fundamental issue: You can't calculate anything and you can't make projections unless you have the raw data with which to start. Information is a valuable commodity; you shouldn't start off with any illusions that good information will fall into your lap without some effort on your part.

These guidelines are necessarily somewhat general. Data will be easier to find in some localities than in others, even within some transactions than in others. Still, if stock market debacles like Enron and WorldCom have taught us anything, it's that investors need to know what's really going on. You owe it to yourself to get the facts. The consequences of doing less can be unpleasant.

Property-Related Data

If you're considering the purchase of an income property, you need to know as much as you can about its income and expenses. As we will emphasize throughout this book, you are not really buying a physical property so much as you are buying its income stream. The beauty is in the bottom line.

If you're considering the purchase of an income property, the information you receive will probably come either directly from the seller or indirectly through the seller's agent. In the next chapter, you'll see in considerable detail how to analyze the basic income and expense numbers, but your first concern here is, "Are they accurate?" Here are some ways that can help you find out.

Ask to See the Leases

There are a lot of good reasons to do this. For one, if you buy the property, you are going to be subject to the terms of those leases, so it's a very good idea to know what they say. More to the immediate point, however, is the question of the rental rates. Do the leases agree with the seller's representations? How long does each lease run? Do tenants have options to renew and at what rates? The answers to these questions will have an important effect on your analysis of the current figures and on the forecasts you'll make about the property's future performance.

Look at the Property Tax Bill

That's one way to confirm the accuracy of this expense; but also look to see if the current owner has received some sort of tax abatement (perhaps a development incentive) that may expire or may not apply at all to a new owner. Also, look for evidence of a "phase-in" of a new assessment. Some cities, in order to mitigate the impact that the periodic reassessment of property values can cause, will choose to implement a new assessment in phases. This can mean that the current taxes are accurate but that there is also the certainty of higher tax bills as the new assessment comes online.

Spot-Check Utility Bills

Most gas, electric, and water companies will give you usage information if you call. This is not the most efficient way to collect expense data on a property, but it can still serve a useful purpose. If what you find matches what the seller has told you, then you can have some reasonable hope that other representations will also be accurate. If, on the other hand, you discover discrepancies, you can ask for an explanation. Even if what you uncovered turns out to be an honest mistake, you've served notice that you are not to be trifled with when it comes to truth and accuracy.

Ask to See the Appropriate Sections of the Seller's Tax Return

You'll have to cover your ears when you try this, because the screaming can be painful. When the din subsides, point out that you don't need to see anything unrelated to the property. If the owner holds the property as an individual, then the income and expense information probably appears on Schedule E, and he or she can show you just that form. The owner may own the property as a limited liability company (LLC) or some other form of partnership, in which case the property has its own tax return. It is quite unlikely that an owner will claim too much income or too little expense on a tax return, so this can be an illuminating source of information.

Recite the Representations About the Leases and the Schedule of Rent Income in the Offer to Purchase

Check with an attorney about the proper language, but put into the offer to purchase something along the lines of "The Seller warrants and represents that as of the date of this agreement, the leases are for [such and such amounts] and the expiration dates and renewal options are [whatever]." Then ask the lawyer about adding, "and that these warranties will survive the delivery of the deed." The first part means the seller swears to tell nothing but the truth, and the second part means that he or she is not off the hook if you discover the lie after you complete the purchase. It's amazing how many sellers get religion when faced with having their words immortalized in a contract.

Rule of Thumb: Forget the lawyer jokes and find yourself a good attorney. You need someone with expertise in investment real estate, not necessarily the person who did your last house closing (single-family closings are to attorneys what oil changes are to auto mechanics). A tight purchase contract or a good lease can save you money and grief. I learned the technique described in the preceding paragraph many years ago from a good friend and attorney. I used it in a purchase offer where the seller was a pleasant, white-haired grandmother with tenants who rented month to month. When I presented a purchase offer with an attached rent schedule and a statement warranting that the rents were true, all pleasantries promptly disappeared and I was informed that "Tenant A would be paying such and so, but he takes out the trash for the building so I charge him less, and Tenant B could be paying what I quoted, but he shovels the snow, etc."

Market-Related Data

Investigate Comparable Sales

If you were contemplating the purchase of a home, you would want to know how much other homes in the neighborhood had sold for. Sales of comparable properties don't tell you as much about an investment property as they do about home sales, but they can sometimes provide a useful insight. There are some obvious problems with trying to use raw "comps" data that you typically get from a real estate agent. One problem is simply the lack of enough comparables to be meaningful. Let's say that you're looking at a 10,000 square foot shopping center. How many recent sales of centers the same size in the same market area are you likely to find? Probably not enough to provide a significant sample.

Your search might be a bit more productive if you look at some additional factors in regard to these comparables. Total square footage is one. You may find that three strip centers have sold in the last year, but each was a different size. You could examine the selling prices per square foot to see if you can discern a trend. You could also consider each property's gross rent. Dividing the selling price by the gross rent gives you something called the gross rent multiplier (more on this in Part II, Calculation 5). Perhaps you'll get lucky and see that these other three sales occurred at 7.1, 7.2, and 7.3 times each property's gross rent.

Where do you find information like this? Public records from the tax assessor and city clerk will probably yield sale prices and property dimensions, but digging this out may be a chore. A growing number of Internet sites are dedicated to aggregating information about commercial properties sold and for sale. We could name some here, but we won't because their Internet addresses will probably change before the ink dries on this page. Nonetheless, a web search should quickly point you to current sources. Also, check the websites of trade organizations like the Appraisal Institute (http://www.appraisalinstitute.org); they will almost certainly direct you to sources of data. Keep in mind, however, that you are not likely to find this kind of information online without having to pay for it.

If you're dealing with a broker, he or she should be a great source of information. Even before computers made it easy to keep property records, good commercial brokers always accumulated data about every property they came in contact with. Ask for the information.

One final word on comparable sales data as they relate to income-producing real estate. Remember your mantra: You're really buying the income stream. Comparable sales data are useful insofar as they give you a feel for your market. Data seldom tell you enough by themselves, however, to lead you to a decision about buying or selling.

Look for Lease Rates and Operating Expense Data

As you get into serious property analysis and projections, you need to know what tenants are willing to pay for space and how much owners are obliged to pay for operating expenses. Once again, you can ask the commercial broker to share that information. It would be a good idea to cozy up to a property manager as well (you may need his or her services later) because a manager will have firsthand knowledge of what it really costs to run a particular kind of property.

Find Out About Local Capitalization Rates

Unless you read this book from the back to the front, you may not know yet what a capitalization rate is. Suffice it to say for now that it's one of several rate-of-return measurements that you will want to know. For the type of financial forecasting you'll learn to perform, it's very valuable to know what the typical capitalization rate is for a particular kind of property in a particular geographic area. Once again, your commercial broker is the first person to ask. This information is more difficult to find online, so despite our reluctance to name commercial websites, we will mention http://www.realtyrates.com as a current source of such data.

Armed with the confidence that you can dig up the data you need to perform a sensible property analysis, turn your sights now onto some real numbers.

2

Financial Detective Work Before You Buy: Finding the Truth Behind What the Seller Is Telling You

Whether you own a shopping mall in the suburbs or a duplex around the corner, the basic principle of income property remains essentially the same. You expect to collect money, mainly in the form of rent, and you expect to spend money to pay for the operating expenses and the loans against the property. When you're done for the year, you hope to have a surplus and to keep as much of it as you can in your own pocket and out of the hands of the tax collector. Perhaps someday you can also sell the property at a handsome profit. In other words, you're looking for cash flow, appreciation, amortization, and tax shelter—the four basic returns.

To achieve these goals, you, as an investor, need to take a careful and critical look at the income and expense data of any property you consider purchasing. Later, when you're ready to sell, a buyer can examine your own figures with the same critical eye to get a fairly realistic picture of the price your property may then command.

In this chapter, you'll take a detailed look at the income-and-expense statement for real estate, commonly called the *Annual Property Operating Data* (APOD). You'll consider how these data can be used as a guide in evaluating the performance of a property and how they can serve to signal the presence of possible problem areas.

Basic Definitions

Begin your analysis of income and expenses by reviewing a few terms:

- **Gross scheduled income** is the total annual rent value of all units in the property. This amount includes the actual rent generated by occupied units, as well as the potential rent from vacant units.
- **Vacancy allowance** is usually expressed as a percentage of the gross scheduled income. As its name suggests, it is an estimate of the amount of potential income that will be lost due to vacancy. Some investors prefer to call this category "vacancy and credit loss" so that it also accounts for uncollectible rent.
- **Gross operating income (GOI)** is the gross scheduled income less the vacancy allowance. It is also known as effective gross income. In short, it is the amount you actually collect.
- **Operating expenses** are items such as property insurance and taxes, repairs, utilities, and management fees. Operating expenses include any costs that are necessary to keep the revenue stream flowing. Mortgage payments and depreciation are not considered operating expenses, nor are capital improvements.
- **Net operating income (NOI)** is the gross operating income less the operating expenses. In other words, it is what is left of your total potential income after all vacancy and expense items have been subtracted. Again, mortgage payments and capital expenditures have no impact on the NOI.

- **Annual Property Operating Data** is the real estate equivalent of an income-and-expense statement. You'll use the terms *APOD* and *income and expense* interchangeably.

Let's take these definitions and see how they might fit into an actual property analysis. Suppose that you're considering the purchase of Property A, a four-unit apartment house. The present owner tells you that each apartment rents for $400 per month and that his operating expenses last year totaled $5,200. You might organize your information in this fashion:

Gross Scheduled Income	19,200
less Vacancy Allowance (3%)	576
Gross Operating Income	18,624
less Operating Expenses	5,200
Net Operating Income	13,424

The gross scheduled income of $19,200 represents 4 units at $400 per month for 12 months. Your vacancy allowance is an estimate, as it almost always will be. Ideally, you should base this estimate on your knowledge of market conditions and of comparable properties in the area.

Rule of Thumb: In the absence of usable market data, many investors like to use a vacancy allowance in the range of 3 to 6%. An exception to this rule of thumb usually occurs in the case of a newly built project that is being leased for the first time. Vacancy during the initial lease-up period can be much higher.

Conventional wisdom also has it that a property whose actual vacancy history is close to zero has probably been rented at less than market rates. In other words, if you don't experience some vacancy, you're just not charging enough.

Subtracting a vacancy allowance of 3% from the gross scheduled income gives you a GOI of $18,624. Subtracting your operating expenses of $5,200 then yields an NOI of $13,424.

You might draw some useful inferences from these basic facts, but you probably should first take a closer look at how this property operates. The next question you would certainly ask is, "Just how was that $5,200 spent?" The seller responds by telling you he spent $2,550 on fuel oil, $130 on electricity, $200 on water, $250 on repairs, $1,270 on property taxes, and $800 on fire and liability insurance.

Now your APOD looks like this:

Gross Scheduled Income	19,200
less Vacancy Allowance (3%)	576
Gross Operating Income	18,624
less Operating Expenses	
Insurance	800
Repairs	250
Taxes	1,270
Utilities	
Electricity	130
Fuel Oil	2,550
Water	200
Total Operating Expenses	5,200
Net Operating Income	13,424

You can help yourself understand more about this property if you go a step further. You know that your actual collected rent, the GOI, is partially eaten up by your operating expenses. You can determine how big a bite each expense takes out of your income by computing the percentage of GOI that each expense represents. You accomplish this by dividing each expense by the GOI and multiplying the result by 100:

Gross Scheduled Income	19,200	
less Vacancy Allowance (3%)	576	
Gross Operating Income	18,624	
less Operating Expenses		
Insurance	800	4.30%
Repairs	250	1.34%
Taxes	1,270	6.82%
Utilities		
Electricity	130	0.70%

Fuel Oil	2,550	13.69%
Water	200	1.07%
Total Operating Expenses	5,200	27.92%
Net Operating Income	13,424	

Analyzing Similar Properties

It would be nice if you had some hard-and-fast rules to measure this property against (something like "Heat should not exceed 11% of GOI—this building must need a new furnace"). The fact that there are no such neat, fixed rules doesn't mean there are no rules at all, however. The piece of real estate in this example doesn't exist in a vacuum, and as a potential buyer, you are sure to ask how the operating statement of this property compares with those of other potential investments. At least, that's what you ought to be asking.

What you really want here is the ability to compare your data to some kind of norms. Your expense percentages may not tell you very much in an isolated example, but they might shed a good deal of light if you could compare them to some reasonable expectations.

Where are you going to get these norms? We discussed a few sources in the previous chapter. You can ask the real estate broker who is trying to sell you this property. He or she may have compiled data on similar buildings in the area and should certainly be interested in giving you the data you need to make an informed decision to buy. You might talk to a property manager in the area, someone who would have firsthand experience with the costs of operating such a building. You may be fortunate enough to own other properties, whose track records you can turn to for guidance. At the very least, you can go back into the marketplace, look at other properties currently for sale, and examine the operating statements of these other properties that are competing for your investment dollar.

Let's consider Properties B, C, and D, which are all small multiunit apartment buildings, and Property E, which is a small commercial piece with two stores and an office. Using the same format as before, you can develop income-and-expense statements for each:

Property B:

Gross Scheduled Income	29,000	
less Vacancy Allowance (3%)	870	
Gross Operating Income	28,130	
less Operating Expenses		
Insurance	2,650	9.42%
Repairs	800	2.84%
Taxes	1,575	5.60%
Utilities		
Electricity	0	0.00%
Fuel Oil	5,680	20.19%
Water	330	1.12%
Total Operating Expenses	11,035	39.29%
Net Operating Income	17,095	

Property C:

Gross Scheduled Income	16,800	
less Vacancy Allowance (3%)	504	
Gross Operating Income	16,296	
less Operating Expenses		
Insurance	800	4.91%
Lawn/Snow	250	1.53%
Repairs	1,000	6.14%
Taxes	1,150	7.06%
Utilities		
Electricity	150	0.92%
Fuel Oil	2,600	15.95%
Water	180	1.10%
Total Operating Expenses	6,130	37.62%
Net Operating Income	10,166	

Property D:

Gross Scheduled Income	26,500	
less Vacancy Allowance (3%)	795	
Gross Operating Income	25,705	
less Operating Expenses		
Advertising	95	0.37%

Insurance	1,340	5.21%
Lawn/Snow	360	1.40%
Repairs	1,875	7.29%
Taxes	1,735	6.75%
Trash Removal	150	0.58%
Utilities		
Electricity	360	1.40%
Fuel Oil	3,875	15.07%
Gas	300	1.17%
Water	720	2.80%
Total Operating Expenses	10,810	42.05%
Net Operating Income	14,895	

Property E:

Gross Scheduled Income	16,800	
less Vacancy Allowance (6%)	1,008	
Gross Operating Income	15,792	
less Operating Expenses		
Insurance	1,100	6.97%
Repairs	300	1.90%
Taxes	1,250	7.92%
Utilities		
Electricity	0	0.00%
Fuel Oil	0	0.00%
Water	0	0.00%
Total Operating Expenses	2,650	16.78%
Net Operating Income	13,142	

The most obvious difference among these statements is that the commercial parcel, Property E, has the fewest expense categories and the lowest total expense ratio. This shouldn't surprise you, since it is quite typical for a commercial tenant to be responsible for its own utilities and interior repairs and often for any increase in property taxes. That's very nice for the landlord, of course, but before you allow yourself to become too euphoric, you'd better make a note to examine the leases on this property to be sure that those costs are indeed being borne by the tenant and not just hidden from view. ("Well, ya know I coulda shoulda woulda passed those expenses through, but my dog ate the leases. You can do it right after you buy the place, no problem.")

Also, you might be wise to allow yourself a bit larger vacancy allowance than you do with your residential properties, since an empty store can often take a lot longer to rent than an empty apartment.

What's most important here, however, is the fact that the character of this property is essentially different from the others under consideration. You shouldn't try to draw inferences from a property that is not really comparable to the subject. If you attempt to use a commercial piece in developing norms for the residential parcel, you risk the mistake of an "apples-oranges" comparison. This may very well be a worthwhile investment, but it is not a suitable yardstick for measuring Property A.

Comparing Expense Ratios

Let's turn instead to the residential investments and see how they compare with each other and with your original proposition. Begin by scanning the operating statements for Properties A through D, looking for similarities in the expense ratios. In doing so, you discover the following:

1. Three of the four properties show insurance expense to be about 4 to 5% of GOI.
2. Two of the four show lawn/snow expense to be about 1.5%.
3. Two of the four show repairs to be about 6 to 7%.
4. All four indicate property taxes in the 5.5 to 7% range.
5. Three show electricity costs under 1.5%.
6. Three of the four properties expended 13.5 to 16% of their GOI on heating fuel.
7. The cost of water fell between 1 and 1.5% on three properties.
8. Total operating expenses ranged from about 37 to 42% on three of the properties.

What about differences? Obviously, almost every parcel shows one or more expense categories with a ratio inconsistent with that of the other properties. Also, you notice that lawn/snow appears only on two operating statements and that advertising, trash removal, and gas each appear only on one.

To what use can you put this information? To good use indeed if you keep in mind the first and best way that an APOD form can benefit you: The APOD is not just a source of answers about an investment property, but rather the source of the most important questions. Read carefully, it can provide the clues that guide you directly to the most revealing line of inquiry about how a property really functions now and how it is likely to function for you in the future.

Look at the facts that you have, and see where the clues lead you.

Property B, which shows the highest GOI, presents you with several odd expense percentages. You notice that insurance and heat costs use up a larger portion of your income. Repairs, on the other hand, consume a low percentage of income. Electricity costs are nonexistent; this is because the tenants have their own meters and thus pay for their own electricity. The same is true of all the buildings. But why are there entries of $130, $150, and $360 on the other statements?

When you ask each building owner, you learn that the electricity expense is for a separate meter governing the lighting of common areas, such as hallways and entryways. You would definitely want to know why such an expense hasn't been listed for Property B. Has it simply been overlooked, or is there no separate meter? If the latter is the case, does the absence of such a meter violate local codes or ordinances, and would you, as the new owner, be compelled to correct that violation at your expense?

The fact that insurance costs are higher here than on the other properties would tend to support your suspicion that building code violations may exist. It's always a good practice for you to get a quote on insurance from your own agent rather than relying on the current cost. After all, it's your own agent's bill that you'll have to pay. In this case, since you're starting to feel a bit suspicious, you might want to go one step further and have someone from your insurance company do a field inspection and advise you of violations that might affect insurability.

You may want to ask your agent if the condition of the heating system has anything to do with the high insurance costs. Also, you should always verify heating and other utility costs by contacting the utility suppliers directly. If the costs are higher than you might expect, as they are here, you want to know why. Is the condition of the heating system suspect? Where are the thermostats? Who controls their setting? Can you correct certain deficiencies and cut your costs? You can answer many of these questions with a careful inspection.

Finally, on the issue of repairs, you notice that less has been spent here than on some of the other properties. Several explanations are possible, and you need to make it your business to find out which one (or perhaps, which combination) is true:

1. The property really did not require much maintenance this year. If that is truly the case this year, it is unlikely to be the case next year.
2. The owner actually spent a bundle keeping the place together this year. In fact, so unusual were his expenditures that the owner feels it would be misleading unless he gave the "typical" annual repair costs instead. In this case, you might wonder what other unpleasant surprises you're being shielded from.
3. The owner spent the amount stated, but it was not enough to care for the building properly. Investors call this phenomenon "deferred maintenance," a polite term that means the owner is letting the property go to the dogs and someone is going to have to pay for the repairs sooner or later. Unfortunately, the longer those repairs are postponed, the higher the cost and the greater the likelihood of management problems and lost income. A building that has uncommonly low repair costs must be scrutinized at least as carefully as one that has costs that appear too high.

By doing little more than taking note of atypical expenditures, you have uncovered plenty of questions to investigate if you want to consider this property further. As an interesting postscript, you should notice that the total operating expenses for Property B represent 39.29% of the GOI, clearly within the range that you thought typical. It's only because you examined the breakdown of those expenses that you were alerted to the possibility of several problem areas.

If you turn next to Property C, you don't find any red flags waving in the expense percentage column. Your attention is drawn, however, to an expense category you haven't seen before: lawn/snow. This example contains a lesson that is as important as it is simple. You may focus so intently on the information that is provided that you may easily forget to notice the information that is missing. It's not enough just to evaluate the expense figures, as you did in analyzing Property B. You must always remember to ask yourself, "When you own this property, what else are you going to have to spend money on?" If there is a sidewalk in front or a parking lot in back, and if it snows in your part of the country, you will probably have a snow removal cost.

The statement for Property D adds advertising and trash removal to the list of expenses. In fact, you should keep in mind a number of expense categories in addition to those you have considered so far. You will look at these shortly, when you reconstruct the income statement for Property A.

The owner of Property D is the only one to report an expenditure for gas. You also notice that the water bill for this property is significantly more than that of the other properties. Does the plumbing leak? No—and it's worth pointing out that, while every departure from the norm should be explained, not every one spells trouble. In this case, you find that the owner of the building has installed a clothes washer and dryer in the basement for the tenants and that these appliances account for both the gas and the water use.

Now that you have a frame of reference, go back and examine Property A, the parcel whose purchase you're considering. What you'll do is reconstruct your original operating statement to reflect what you realistically expect to happen over the next 12 months.

The Annual Property Operating Data Form

Let's get used to working with an APOD form similar to what an experienced investor might use. You can put the form on the following page on your office copy machine and make some worksheets to follow along with your examples here. If you prefer, you can also go to http://www.realdata .com/book and download a spreadsheet of this form. The spreadsheet will calculate totals and percentages for you. To make the following examples more compact, we'll show just the rows that you need to use.

Take a look at the operating statement for this investment with the same critical eye that you applied to Properties B through D.

Annual Property Operating Data

Property Address:
Date:
Prepared by:

INCOME	$	%	Comments
Gross Scheduled Rent Income			
Other Income			
TOTAL GROSS INCOME			
VACANCY & CREDIT ALLOWANCE			
GROSS OPERATING INCOME			
EXPENSES			
Accounting			
Advertising			
Insurance (fire and liability)			
Janitorial Service			
Lawn/Snow			
Legal			
Licenses			
Miscellaneous			
Property Management			
Repairs and Maintenance			
Resident Superintendent			
Supplies			
Taxes			
Real Estate			
Personal Property			
Payroll			
Other			
Trash Removal			
Utilities			
Electricity			
Fuel Oil			
Gas			
Sewer and Water			
Telephone			
Other			
TOTAL EXPENSES			
NET OPERATING INCOME			

INCOME

Gross Scheduled Rent Income	19,200	100.00%
TOTAL GROSS INCOME	19,200	100.00%
VACANCY & CREDIT ALLOWANCE	576	3.00%
GROSS OPERATING INCOME	18,624	97.00%
EXPENSES		
Insurance (fire and liability)	800	4.30%
Repairs and Maintenance	250	1.34%
Taxes		
Real Estate	1,270	6.82%
Utilities		
Electricity	130	0.70%
Fuel Oil	2,550	13.69%
Sewer and Water	200	1.07%
TOTAL EXPENSES	5,200	27.92%
NET OPERATING INCOME	13,424	72.08%

As you look through the expenses, the insurance cost seems to be in line with the other properties, although you must still remember to get a quote from your own agent. Taxes also appear normal, and a quick telephone call to the assessor's office will determine whether any change can be expected soon. You must not forget that a revaluation or a change in the tax rate can affect you next year, even if last year's figures are accurate. The fuel oil costs are near the low end of your typical range, and the seller's oil dealer confirms the number of gallons delivered. Multiplying the gallons used by this season's prevailing rate for oil confirms the heating cost (see the following table).

The cost of electricity is lower here than in most of the other buildings, and the owner can provide you with no reason that it should be. For the purpose of your reconstructed analysis, then, you decide to increase your estimate of that cost to conform to your expectation of about 1.5% of gross income, or $280. Now your APOD form looks like this:

INCOME

Gross Scheduled Rent Income	19,200	100.00%
TOTAL GROSS INCOME	19,200	100.00%
VACANCY & CREDIT ALLOWANCE	576	3.00%

GROSS OPERATING INCOME	18,624	97.00%
EXPENSES		
Insurance (fire and liability)	800	4.30%
Repairs and Maintenance	250	1.34%
Taxes		
Real Estate	1,270	6.82%
Utilities		
Electricity	280	1.50%
Fuel Oil	2,550	13.69%
Sewer and Water	200	1.07%
TOTAL EXPENSES	5,350	28.73%
NET OPERATING INCOME	13,274	71.27%

The most dramatic departure from your tentative norms is in the area of repairs. The property does not look shabby, and yet 1.34% is quite a bit less than the 6 to 7% spent at the other buildings. You certainly need to ask the owner to explain this, and you might even be bold enough to ask to see a copy of Schedule E of his previous year's income tax return, which will show you how much he claimed as taxable income and deductible expenses on this property.

An explanation does come forth. All the apartments have been remodeled within the last 18 months, and the owner's accountant advised him that the work done must be classified as capital improvements, not as expenses. Thus, the costs are not listed as current repairs. The actual repairs for the year were quite minor since each of the rental units had recently been restored to excellent condition. In fact, the last unit was renovated just recently, in January and February of this year.

In addition to answering your question, the owner has also given you some more to think about. First, these apartments will not remain new forever. The owner may have enjoyed low repair costs last year, but he paid for that privilege with his remodeling expenses. You should count on something more realistic for repairs and maintenance for next year, perhaps 6%, which would be the low end of your typical range.

INCOME		
Gross Scheduled Rent Income	19,200	100.00%
TOTAL GROSS INCOME	19,200	100.00%
VACANCY & CREDIT ALLOWANCE	576	3.00%

GROSS OPERATING INCOME	18,624	97.00%
EXPENSES		
Insurance (fire and liability)	800	4.30%
Repairs and Maintenance	1,117	6.00%
Taxes		
Real Estate	1,270	6.82%
Utilities		
Electricity	280	1.50%
Fuel Oil	2,550	13.69%
Sewer and Water	200	1.07%
TOTAL EXPENSES	6,217	33.38%
NET OPERATING INCOME	12,407	66.62%

The next point to consider is the fact that one apartment was unoccupied for two months during renovation. It would be prudent for you to assume that less heat was used than would have been if a tenant occupied the unit during January and February. You cannot expect to be very precise in estimating the amount of fuel saved, but you might want to take the current heating cost and add a few percent to it. To assume an increase in total heating costs seldom turns out to be a far-fetched conjecture.

INCOME		
Gross Scheduled Rent Income	19,200	100.00%
TOTAL GROSS INCOME	19,200	100.00%
VACANCY & CREDIT ALLOWANCE	576	3.00%
GROSS OPERATING INCOME	18,624	97.00%
EXPENSES		
Insurance (fire and liability)	800	4.30%
Repairs and Maintenance	1,117	6.00%
Taxes		
Real Estate	1,270	6.82%
Utilities		
Electricity	280	1.50%
Fuel Oil	2,900	15.57%
Sewer and Water	200	1.07%
TOTAL EXPENSES	6,567	35.26%
NET OPERATING INCOME	12,057	64.74%

Finally, the owner mentioned his accountant's advice. Unless you intend to be a rugged individualist and contend with the vagaries of your own income tax returns, you'd better assume that this venture will add a few dollars to the cost of your tax preparation.

INCOME		
Gross Scheduled Rent Income	19,200	100.00%
TOTAL GROSS INCOME	19,200	100.00%
VACANCY & CREDIT ALLOWANCE	576	3.00%
GROSS OPERATING INCOME	18,624	97.00%
EXPENSES		
Accounting	150	0.81%
Insurance (fire and liability)	800	4.30%
Repairs and Maintenance	1,117	6.00%
Taxes		
Real Estate	1,270	6.82%
Utilities		
Electricity	280	1.50%
Fuel Oil	2,900	15.57%
Sewer and Water	200	1.07%
TOTAL EXPENSES	6,717	36.07%
NET OPERATING INCOME	11,907	63.93%

Your final task is to look over the expense categories (on the generic APOD form, above) that you have not yet used and to consider whether you might incur any of these costs.

You plan to manage the building yourself, so you don't feel that you need to budget for either a resident superintendent or a professional property manager. Janitorial service is unnecessary in this small building, and you have a standard lease you have used before, so you're expecting to have no legal costs. Should a vacancy occur, you intend to show the unit yourself, so there will be no rental commissions. If you need to find a new tenant, you will have to advertise, so you should allot a small amount, perhaps $75, for that purpose.

Finally, there is lawn/snow and trash removal. The present owner lives a block away and takes care of these items. You will have to hire someone to care of the yard, shovel the snow from the sidewalk, and take the trash cans to and from the curb on collection days. A cost of $250 for lawn/snow would be consistent with the other properties you examined, and $5 per week (a total of $260) seems fair for the trash.

Your final reconstructed APOD form should now look like this:

INCOME		
Gross Scheduled Rent Income	19,200	100.00%
TOTAL GROSS INCOME	19,200	100.00%
VACANCY & CREDIT ALLOWANCE	576	3.00%
GROSS OPERATING INCOME	18,624	97.00%
EXPENSES		
Accounting	150	0.81%
Advertising	75	0.40%
Insurance (fire and liability)	800	4.30%
Lawn/Snow	250	1.34%
Repairs and Maintenance	1,117	6.00%
Taxes		
Real Estate	1,270	6.82%
Trash Removal	260	1.40%
Utilities		
Electricity	280	1.50%
Fuel Oil	2,900	15.57%
Sewer and Water	200	1.07%
TOTAL EXPENSES	7,302	39.21%
NET OPERATING INCOME	11,322	60.79%

Based on the facts you know about Property A, the trends you observe among similar buildings, and the fact that your physical inspection reveals no structural problems or deferred maintenance, you can now feel reasonably confident that your projections for income and expenses are as realistic as you can make them.

Where does that leave you? Is this a worthwhile investment? To answer that question fully, you will have to go beyond the APOD to analyze cash flows, value, and rates of return, topics you'll read about in upcoming chapters. You've uncovered nothing about the property to scare you off (no lead paint, asbestos, leaky oil tanks, or ghosts). You've also completed the formidable task of taking raw data and distilling from those data a realistic operating budget for an income-producing property. With that budget—your reconstructed APOD—you can begin to evaluate at what price and on what terms this property will make sense as an investment.

3

How the "Time Value of Money" Should Influence Your Real Estate Investing Decisions

It may seem that the subject of compound interest belongs strictly to the world of savings accounts and certificates of deposit and has little to do with real estate. The truth, of course, is that compound interest is a way of understanding how the value of your investment is increasing (or decreasing!) over time. Understanding how this works is critical to understanding the value of any real estate investment.

The compounding with which you're most familiar occurs when you deposit cash in a bank. Your money earns interest at a specified rate, and that interest is compounded at regular intervals. For example, suppose you deposit $1,000 at an annual interest rate of 12%, compounded monthly (at that high rate you will not be getting a free toaster, but it does make this example easier to follow).

By the end of the first month, your $1,000 grows by 1% (1/12 of the annual rate). You now have $1,010. This 1% is called the periodic interest rate because it is the rate at which interest accrues for each compounding period. By the end of the second month, your $1,010 increases by 1% again, or $10.10, giving you a total now of $1,020.10.

If you continue this process for 10 more months, you'll find your account balance has grown to $1,126.83. A simple 12% of your original $1,000 would have been just $120, but you can see here that your total interest is more—$126.83. This difference occurs because, thanks to compounding, you earn interest on your interest. The more frequently compounding occurs, the more dollars of interest will be generated by a given rate. In this example, if your deposit had compounded daily, you would have ended up with even more for the year—$127.47 in interest.

Notice that, in total, four variables are involved in this or any other compound interest calculation. The initial dollar amount is called the *present value* (PV). It grows by applying a periodic interest rate (written as *i* or %*i*) for some number of compounding periods (NPER, or sometimes just *n*). The end result, the amount to which it grows by the time you've gone through all the compounding periods, is called the *future value* (FV).

As you'll see in the next section, bank accounts aren't the only asset that can grow from a PV to an FV. Real estate can do that too.

And FV is not the only one of the four variables you can calculate. If you know any three of the variables, you can calculate the fourth. Why do you care? Because sometimes you may want to estimate how long it will take a piece of property to grow from its original purchase price to a targeted resale price at a given rate of growth. In that case, you'll start off knowing the PV, FV, and periodic rate and will want to figure out the number of periods. Or maybe you're looking at a piece of property that was bought some years ago and sold recently for a higher price. You'll want to know what the annual growth rate was for that property. Again, you have three of the variables and can calculate the fourth, in this case the periodic interest rate.

Real Estate Applications

In the Introduction, we described appreciation—the growth in value of a property over time—as one of the four ways you make money in real estate. Appreciation is a perfect example of the use of the time value of money (and compound interest) in real estate.

Let's look at an example. You're considering the purchase of a home for $100,000 and want to keep it until it appreciates in worth to $200,000. Past history suggests that you can reasonably expect properties to grow in value in this location at a rate of about 3% per year. You want to know how many years it will take for the value to appreciate from $100,000 to $200,000.

To pose the same question mathematically, you know the PV ($100,000), the FV ($200,000), and the periodic rate (3%). You need to calculate the number of periods, given the other three variables.

There are several approaches you can take to get to the result. As you work through the material in this book, you'll find that to be true of many of the calculations we present. Some lend themselves to easy paper-and-pencil solutions, either with a formula, a fill-in-the-blanks form, or the use of one of the tables provided in the Appendix. For others, particularly those where the math is a bit of a chore, we provide more automated solutions in the form of basic computer spreadsheet models that you can download to perform each task. One option that we won't discuss in this text is the use of a financial calculator—a perfectly reasonable method, but instructions vary, of course, from model to model.

Let's look at a few ways to calculate the number of periods in a compound interest problem.

Method #1   This first is the classic but really hard way:

Number of periods = log (FV / PV) / log (1 + i)

where

PV = Present Value
FV = Future Value
i = Periodic Interest Rate

This technique requires a table of logarithms. If you have such a table and know where to find it, then you know what to do; and in fact, you should probably be writing this book, not reading it. You're dismissed.

Method #2   The formula above works fine, but even if you know how to apply it, it's tedious and hardly the best use of your time as an investor. A much easier method is to use a spreadsheet program on your personal computer. We'll assume that you have Microsoft Excel available. Excel provides a wealth of financial functions that can help you with virtually anything you need to accomplish in regard to real estate calculations. You can use one of those functions here.

Using Excel to Make Real Estate Calculations

We're going to spend some extra time on what would otherwise be a fairly uncomplicated example. As we do so, you'll see how to use Excel in a basic way to perform some of the calculations that would otherwise be time-consuming to do by hand. If you're already familiar with Excel, please be patient; we'll go through this in small steps for the purpose of this first example.

Let's start. You want to calculate the number of periods it will take your $100,000 property to grow in value to $200,000 if real estate values rise at 3% per year.

1. Open a blank Excel worksheet.
2. Pull down the "Insert" menu and choose "Function." You'll see a window that looks like this (Figure 3.1).
3. In the left-hand pane, you'll see function categories. Choose "Financial." Excel has a financial function called NPER for calculating the number of periods in a lot of different investment scenarios. Select that function in the right-hand pane and click "OK."
4. You will next see a window where you can enter amounts for each of the variables that might be used with this function. Not all of the variables are necessary for our example. You have no payments, so that can be ignored. The "Type" refers to whether payments are made at the beginning or end of each period; the function defaults to the typical choice, so you can ignore that also. You need to enter:

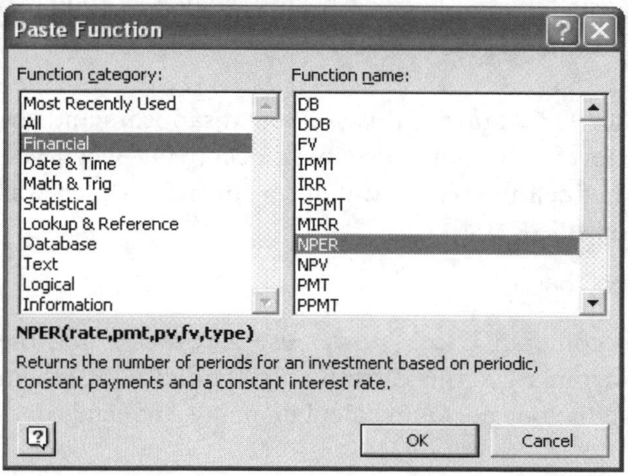

FIGURE 3.1
Excel functions.

   a. The "Rate" as .03 (the decimal equivalent of 3%)
   b. The "PV" as -100000 (notice that you must express the PV as a negative number because, from the function's flow-of-funds investment perspective, PV is money going out and FV is money coming back in; note also that you don't enter commas within the numbers)
   c. The FV as 200000
5. At the bottom of the window (Figure 3.2), you'll see the formula result, 23.44977225. This means it will take about 23.45 years for

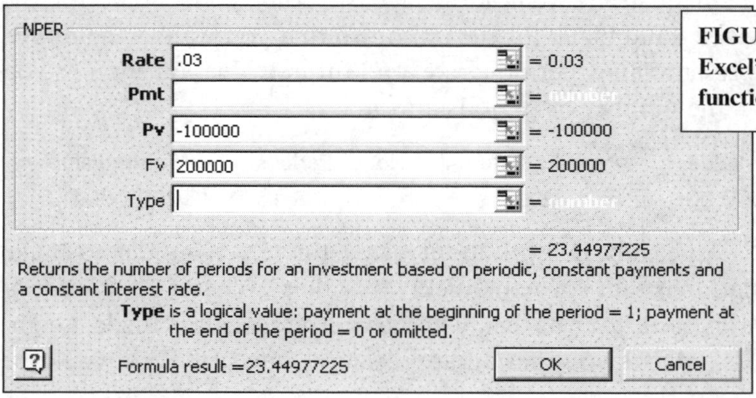

FIGURE 3.2
Excel's NPER function.

the value of this property to appreciate from $100,000 to $200,000 at an annual growth rate of 3%.

When you click the "OK" button, this window disappears and the result displays in whatever cell your cursor was occupying when you began this exercise. That cell now also contains a formula, which was created by the form you filled:

```
=NPER(0.03,,-100000,200000)
```

If someday you become an Excel "power user," you can skip the form and just type a formula like this directly into the cell. Until then, you can use a form like the one above to calculate many financial functions.

Method #3   You don't have to be a mathematician or a computer whiz to succeed as a real estate investor. Being comfortable using a spreadsheet can be a real benefit, but if you don't want to dig too deeply into the functions and formulas, that's all right too. A third and painless way to perform these calculations is to use the collection of Excel templates that we've written to accompany this book. You can download them from http://www.realdata.com/book. These Excel sheets make it easy not only to perform the calculations but also to visualize the examples.

When you open the Excel file for "Compound Interest," you'll find a section where you can calculate the number of periods. If you use this spreadsheet, the task of performing this calculation is really easy. Within the spreadsheet, we'll adopt a basic color code—blue for the known variables and black for the unknown that you want to compute. Enter the present value, periodic rate, and future value. As soon as you do, presto—the number of periods appears:

Present Value	Periodic Rate	No. of Periods	Future Value
$100,000.00	3.00%	23.45	$200,000.00

What is especially helpful about using this Excel model to make your calculation is that you can quickly try other "What if . . . ?" propositions. In this case, your barber, who has correctly called the last eight Super Bowls, advises you that an appreciation rate of 3.75% would be more realistic. Change the periodic rate, and the worksheet recalculates instantly:

Present Value	Periodic Rate	No. of Periods	Future Value
$100,000.00	3.75%	18.83	$200,000.00

Now you're looking at a little less than 19 years for your property to double in value.

You may want to consider this problem from a different perspective. You're not getting any younger, so you decide that you can wait nine years at most to double your money. What growth rate would be necessary to accomplish that goal?

Once again, you could seek your answer using the following formula:

Periodic interest = $(FV / PV)^{(1/N)} - 1$

But as before, this is a difficult and time-consuming process.

You could also build an Excel formula to do the job, using the financial functions window shown in Figure 3.1. If you do so, you'll run through these inputs for RATE—nper, pmt, pv, fv, type, guess—and get a formula like this:

```
=RATE(9,,-100000,200000,,0.1)
```

The easiest way is simply to stay with the same Excel worksheet and use this handy section:

Present Value	Periodic Rate	No. of Periods	Future Value
$100,000.00	8.01%	9.00	$200,000.00

You still have a PV of $100,000 and an FV of $200,000. This time, instead of entering the rate and getting back the number of years as your answer, you enter the number of years, and the model tells you what rate is necessary to achieve your goal. You'll need an appreciation rate of about 8% to double the value of this property in nine years.

Now suppose that you want to speculate on what the value of this property might have been three years ago. Assume that property values grew at 4% annually during that period. Do you need a template for "past value"? No, as Figure 3.3 shows, you just have to orient yourself correctly on the economic timeline.

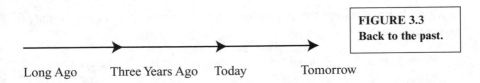

FIGURE 3.3
Back to the past.

Long Ago   Three Years Ago   Today   Tomorrow

To figure out what this property must have been worth three years ago, you have to imagine yourself back then looking toward today as the future. Once again, you find yourself in a situation where you know three of the four variables and want to calculate the fourth. You know that the periodic rate is 4% per year, the time is three years, and the FV is $100,000 (Figure 3.4).

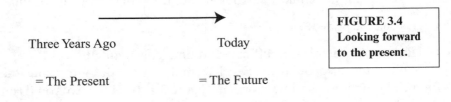

FIGURE 3.4
Looking forward
to the present.

Three Years Ago   Today

= The Present   = The Future

Present Value Is Unknown   Future Value Is $100,000

You want to calculate the PV. Remember, you're standing back in time three years ago (that's the "Present") looking forward to today (the "Future").

By now you know the drill. The formula is ugly—Present Value = $FV / [(1 + i)^N]$—so forget it. You can use Excel's financial functions menu to fill out a form for the PV function with these entries: rate, nper, pmt, fv, type. You get back a formula that says =PV(0.04,3,,-100000).

That's all right, but easiest of all is to return to the Excel spreadsheet and use the mini-template that we've created for you. This basic template for computing the PV will do the trick. You enter the data, and the sheet calculates as follows:

Present Value	Periodic Rate	No. of Periods	Future Value
$88,899.64	4.00%	3.00	$100,000.00

If your assumptions are correct, you can reasonably estimate that, all other factors being equal, the property was worth about $89,000 three years ago.

What Every Investor Needs to Know About Cash Flow: Calculating the Present Value

You'll recall that the first item we talked about in the Introduction, "The Four Ways to Make Money in Real Estate," was cash flow. Invariably, you are pleased when more cash comes in than goes out. However, the cash flow from an income-property investment does not all come suddenly in a single rush. You would like to have a positive cash flow each year that you operate the property, but that cash flow will almost certainly be greater some years than others. When you eventually sell the property, you'll consider the proceeds to be part of your overall cash flow for the sale year.

The time value of money plays a critical role when you consider just how valuable your property's cash flows really are. Timing is everything. Cash you receive sooner is more valuable than cash you receive later because the sooner you have it, the sooner you can put it to work earning more cash.

When you look at the cash flows from a real estate investment, you want to calculate the PV of those cash flows. Essentially, this calculation presents the same situation you saw in the previous compound interest example, except you are viewing it from the other end of the telescope. Instead of watching the smaller value get larger, you watch the larger value get smaller.

When you find the PV of a future cash flow, you are finding what it is worth right now in today's dollars. When you find the PV of a series of cash flows, you are finding the present worth of each of them and then totaling those individual PVs. The sum of the PVs of each individual future cash flow is the PV of the whole stream of future income.

Let's start by looking at just one cash flow that occurs in the future. In Figure 3.5, you can see that if you have a single $100,000 cash flow that occurs five years in the future, its value today, discounted at 10% per year, is $62,092.13. Following the figure from right to left, you can track how the $100,000 steps down each year until it reaches the present.

Why is this procedure so important to you as a real estate investor? It may be fine to know that you can take $100,000 out of your venture five years from now, but as an investor, you recognize that money has a time value. A dollar to be received in five years has less value than one

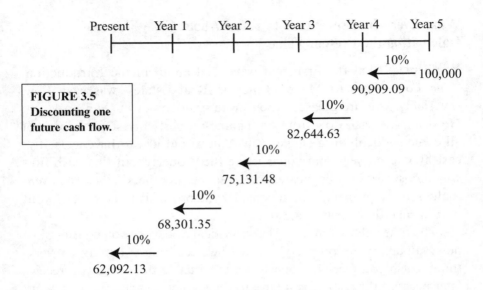

FIGURE 3.5
Discounting one
future cash flow.

you can have today. The dollar will typically lose buying power each year, so you can't expect in five years to purchase goods and services with a current value of $100,000. Perhaps more importantly, if you don't have the cash in hand today, you can't put it to work for you. For this reason, even individuals who may not think of themselves as investors will certainly put any significant amount of cash received today into a certificate of deposit, money market fund, hot Internet stock, or some other form of investment. Similarly, professional investors look at their return as the subject of reinvestment. The longer they must wait for it, the less it can earn.

Discounting is a way of measuring the loss of value caused by the deferral of a return. In the typical real estate venture, you expect some kind of return each year that you operate the property, and you expect an additional benefit from the eventual sale. Each of these returns will have its own timing and therefore will require its own discounting.

Let's look at a specific example. Using a $90,000 down payment, you plan to purchase a property that yields the following cash flows each year. These amounts represent what remains after paying all operating expenses and debt requirements:

Year 1	$9,000
Year 2	$11,000

Year 3	$11,500
Year 4	$12,500
Year 5	$15,000

You expect to sell the property at the end of year 5, realizing cash proceeds of $100,000. Your overall cash flow now looks like the following, where the final year includes cash from both the operation and the resale of the property:

Year 1	$9,000
Year 2	$11,000
Year 3	$11,500
Year 4	$12,500
Year 5	$115,000

To determine the PV of all the benefits of this proposed investment, you calculate the PV of each cash flow, including the sale proceeds, and then sum these amounts. You can consider the investment profitable if the PV of the benefits exceeds their cost (the down payment).

Perhaps you're confident that you could earn 10% if you invested your money in a similar property presenting a similar risk. Why? Because that's what other investors in your area are earning with those similar properties. For that reason, you feel that cash received in the future from this property must be discounted in value at no less than 10%.

> **Rule of Thumb:** When you try to decide whether it makes sense to buy a particular income property at a given price, you should typically discount all future returns from that property at a rate that is no less than what is being achieved by other similar properties. We'll discuss the mechanics of how to do this as we move on, but for now, recognize the reason for this rule. The value and the rate of return are like a seesaw. If you choose a discount rate lower than the prevailing rate, you'll overestimate the value of the property and perhaps pay a price that is higher than what the market requires.

Let's put this example in a more visual form (Figure 3.6).

Your first-year cash flow of $9,000 is discounted back one year at 10%; its PV is $8,182.82. Your second-year cash flow of $11,000 is dis-

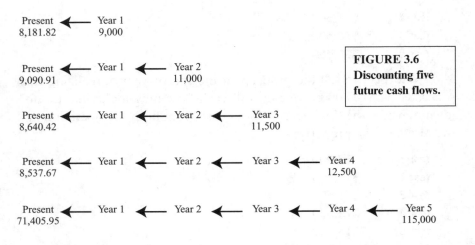

FIGURE 3.6
Discounting five
future cash flows.

counted back in two steps, 10% each year, and its PV equals $9,090.91. This pattern continues until your final cash flow, which represents both the cash from operating the property and the cash from its resale in the fifth year. You must discount the $115,000 for five years at 10% per year, giving that cash flow a worth of $71,405.95 today.

If you sum the PVs of each of these cash flows, you get $105,856.47. Assuming your discount rate of 10% is reasonable, you can think of this sum as the value today of this property's expected future benefits.

What does this figure tell you about the merits of this property as an investment? Don't expect this calculation or any other single measure to give you a simple and definitive "good deal/bad deal" answer. You need to look at each measurement as part of a larger picture and apply your judgment to determine if the deal makes sense to you.

Keep in mind that the PV represents the present worth of all future benefits. If that's so, then you should compare the PV to what it cost you, namely the cash required to purchase the property. You find that the value of what you expect to receive ($105,856.47) is greater than that of what you had to invest ($90,000) to get it. As a successful developer once said to me, you can't lose money making a profit.

The difference between these two is called the net present value (NPV). In this case, the NPV is $15,856.47.

> **Rule of Thumb:** Whenever the NPV is greater than zero, it means that the discounted value of the future cash flows is greater than your original cash investment. **Translation:** Your real rate of return is actually higher than the discount rate you used.

How do you perform this kind of discounted cash flow analysis? Once again, there's the hard way and the easy way.

The hard way is to begin with any of the methods discussed previously for calculating PV. Then do the following:

1. Use that method to figure out the PV of each of the cash flows.
2. Add those PVs up to get the PV of all the cash flows combined.
3. Subtract the initial investment to get the NPV.

The easy way is to use a spreadsheet like the one called "Net Present Value," available for download. The model uses a built-in Excel function called @NPV. This function allows you to specify a periodic discount rate and a range of spreadsheet locations for the cash flows. The first location is discounted once at the periodic rate, the second location is discounted twice, and so on.

Discount Rate	10.00%
Initial Investment	(90,000)*
Cash Flow #1	9,000
Cash Flow #2	11,000
Cash Flow #3	11,500
Cash Flow #4	12,500
Cash Flow #5	115,000
Cash Flow #6	
Cash Flow #7	
Cash Flow #8	
Cash Flow #9	
Cash Flow #10	
Net Present Value	15,856

*Your initial investment is a cash outflow. It will be shown as a negative number when displayed as part of a table.

Because your initial investment occurs on day 1 (and not at the end of the first period), you don't want to discount that number. So you use the NPV function to discount just the cash flows and then subtract the initial investment as you did in the preceding example.

After you enter the data as shown, you find that the answer is the same as with your earlier computation. The template's "What if . . . ?" capabilities are now at your disposal. For example, suppose you discover that 10% is not a suitable discount rate to use for properties in your area and you need to refigure these cash flows at 12%. By simply changing the discount rate to 12%, you can determine that your income stream has a NPV of only $8,188 if discounted at that rate.

Evaluating Leases

You can use your discounting skills for yet another type of analysis. Just as you may be interested in the PV of the income stream from an entire property, you may also be interested in the PV of the income from an individual lease.

Why would you want to determine the value of a lease? First of all, a lease is an asset, something of value, much like a promissory note. It can be useful for you to know what it's worth because you may want at some time to sell your rights under a lease. In order to raise immediate cash, for example, you might try to sell the right to collect the payments due under a lease you currently own.

Perhaps more common is the situation where you are negotiating terms with a prospective tenant. If you're dealing with commercial property, there may be many matters to settle. You need to agree not only on the initial rental amount and the length of the lease, but also on the rate and timing of rent increases and on the amount and timing of other payments such as the tenant's contribution to real estate taxes, utilities, or insurance.

The lease proposals you make or receive could involve a number of possible combinations of these variables. The value in finding the present worth of a lease really lies in the ability it gives you to compare different lease proposals. Keep in mind the theme of this chapter: the time value of money. As the owner of a property, you may be able to seal the deal with a tenant by agreeing to a lease that provides for a small rent increase each year rather than just one, much larger increase that kicks in at a later time. A quick discounted cash flow analysis of the lease payments may be able to show you that the concession that convinces the tenant to sign on the dotted line really costs you little or nothing in discounted dollars.

How does this calculation differ from what you've already done? First, it's common practice when evaluating a property to annualize the cash flows. By that, we mean we usually look at income and expenses as though they were received and disbursed in lump sums at the end of each year. You know, however, that lease payments are typically made monthly and in advance. They're defined by contract; unlike property cash flows, their timing and amount are reasonably predictable. When you evaluate a lease, you can be a bit more precise if you look at a lease's income stream in terms of monthly amounts; and doing so is not impractical.

One decision you may face with a small commercial property concerns terms for a tenant who has just started in business. Do you begin at a low rent to give the tenant a chance to get established and then escalate quickly to make up for lost time? Or do you start off high, assuming that you'd better collect as much as you can while the tenant is still solvent, and not worry about a long term that may never occur?

You can use a basic Excel model (see http://www.realdata.com/book for "Value of a Lease") to analyze such a situation. The model treats each monthly payment as a periodic cash flow. Since lease payments are made at the beginning rather than at the end of each period, it leaves the first payment undiscounted and applies Excel's NPV function to the remaining payments. It also divides the discount rate by 12, so that it's applying a monthly rate to the monthly payments.

Suppose you have a prospective tenant for a retail space in your strip shopping center. Your advertised price is $2,000 per month on a five-year lease beginning in April. The tenant is responsible for a share of the real estate taxes, payable in July of each year. This year's share is $1,000, and your experience has been that taxes in this location increase about 10% per year.

(Take a quick side trip to figure out the tenant's share of the property tax bill. You know it's $1,000 in year 1, and it will increase 10%

each year. Does this sound like something you've read about recently? If you said "compound interest" or "future value," go to the head of the class. Scribble a few notes in the margin now to see if you get the right amounts for years 2 through 5. You'll find the answers in the discussion below.)

The tenant counters with a proposed five-year lease under which he will pay $1,000 per month for each of the first two years, $2,000 per month the third year, and $3,000 for the fourth and fifth years. He makes no mention of paying a share of property taxes. How does his proposal compare in value with yours?

To calculate the PV of each scenario, you must enter your data into the model. Start with the first blue cell, which is the discount rate. You decide to choose an annual rate of 9%. Next, enter on the appropriate line each monthly rent amount that the tenant has proposed.

Discount Rate: 9.00%

Monthly Rent		◄─────────── month ───────────►						
	1	2	3	4	5	6	7	8
Year 1 1,000	1,000	1,000	1,000	1,000	1,000	1,000	1,000	1,000
Year 2 1,000	1,000	1,000	1,000	1,000	1,000	1,000	1,000	1,000
Year 3 2,000	2,000	2,000	2,000	2,000	2,000	2,000	2,000	2,000
Year 4 3,000	3,000	3,000	3,000	3,000	3,000	3,000	3,000	3,000
Year 5 3,000	3,000	3,000	3,000	3,000	3,000	3,000	3,000	3,000

Present Value of lease payments: $91,868

As you can see, the PV of the lease proposed by the tenant is $91,868. It's an easy matter to change the monthly rental amount now to $2,000 for each year, as you had originally proposed. In this new example, you need to account for the tenant's contribution to property taxes. Remember that the tenant is also responsible for paying a share of the property taxes. When a tenant is obligated by the terms of the lease to pay all or part of some property operating expense, that obligation is called an "expense pass-through." Did you calculate the pass-through for property taxes correctly? Year 1 is $1,000, and each subsequent year increases by 10%: $1,100 for year 2, then $1,210, $1,331, and $1,464.

The taxes are payable in July, which is the fourth month of the lease year. In month 4 (recall that the lease is scheduled to begin in April, so calendar month July is month 4 in your model), you need to change the amount to include combined rent and taxes.

Discount Rate: 9.00%

	Monthly				month				
	Rent	1	2	3	4	5	6	7	8
Year 1	2,000	2,000	2,000	2,000	3,000	2,000	2,000	2,000	2,000
Year 2	2,000	2,000	2,000	2,000	3,100	2,000	2,000	2,000	2,000
Year 3	2,000	2,000	2,000	2,000	3,210	2,000	2,000	2,000	2,000
Year 4	2,000	2,000	2,000	2,000	3,331	2,000	2,000	2,000	2,000
Year 5	2,000	2,000	2,000	2,000	3,464	2,000	2,000	2,000	2,000

Present Value of lease payments: $102,014

The PV of your original proposal is a good deal greater than that of the tenant, so you must decide whether you are willing to accept a decrease in the cash flow expected from this lease. As a landlord, you need to consider whether it's better to take the offer, make a counteroffer, or wait until a better proposition comes along.

In this situation, you can evaluate several possible counterproposals in seconds. Perhaps you can find one that's acceptable to your prospective tenant, yet close enough to your own requirements that the risk of waiting for a better deal isn't justified.

Consider five different rent options you might propose:

	Monthly Rent				
	Option 1	Option 2	Option 3	Option 4	Option 5
Year 1	1,000	1,000	1,500	1,000	1,000
Year 2	1,500	2,000	1,500	1,000	1,500
Year 3	2,000	2,000	2,000	2,000	2,000
Year 4	3,000	3,000	2,000	3,000	2,500
Year 5	3,000	3,000	3,000	4,000	3,500

Use the model and try out each of these scenarios. Don't forget to add the property tax pass-through into month 4 of each proposal. You should discover that you end up with the following results:

Option 1	102,079
Option 2	107,346
Option 3	99,036
Option 4	104,861
Option 5	101,702

The PVs of the first and fifth alternatives are virtually the same as that of your original proposed lease, while the second and fourth have higher values, and the third has a lower value.

You begin to appreciate here the enormous benefit you can derive from working the numbers on a real estate deal. Compared with your original proposal, any one of these five options might actually be more appealing to your start-up tenant because each offers a significant concession in the first year. Four of the five options offer a break in the second year as well. Only option 3 would cost you any real money; 2 and 4 would actually give you more than you originally expected. Just a few minutes of playing with PV calculations has given you four new ways to make this deal work.

You can continue to juggle these rent amounts—and any of the variables involved—looking for still other recipes that might make this deal work. Perhaps you want to consider breaking the tax payment into two installments or forgoing it altogether in the first year. Or you might want to try some other combination of rental amounts. Whatever you want, it's easy to try. The easier it is for you to know and understand your options, the better your decision will be.

Mortgage Calculations

One of life's few certainties, in addition to death and taxes, is that you should buy real estate, whenever possible, with other people's money. The other people may be banks, insurance companies, private lenders, or the property sellers themselves. Just avoid lenders who disburse funds from the trunks of their cars.

The money is loaned most often in the form of a mortgage—an interest-bearing note secured by the property and repaid typically in equal monthly installments.

Because mortgage financing is an integral part of real estate investing, there are probably no calculations performed more often than those that pertain to such financing. It's a rare transaction that doesn't cause you to ask, "What will it take to service the debt? How much interest will I pay? How much will I owe when I sell?"

The typical amortized mortgage is structured as something called an ordinary annuity. That's a series of regular, equal amounts disbursed at the end of each payment period. Four variables are involved in any mortgage calculation: the principal amount (or PV), the periodic interest rate, the number of payment periods, and the payment amount.

You can calculate the monthly payment using a mathematical formula that is about a yard and a half long. Let's take the liberty of assuming that you'd rather go directly to the simpler methods.

First, turn to the Appendix in the back of the book where you will find the first few pages of a table called "Monthly Mortgage Payment per $1." The rest of the table can be found at http://www.realdata .com/book. The chart runs from 1% to 14.375% and from 1 to 30 years in 1-year increments. The following is a segment of that table.

Monthly Mortgage Payment per $1—Mortgage Constant

Years	4.500%	4.625%	4.750%	5.500%	5.625%
20	0.00632649	0.00639417	0.00646224	~ 0.00687887	0.00694966
21	0.00614117	0.00620956	0.00627836	~ 0.00669970	0.00677133
22	0.00597386	0.00604296	0.00611248	~ 0.00653849	0.00661095
23	0.00582221	0.00589201	0.00596225	~ 0.00639288	0.00646615
24	0.00568425	0.00575475	0.00582580	~ 0.00626089	0.00633497
25	0.00555832	0.00562951	0.00570117	~ 0.00614087	0.00621575
26	0.00544304	0.00551491	0.00558727	~ 0.00603143	0.00610709
27	0.00533720	0.00540976	0.00548281	~ 0.00593137	0.00600780
28	0.00523980	0.00531302	0.00538675	~ 0.00583966	0.00591685
29	0.00514993	0.00522382	0.00529823	~ 0.00575542	0.00583336
30	0.00506685	0.00514140	0.00521647	~ 0.00567789	0.00575656

Say that you are applying for a mortgage of $200,000 for 30 years at 5 5/8% (that's 5.625% for the fractionally challenged). Find the column for the rate 5.625 and follow it down to the row for 30 years. There you see 0.00575656. This is the monthly payment amount for $1 at

5.625% for 30 years. Multiply the total dollar amount of the mortgage by this factor to calculate the monthly payment:

200,000 × 0.00575656 = 1,151.31

> **Rule of Thumb:** Sometimes you need to make a quick estimate without the benefit of a calculator. Look up the factor and move the decimal point four places to the right so that you are dealing with mortgages in the tens of thousands, or move it five places for hundreds of thousands. In the preceding example, the factor becomes 575.656 per 100,000. For two "hundreds of thousands," double the 575, and you have a quick estimate of 1,150.

Try another example. You want to borrow $127,650 at 6% for 25 years. What is the monthly payment? This time we'll let you find the right page in the table by yourself. Come back when you're ready.

You should have discovered that 6% for 25 years requires a monthly payment of 0.00644301 per $1.

127,650 × 0.00644301 = 822.45

Once again, Excel has a function for computing each of the variables, so you'll find that a spreadsheet template is the fastest and easiest way to perform mortgage calculations. Just as you saw in the compound interest calculations earlier, if you know three of the mortgage variables, you can calculate the fourth.

Let's use an Excel model (see http://www.realdata.com/book for "4 Annuity Functions") to figure a payment amount.

N	%i	Pmt	PV	
300	0.75%	839.20	100,000.00	calculate payment

As you can see, you have the four variables: N, the number of payment periods; %i, the interest rate per period; Pmt, the payment per period; and PV, the present value.

Suppose that you want to find the monthly payment amount needed to amortize a $100,000 loan at 9% per year for 25 years. If you want your answer—the payment—to be the correct *monthly* amount, then it's necessary for you to express the number of payment periods and the periodic interest rate as monthly amounts also. Similarly, if you were seeking the quarterly payment, you would have to express N as the number of quarters and %i as the quarterly rate.

To solve the problem, you enter 300 under N. This is the number of payments you would make in 25 years. (You can also type =25*12, and Excel will act as a calculator, placing the product of these two numbers in the active cell.) If your annual interest rate is 9%, you must divide 9% by 12 for the monthly rate. To do so, you can enter =0.09/12, or .0075 under %i. The amount of the loan is $100,000, so you enter 100000 under PV.

Your results should look like the example above, which shows that the monthly payment is $839.20.

Now suppose you want to know how your situation might improve if you succeeded in negotiating this loan at 8% instead of 9%. You can simply change the %i figure to .0067 (8% annually divided by 12 months) and view the results immediately. The change in the interest rate lowers the monthly payment from $839.20 to $771.82.

As a final consideration, let's say that you want to consider a 30-year term. Change N to 360 (the number of months in 30 years) and note that your payment now drops to $733.76.

N	%i	Pmt	PV	
360	0.67%	733.76	100,000.00	calculate payment

As we mentioned earlier, you can compute any sort of periodic payment as long as you are consistent about your input. For example, what is the quarterly payment needed to amortize $80,000 at 10% per year for 15 years? You enter 80000 under PV. Under N, you enter 60, the number of quarters in 15 years. Under %i, you enter the quarterly interest rate—10% per year divided by 4, or .025. Since you have expressed N and %i in terms of quarters, Pmt will now be calculated as a quarterly amount:

N	%i	Pmt	PV	
60	2.50%	2,588.27	80,000.00	calculate payment

Now let's expand the model to calculate the PV when the other three variables are known. As an example, let's say that you have a 25-

year note bearing interest at 15% per year. It requires monthly payments of $1,408.92. What is the principal amount of the note?

The solution is easy to obtain. Look one row down in the spreadsheet template, and you'll see that the next row is designed to calculate PV. You enter 300 under N, .0125 (0.15/12) under %i, and 1408.92 under Pmt and find the following:

N	%i	Pmt	PV	
60	2.50%	2,588.27	80,000.00	calculate payment
300	1.25%	1,408.92	110,000.49	calculate present value

An important application of the PV portion of this model lies in computing the balance of a loan that has been partially paid down. You need merely to consider N as the number of payments remaining. If you're dealing with a new loan, N is the full number of payments because they are all still outstanding.

A $60,000 note for 25 years at 15% requires monthly payments of $768.50. You would like to pay off the loan at the end of four years. What will the balance be? Remember that you need only three facts: N, the number of payments remaining; %i, the periodic rate; and Pmt, the monthly payment.

If 48 months have elapsed on a 300-month note, then there are 252 left; N is 252. Your %i is 1.25, and the payment is $768.50.

N	%i	Pmt	PV	
60	2.50%	2,588.27	80,000.00	calculate payment
252	1.25%	768.50	58,793.51	calculate present value

You see that your payoff amount is $58,793.51.

From time to time, you may want to know how many payments are needed to amortize a given principal amount or how many payments remain on a loan. Go down yet one more row in this spreadsheet to find another Excel financial function. You are paying $1,184.87 per month on a loan that bears interest at 14% annually. The lender advises that your loan balance is currently $76,312.16. How many payments remain? You enter these three facts in the appropriate locations and find that your answer is 120.

N	%i	Pmt	PV	
60	2.50%	2,588.27	80,000.00	calculate payment
252	1.25%	768.50	58,793.51	calculate present value
120	1.17%	1,184.87	76,312.16	calculate number of periods

Finally, you may want to know what interest rate is being charged on a particular note. You'll need one more spreadsheet row with a formula that computes %i. Scroll down the Excel file, and you'll find that it's there, ready to use. Suppose that a seller offers you a purchase money mortgage of $42,000 for five years. The seller is fond of round numbers, having discovered that they make his checkbook easier to balance, and so he insists on a monthly payment of exactly $1,000. What rate of interest are you paying for this loan?

The input is straightforward and reveals the following:

N	%i	Pmt	PV	
60	2.50%	2,588.27	80,000.00	calculate payment
252	1.25%	768.50	58,793.51	calculate present value
120	1.17%	1,184.87	76,312.16	calculate number of periods
60	1.25%	1,000.00	42,000.00	calculate periodic rate

Don't forget, however, that the 1.25% here is the monthly interest rate. You need to multiply that rate by 12 to get the annual rate, which is 15%.

Now that you have established a good foundation in performing basic financial calculations, you'll turn your attention in the next few chapters to learning valuable lessons about income, value, cash flow, resale, and rates of return.

4

How to Estimate What an Income Property Is Really Worth

Whether you're a buyer, a seller, or a mortgage lender, one of the most important questions you need to answer is, "What is this property really worth?" It may be argued that value, like beauty, is in the eye of the beholder. This argument tends to ring true in regard to single-family homes, where conventional wisdom has always held that a house is worth what someone is willing to pay for it. Income-producing property, however, is different. Value is determined by the numbers. The owner of the Yankees may admire a batter's graceful swing, but he pays for that player's batting average.

Let's begin this discussion with a subject that always warms your heart: income.

Everyone in business or finance has encountered the term "net income" and understands its general meaning (i.e., what is left over after expenses are deducted from revenue). With regard to investment real estate, however, the term "net operating income" (NOI) represents a minor variation on this theme and has a very specific meaning. You might think of NOI as the number of dollars a property returns in a given year if the property is purchased for all cash and if there is no consideration of income taxes or depreciation. By more formal definition, it is a property's gross operating income less the sum of all operating expenses.

You saw these terms in Chapter 2, but they're critical to your understanding of virtually everything that follows. Let's review them briefly:

- **Gross operating income.** Definitions are like artichokes. You need to peel the layers off one at a time. In this case, start with the gross scheduled income, which is the property's annual income if all space were in fact rented and all the rent actually collected. Subtract from this amount an allowance for vacancy and credit loss. The result is the gross operating income.

  Gross Scheduled Income
  less Vacancy & Credit Loss
  = Gross Operating Income

- **Operating expenses.** This is the term that causes the greatest mischief. Many people say, "If I have to pay it, then it's an operating expense." That is not always true. To be considered a real estate operating expense, an item must be necessary to maintain a piece of a property and to ensure its ability to continue to produce income. Loan payments, depreciation, and capital expenditures are not considered operating expenses.

  For example, utilities, supplies, snow removal, and property management are all operating expenses. Repairs and maintenance are operating expenses, but improvements and additions are not—they are capital expenditures. Property tax is an operating expense, but your personal income tax liability generated by owning the property is not. Your mortgage interest may be a deductible expense, but it is not an operating expense. You may need a mortgage to afford the property, but not to operate it.

  Subtract the operating expenses from the gross operating income, and you have the NOI.

> Gross Operating Income
> less Operating Expenses
> = Net Operating Income

Why all the nitpicking? Because NOI is essential to your understanding the market value of a piece of income-producing real estate. That market value is a function of the property's "income stream," and NOI is at the core of that income stream. As unfeeling as it may sound, a real estate investment is not a handsome assemblage of bricks, boards, bx cables, and bathroom fixtures. It is an income stream generated by the operation of the property, independent of external factors such as financing and income taxes.

Investors don't decide to buy properties; they decide to buy the income streams of the properties. This is not such a radical notion. When was the last time you chose a stock based on the aesthetics of the stock certificate? ("Broker, what do you have with a nice mauve filigree border?") Never. You buy the anticipated economic benefits. The same is true of investors in income-producing real estate.

Those readers who have not yet been lulled to sleep by this discussion will alertly point out that they have in fact observed changes in the value of income property brought about by changes in mortgage interest rates and in tax laws. Doesn't that observation contradict our assertion about external factors?

If you're familiar with the concept of capitalization rate (which we'll discuss again below), you recognize that there are two elements to a property's value equation: the NOI and the cap rate (universal shorthand for capitalization rate). The NOI represents a return on the purchase price of the property, and the cap rate is the rate of that return. Hence, a property with a $1,000,000 purchase price and a $100,000 NOI has a 10% capitalization rate. However, the investor will purchase that property for $1,000,000 only if he or she judges 10% to be a satisfactory rate of return.

What happens if interest rates go up? In that case, there may be other opportunities competing for the investor's capital—bonds, for example—and that investor may now be interested in this same piece of real property only if its return is higher, say 12%. Apply the 12% cap rate (PV = NOI / Cap Rate), and now the investor is willing to pay about $833,000. External circumstances have not affected the operation of the property or the NOI. They have affected the rate of return—the so-called market cap rate—that the buyer will demand, and it is that change that impacts the market value of the property.

In short, the NOI expresses an objective measure of a property's income stream, while the required capitalization rate is the investor's subjective estimate of how well his or her capital must perform. The former is mostly science, subject to definition and formula, while the latter is largely art, affected by factors outside the property, such as market conditions and federal tax policies. The two work together to give you your estimate of market value.

Cash Flow and Taxable Income

So far, our discussion has focused on the meaning of NOI—what it includes, what it does not include, and what significance it has to your understanding of the worth of an income property. As Figure 4.1 shows, the topics of cash flow and taxable income are natural exten- sions of NOI.

When you look back at a year of operating your property, a reason- able question for you to ask is, "How much did I make this year?" The answer lies in a review of the property's cash flow and taxable income.

NOI is the starting point of our discussion here. Once you know the property's NOI, you branch off in one direction to figure its taxable income and in another to figure its cash flow.

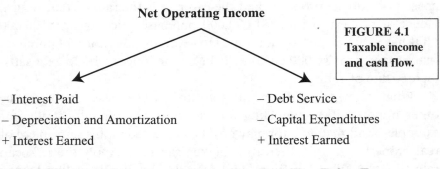

Net Operating Income

FIGURE 4.1
Taxable income
and cash flow.

– Interest Paid   – Debt Service

– Depreciation and Amortization   – Capital Expenditures

+ Interest Earned   + Interest Earned

Taxable Income or Loss   **Cash Flow Before Taxes**

As you'll see shortly, these two branches eventually reconnect to give you your true bottom line. First, let's look at these two branches to see how they differ.

Taxable Income or Loss

Both branches start with NOI. Remember that mortgage payments play no part in the NOI calculation, so it is now, below the NOI line, that you will at last take financing into account.

When you make your taxable income calculation, you can deduct only the interest portion of the loan payments. Likewise, if you earn interest (on your escrow account, for example), you must add that back into your income.

You also make deductions for depreciation and amortization. When you purchase a piece of investment real estate, you can't just deduct its full cost immediately as an investment expense. Instead, you can deduct each year a portion of the value of the depreciable asset, until finally you have written off the entire amount. With real estate, you are allowed to treat the physical structures (i.e., the buildings) as the depreciable asset for tax purposes, but not the land.

(*An editorial aside:* The author, having learned the commercial real estate business in the Pleistocene Age, still uses the traditional term "depreciation." In the Modern Age of unrelenting political correctness, you will frequently find this same concept referred to as "cost recovery." Congress, ever the subtle wit, no doubt became uncomfortable with an economic term that conveyed the notion of unremitting decay and collapse and chose to replace it with one that conveyed a sense of a rise-from-the-ashes return to health and well-being. No political agenda here, of course. It is interesting to note that Congress could not let go of the term "depreciation recapture," which seems to conjure up subliminal images of the taxpayer as escaped convict, once again ensnared.)

At this writing, you can depreciate a residential income property over 27.5 years and a nonresidential property over 39 years. Since not everyone buys or sells on the first of the month, the tax code tries to even matters out with a so-called half-month convention, which allows the taxpayer to claim only half the normal amount of depreciation in the month that the property is placed in service and half in the month when it is sold. Of course, the authors of the tax code could have made matters more precise by simply asking you to prorate your partial month of depreciation, just as your bank does with per diem mortgage interest when you buy or sell. But they didn't.

Another item that affects your taxable income is amortization. It is important to understand that the term, as used here, does not refer to the principal portion of a loan payment. Instead, it refers to the process of taking a partial annual tax deduction for an item you are not allowed to expense in a single year. A good example of a cost that must be amortized is the premium you pay for securing a loan, commonly called "points." You typically pay this premium in one lump sum on the day you close the loan, but you must amortize it over the life of the loan. So, if you take out a 240-month investment-property loan for $720,000 that requires payment of 2 points (2%, or $14,400), you can deduct $60 per month, or $720 for each full tax year.

You may also earn some interest income on your property bank accounts or on an escrow account that your lender may require for real estate taxes and insurance.

To review, your taxable income is your NOI less interest payments, less your allowable write-offs for depreciation and amortization, plus any interest earned (Figure 4.2).

Net Operating Income

FIGURE 4.2
Taxable income
or loss.

– Interest Paid

– Depreciation and Amortization

+ Interest Earned

_____

Taxable Income or Loss

Cash Flow Before Taxes

Cash flow is even more straightforward. As we suggested in the Introduction, think of it as your property's checkbook. It is everything that comes in less everything that goes out. By starting with NOI, you have already accounted for all the rent revenue, credit losses, and operating expenses. Where else do you spend or receive money?

You make mortgage payments, and now you can count the entire payment amount. You may also make capital improvements to a property. An improvement prolongs the life of a property. It's different from a repair, which maintains, rather than increases, that life expectancy. The cost of the improvement affects your cash flow as soon as you spend the money, even though you may typically have to write it off over 27.5 or 39 years.

Again, here you may earn interest income on your property bank accounts, which also adds to your cash inflows.

The short version of our discussion now boils down to this (Figure 4.3): To derive your property's taxable income, you take its NOI, subtract everything that is properly tax deductible, and add any nonrental income such as interest. To calculate its cash flow, you take its NOI and subtract everything that was actually spent but not already accounted for in the NOI computation itself. Again, add any nonrental receipts.

Cash flow and taxable income are closely related but still have important differences. Cash flow is real. Money comes in; money goes out. You earnestly hope the difference will always be a positive number, and if it is, you can take it with you; you can even spend it.

FIGURE 4.3 Cash flow before taxes.	**Net Operating Income**
	− Debt Service
	− Capital Expenditures
	+ Interest Earned
	Cash Flow Before Taxes

With all due respect to the considerable industry that is built around tax planning and preparation, taxable income is not quite so real. It's whatever the tax code du jour says it is.

If tomorrow the House of Representatives should decide that the useful life of commercial real estate ought to be 100 years instead of 39, then your property's taxable income will rise without your experiencing a single additional dollar in rental income. Why? Because the longer write-off period would mean smaller annual deductions for depreciation, and fewer deductions mean higher taxable income—despite the fact that your gross and net incomes remain unchanged.

Likewise, if mortgage interest were no longer deductible, the effect of the mortgage payment on your cash flow would remain unchanged, but the effect of the lost deduction would be to increase your taxable income and hence your taxes.

Cash Flow After Taxes

All this talk of deductions brings you to the fulfillment of an earlier promise, to reconnect the two branches of our diagram. Up until now, we have been discussing cash flow before taxes (CFBT), but a more meaningful bottom line to you as an investor may be cash flow after taxes (CFAT, Figure 4.4).

While taxable income is a somewhat artificial notion, the tax liability it provokes feels very real indeed. Taxable income creates one last cash flow item: income tax, which must be subtracted from your CFBT to give you your bottom line, CFAT.

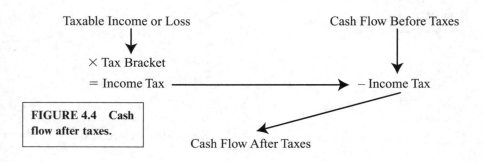

FIGURE 4.4 Cash flow after taxes.

Again, recall our discussion in the Introduction of the four ways to make money in real estate. Your taxable income may be negative as well as positive. If it is negative, then it may actually result in a negative tax liability and can increase your CFAT by sheltering other earnings.

A Case Study

A comprehensive example will demonstrate how all these numbers interact. For readability, let's make projections that go out just five years. If you would like to work out any of the calculations in longhand, you'll find forms for taxable income and cash flow in their respective chapters in Part II.

In this analysis, you plan to acquire a small strip shopping center for $1,250,000. Your cavalier attitude toward debt leads you to take on three mortgages. The first mortgage is for $720,000 with an interest rate of 8% for 20 years. You must pay 2 points ($14,400) to secure the loan. The second mortgage is a 10-year note for $100,000 at a fixed interest rate of 9%. It also requires 2 points (in this case, $2,000). The third loan is from the seller for $10,000, interest only, at 10% fixed and due to mature in 10 years. It requires a single interest-only payment annually until then.

For purposes of calculating depreciation, you look at the municipal tax assessments for the land and the building and conclude that 72% of the property's value lies in the building and the remainder in the land. Therefore, you judge, reasonably enough, that the amount that can be depreciated is 72% of the $1,250,000 purchase price, or $900,000.

The property has an annual gross scheduled income of $208,200 and annual operating expenses of $40,900 for the first year of your projections. You expect both income and the expenses to increase at a rate of 2% per year. You leave an allowance of 3% for possible vacancy and credit loss.

Sorry to get personal, but we also need to know your marginal tax bracket (that is, the rate at which your next dollar of income will be taxed). You whisper it to us discreetly, but we publish it here for the world to see: 28%.

Now you can begin to sort out all this information. What is the NOI for years 1 through 5?

In the first year, your property's gross scheduled income is $208,200. From that amount you subtract a 3% allowance for vacancy and credit loss to get the gross operating income. Next, you subtract $40,900 in operating expenses to find a first-year NOI of $161,054.

To calculate the NOI for the next four years, you'll first need to increase the gross scheduled income by 2% for each year. Once you have done so, you can then compute the vacancy and credit allowance, which is 3% of each year's scheduled gross. After that, figure out the operating expenses by taking the first-year amount of $40,900 and increasing it 2% per year (it's that old compound interest again). Finally, subtract the expenses from the gross operating income to get your NOI.

	Year 1	Year 2	Year 3	Year 4	Year 5
GROSS SCHEDULED INCOME	208,200	212,364	216,611	220,943	225,362
− Vacancy & Credit Allowance	6,246	6,371	6,498	6,628	6,761
GROSS OPERATING INCOME	201,954	205,993	210,113	214,315	218,601
− Operating Expenses	40,900	41,718	42,552	43,403	44,271
NET OPERATING INCOME	161,054	164,275	167,561	170,912	174,330

All that was easier to do than to say. Now, from the NOI, you can follow the first branch of our diagram, which calculates the taxable income. Before you do the math, look at a more detailed representation of that branch:

NET OPERATING INCOME
-    Interest, 1st Mortgage
-    Interest, 2nd Mortgage
-    Interest, 3rd Mortgage
-    Depreciation, Real Property
-    Amortization of Points, 1st Mortgage
-    Amortization of Points, 2nd Mortgage
-    Amortization of Points, 3rd Mortgage
+ Interest Earned
TAXABLE INCOME

From your NOI, you subtract anything that is tax deductible. Mortgage interest falls into that category, so you subtract the interest from each of the three mortgages. Depreciation, even though it is not cash out of pocket, is also deductible. Similarly, you can deduct a portion of the points you paid to obtain each mortgage. If you had income that was not from rent—typically, interest earned on the property's bank or escrow accounts—that interest needs to be added in as additional income.

(*A shameless self-promotion:* If you go to realdata.com, you can purchase software that performs calculations like these and produces elegant presentations. This fact absolutely does not excuse you from reading the rest of this book, however. No amount of automation will benefit you if you don't first get a grip on the basic formulas and techniques presented here.)

Now let's look at this same list with the amounts calculated and filled in:

	Year 1	Year 2	Year 3	Year 4	Year 5
NET OPERATING INCOME	161,054	164,275	167,561	170,912	174,330
– Interest, 1st Mortgage	57,050	55,786	54,419	52,937	51,332
– Interest, 2nd Mortgage	8,738	8,131	7,468	6,743	5,949
– Interest, 3rd Mortgage	1,000	1,000	1,000	1,000	1,000
– Depreciation, Real Property	22,115	23,077	23,077	23,077	23,077
– Amortization of Points, 1st Mortgage	720	720	720	720	720
– Amortization of Points, 2nd Mortgage	200	200	200	200	200
– Amortization of Points, 3rd Mortgage	0	0	0	0	0
+ Interest Earned	0	0	0	0	0
TAXABLE INCOME	71,231	75,361	80,677	86,235	92,052

In regard to the mortgage interest paid out each year, there are several ways to calculate the amount manually or with Microsoft Excel (see Part I, Chapter 3, and Part II, Calculations 28 through 30). You can also download a loan amortization schedule to create a table that will show monthly and annual principal and interest (see http://www.realdata.com/book).

Note, however, that one of the mortgages is not amortized. The third mortgage in this transaction is interest only, paid annually. This is a calculation you can do in your head: $10,000 at 10% requires an annual payment of $1,000.

For purposes of depreciating a piece of investment real estate, you must first identify it as residential or nonresidential. This is a shopping center, so clearly it is nonresidential. You then depreciate it over what the tax code defines as its "useful life"—which, as you might guess, is an artifact of the tax code and has nothing at all to do with its real useful life. If you were to hold and depreciate the property for decades and then sell it to a new owner, that owner could start over with a brand-new useful life.

As of this writing, you depreciate residential property over 27.5 years and nonresidential over 39 years. Although they have been at this level for over several decades, be aware that these periods could change with any revision of the tax code.

You'll recall that we said the depreciable basis of this property is $900,000. Because it is nonresidential, you need to depreciate it over 39 years. Divide 900,000 by 39, and you get 23,077, which is what you find in the example above for year 2 and after. But what about year 1? The "half-month convention" allows you to take only one-half of the normal depreciation for the month that you place the property in service. In year 1, therefore, you are entitled to 11.5 months of depreciation. One month of depreciation would equal the yearly amount divided by 12 (23,077 / 12), or 1,923.08. Multiply this by 11.5 months, and you get the depreciation for year 1 as shown, 22,115.

You paid 2 points on the $720,000 first mortgage for a total of $14,400 (720,000 × 0.02). This is a 20-year note, so you divide the total amount of the points by 240 months to find that you can deduct $60 each month or $720 per year until you have written off the full amount. You refer to this process as "amortizing" the loan points—deducting them not in full when you spent the money, but over time for the length of the loan. If you were to retire the loan before the 240 months ran out (by refinance of the mortgage or sale of the property), you could, under the tax code at this writing, deduct the unamortized balance of the points in the year that you paid off the loan.

The points for the second mortgage, of course, work exactly the same way.

Now let's look at what happens in the cash flow branch. First, the categories:

NET OPERATING INCOME
- Debt Service, 1st Mortgage
- Debt Service, 2nd Mortgage
- Debt Service, 3rd Mortgage
- Capital Additions
+ Interest Earned
CASH FLOW BEFORE TAXES

Again, you start with the NOI. From that amount, you subtract the full amount of all mortgage payments, not just the interest. You did not choose to make any capital additions to the property, but if you had, then you would subtract them as well. You didn't earn any interest on your property checking or escrow accounts.

In this example, you have the same NOI as before, of course, and your disbursements are the payments you make on three mortgages. Using the techniques you learned in the previous chapter, you can calculate the monthly payment for each of the two regularly amortized mortgages. Once you have the monthly payment for each, you simply multiply it by 12 to find the total debt service for each year. The third mortgage is interest only, so the annual debt service is exactly the same as the annual interest.

You subtract these mortgage payments from the NOI to leave you a positive CFBT in year 1 of $72,585. In subsequent years, the debt service remains constant, but your NOI increases, so you forecast that your cash flow will increase every year.

	Year 1	Year 2	Year 3	Year 4	Year 5
NET OPERATING INCOME	161,054	164,275	167,561	170,912	174,330
- Debt Service, 1st Mortgage	72,268	72,268	72,268	72,268	72,268
- Debt Service, 2nd Mortgage	15,201	15,201	15,201	15,201	15,201
- Debt Service, 3rd Mortgage	1,000	1,000	1,000	1,000	1,000
- Capital Additions	0	0	0	0	0
+ Interest Earned	0	0	0	0	0
CASH FLOW BEFORE TAXES	72,585	75,806	79,092	82,443	85,861

To get to your bottom line, you need to estimate your income tax liability in order to figure your CFAT. The calculation of the potential income tax liability can sometimes get complicated, involving issues like passive loss limitations and suspended losses, but we've chosen to make this case study fairly straightforward. As illustrated in Figure 4.4, you have to go back to the taxable income calculation in the previous table to retrieve the year 1 taxable income of $71,231. From that, you calculate the income tax liability that is attributable to your ownership of the property. Multiply the taxable income of $71,231 times your marginal tax bracket of 28% for an estimated tax liability of $19,945.

In short, if you achieve your projected year 1 CFBT of $72,585, you'll have a tax liability of $19,945, leaving a CFAT of $52,640.

	Year 1	Year 2	Year 3	Year 4	Year 5
CASH FLOW BEFORE TAXES	72,585	75,806	79,092	82,443	85,861
– Income Tax Attributable to Property	19,945	21,101	22,590	24,146	25,775
CASH FLOW AFTER TAXES	52,640	54,705	56,502	58,297	60,086

Note that you expect to pay more tax each year because the property earns more taxable income each year. However, your CFBT is growing faster than your tax liability, so your bottom line—the CFAT—becomes greater each year.

Without a positive cash flow, your property becomes like the plant in *Little Shop of Horrors*, greeting you with a baritone "Feed me" at every turn. A positive cash flow is important to all investors and essential to some. Is CFAT, then, the end of your continuing saga of investment analysis? Not at all. Next, you'll look at the ultimate resale of your property and at how value impacts the overall quality of your investment.

Resale—How to Forecast the Appreciation Potential for a Property

We've talked about net operating income, taxable income, and cash flow. One topic that sometimes gets less attention than it deserves from beginning real estate investors, however, is resale. Some investors tend to be dismissive, looking at resale as speculation, but many others simply find it difficult to focus seriously on the matter of selling a property they haven't yet purchased. It may take a little extra discipline to work a consideration of resale into your investment mindset, but it is just such discipline that often separates the successful investor from the sorry. Attention to what your property may be worth in the future is no less important than your concern for its value on the day you purchase it.

You care about the potential cash flow, the financing, the operating costs, and the tax benefits. You'd better care also about whether the property will be saleable after you buy it. Often one hears, "Yes, but I plan to keep it for 15 years, or until my toddlers graduate from med school, or until the Federal Reserve Board performs a synchronized swimming exhibition on reality TV."

That's fine; may all your plans go without a hitch. But what if you need to sell this property next year? What if a better opportunity comes along in five years, and you want to cash out?

> **Rule of Thumb:** Recite this mantra whenever you consider purchasing an income property: *If it's not worth selling, then it's not worth buying.*

The world may not be perfect, but at least it's flat—as in "level playing field." You can reasonably assume that if *you* would scrutinize a property's income, operating expenses, financing, and various measures of return before you purchase, then tomorrow some equally astute investor will apply a similarly jaundiced eye to your numbers when you choose to sell. It pays, therefore, to run tomorrow's numbers today and to see just what this investment will look like to a future buyer.

So, what are the numbers that should concern you when you analyze the potential resale of an income property? The most obvious and the most important is the selling price. What will the property be worth in the future? With most income properties, you can estimate the value by applying a reasonable capitalization rate to the net operating income.

In brief, you first estimate the property's NOI in the year of sale. Next, you have to estimate the capitalization rate (i.e., the rate of return) that the buyer would reasonably expect. The NOI is the *amount* of the return, and the cap rate is the *rate* of return. Hence, if the market expects a 10% return and your property produces an NOI of $12,000, your estimate of its selling price would be $120,000. Another way of articulating the algebra involved is to say, "$12,000 represents 10% of what?"

A curious phenomenon exists in the real world. Buyers and sellers can look at the same information and see different meanings. This, you may suspect, is the closest that commercial real estate will ever come to poetry. Not only might you have a different notion of "reasonable rate of return" as a seller, but you might also change your perspective on NOI. It is common for a buyer to estimate value by capitalizing the current year's NOI and for a seller to capitalize next year's expected NOI. The buyer often takes the position, "I am buying the income stream that just happened, and the property's value is based on that income stream. If the income goes up next year when I own the property, that's my business." The seller, as a rule, will assert, "You didn't own the building last year. You're buying next year's higher income stream. The value of what you're buying should be based on that."

> **Rule of Thumb:** If you're the buyer, you generally prefer to capitalize the current year's NOI when you estimate what a property is worth. If you're the seller, you typically prefer to capitalize your estimate of the coming year's NOI. The buyer prefers the current year because the NOI is likely to be lower and will justify a lower selling price. Similarly, the seller is inclined to predict that next year's income will be higher and thus will justify a higher selling price.

Once you develop your estimate of the resale price, the rest of the analysis of resale is fairly straightforward. You will want to calculate the estimated tax liability at the time of sale. Then, with that number in hand, you can forecast the sale proceeds and the overall rate of return for the holding period.

Let's revisit the property in our case study and see if you can estimate both its value to a new buyer and the cash proceeds you might expect from a sale to that buyer. The case study looked five years into the future, so let's assume that you will sell the property at the end of those five years.

Start with an estimate of its selling price. The most straightforward approach is to capitalize its NOI. When you use a cap rate to forecast a property's value at some point in the future, the first judgment you must make is to decide what rate of return (i.e., what cap rate) will investors then demand. Unless you recently traded in your laptop for a crystal ball, you don't know the answer with certainty. You can, however, make a reasonable guess. As discussed in Chapter 1, you can find out what cap rate investors are typically achieving for similar properties today. Then you behave like a sensible and cautious adult, and you assume that you must use a slightly higher rate to estimate the value of your property in the future.

(The alert reader will recognize that, while we're discussing how to estimate the value of a property five years into the future based on its income, the same approach—capitalizing the NOI—is typically one of the ways we would estimate what it is worth today. See Part II, Calculation 10.)

> **Rule of Thumb: *Fact:*** A higher cap rate yields a lower estimate of value. A lower cap rate yields a higher estimate of value.

You do this because you don't like unpleasant surprises. As the Rule of Thumb proclaims, the higher cap rate yields the lower estimate of value. Why? Because if the property generates a certain number of dollars of income (the NOI), the less you pay for the property, the higher the rate of return on your investment will be. The more you pay, the less the rate of return.

Your research shows that investors are currently buying properties like yours at an 11% capitalization rate. The formula:

Cap Rate = NOI / Value

expresses mathematically what we've been saying. If you made a $10 profit on a $100 investment, you would be able to say almost intuitively, "I made 10% on my money." Perhaps without realizing it, you used the preceding formula.

Rate of Return = $10 profit / $100 investment

Rate of Return = 10%

With some minimal algebra, you can transpose the formula if you want to calculate the value of the investment:

Value = NOI / Cap Rate

Put away the folding money now and get back to your real estate. Say that your property has an NOI of $11,000. If investors are buying property at a 10% cap rate, what will they be likely to pay for yours?

Value = NOI / Cap Rate

Value = 11,000 / 0.10

Value = 110,000

But, as noted above, your research suggests that investors are demanding a higher rate today of 11%. What happens to the presumed value of the property?

Value = NOI / Cap Rate

Value = 11,000 / 0.11

Value = 100,000

As advertised, the value goes down because the investor must pay less for the property in order to get a higher rate of return from the same NOI. Now let's apply this reasoning to the property in the case study. You want to sell it after holding it for five years. If you go back to the example, you'll see that you forecast an NOI for year 5 of $174,330. You want to be conservative, so you assume that investors will expect a higher cap rate that year. Given an NOI of $174,330, what do you think an investor who expects a 12% cap rate would be willing to pay?

Value = NOI / Cap Rate

Value = 174,330 / 0.12

Value = 1,452,750

Rounded to the nearest thousand, 1,453,000

How much of that $1,453,000 will you get to carry home from the closing? Not all of it, of course, because you have debts and expenses to pay:

PROJECTED SELLING PRICE
– Costs of Sale
– 1st Mortgage Payoff
– 2nd Mortgage Payoff
– 3rd Mortgage Payoff
BEFORE-TAX SALE PROCEEDS

In this case, you have three mortgages to pay off. Remember that the third mortgage was interest only, so its balance at the end of five years will be the same as it was at the beginning—you've made no principal payments. In addition to the mortgages, you will incur some costs when selling the property. These will include legal costs related to the closing and a commission if you used a broker to help you sell.

> **Rule of Thumb:** An estimate of 7% of the selling price for cost of sale has traditionally been popular among income-property investors. This amount would presumably be sufficient to cover the legal and brokerage costs of a typical transaction. Before you assume that such a percentage is always sufficient, keep in mind that not all transactions are typical. Stir in a little contaminated groundwater and add a dash of environmental liability insurance, and you may be serving up an altogether different deal.

Let's fill in the numbers now and see what's left in the till:

	Year 5
PROJECTED SELLING PRICE	1,453,000
– Costs of Sale	101,710
– 1st Mortgage Payoff	630,184
– 2nd Mortgage Payoff	61,024
– 3rd Mortgage Payoff	10,000
BEFORE-TAX SALE PROCEEDS	650,082

How does that compare with the cash you invested at the outset? You had to pay for the property and the loan points. You used three mortgages to cover some of that cost, and the balance was your cash investment.

PURCHASE PRICE	1,250,000
+ Points, 1st Mortgage	14,400
+ Points, 2nd Mortgage	2,000
− 1st Mortgage	720,000
− 2nd Mortgage	100,000
− 3rd Mortgage	10,000
CASH INVESTMENT	436,400

So, you went into this deal with $436,400, enjoyed some positive cash flows along the way, and walked away from a closing with a check for more than $650,000 before taxes. Not too shabby.

Speaking of taxes, how big a bite will the government take out of that check? The rules governing the tax on the sale of real estate are moderately complex and subject to change. If the author had a red flag (he does not), he would be waving it vigorously here. The discussion that follows will give you a general idea of how it's done currently without getting bogged down in the fine points. That's what you pay your accountant to do.

To figure the tax on the sale of income property, you must first figure the gain. The gain is the difference between the selling price and the property's "adjusted basis."

We talked about basis earlier in our discussion of depreciation, so what is the adjusted basis? Adjusted basis is the property's original cost, plus capital improvements, plus closing costs and other costs of sale, less accumulated depreciation. Essentially, the adjusted basis is what you spent to purchase, improve, and sell the property less the amount you have already written off. If you sell the property for more than this amount, you have a taxable gain.

The adjusted basis calculation for the property in the case study looks like this at the end of the fifth year:

	Year 5
ORIGINAL BASIS, PURCHASE	
PRICE OF REAL ESTATE	1,250,000
+ Cumulative Capital Improvements	0
+ Costs of Sale	101,710
− Cumulative Depreciation, Real Estate	113,462
− Cumulative Depreciation, Capital Improvements	0
ADJUSTED BASIS AT SALE	1,238,248

Keep in mind that under the current tax code, you can take only one-half month of depreciation deduction in the month that you dispose of the property. This rule mirrors the one that allows only one-half month when you first put the property in service.

What, then, is your gain when you sell this property?

	Year 5
PROJECTED SELLING PRICE	1,453,000
− Adjusted Basis	1,238,248
GAIN OR (LOSS)	214,752

This part of the calculation has survived quite a few changes in the tax code, so you can probably expect that it will hang around awhile longer. Nonetheless, you should never rely on permanence in regard to tax rules, so please heed the warning that we have included the calculations in the next section more for illustration than instruction.

In calculating your tax liability at the time of sale, there are certain deductions that may come into play. For example, you may have had operating losses in prior years that you were not allowed to take because they exceeded your "passive loss allowance." If you could not deduct them earlier, you can deduct them at the time of sale. You may also have had loan points and leasing commissions that you've been amortizing (i.e., deducting over time). If you have an unamortized balance on any of these items, you can deduct it when you sell.

Your sample property does indeed have points that have not yet been fully written off. Recall that you paid $16,400 in points to obtain the first and second mortgages. You have been amortizing $720 of the first mortgage points each year and $200 of the points for the second mortgage. That means you've deducted $920 each year for five years, a total to date of $4,600. If the full amount of the points was $16,400 and you've amortized $4,600, you have $11,800 left to deduct. You can add that amount to your deduction for the fifth year because you are retiring the loan by selling the property.

POINTS PAID	16,400
− Amount Amortized	
1st Mortgage 5 Yrs × 720	3,600
2nd Mortgage 5 Yrs × 200	1,000
UNAMORTIZED BALANCE	11,800

Now you have enough information to compute the tax liability due on sale.

Under the current rules, you as a 28% bracket taxpayer would break your $214,752 gain into two parts: an amount equal to the total depreciation you've taken (which needs to be recaptured at an ordinary income rate, but not more than 25%) and all the rest. So you would break the gain into $113,462 taxed at 25% and $101,290 taxed at the capital gains rate (15% or 20% or sometimes even more under the tax code at this writing, and which could be affected by your modified adjusted gross income, tax bracket, holding period, and year of sale). And recall that you still have those amortized points ($11,800) that you can take as a deduction at your ordinary income rate.

If you find that confusing, you're not alone. Take our earlier advice and have your accountant do this when it gets to be real. Our purpose for including it here is to close the circle and to show your ultimate bottom line at the time of sale, the after-tax sale proceeds.

	Year 5
BEFORE-TAX SALE PROCEEDS	650,082
− Total Federal Tax on Sale	45,438
AFTER-TAX SALE PROCEEDS	604,644

In this chapter, you've developed a good understanding of what a property is really worth in terms of the cash flow and eventual sale proceeds that it can provide. Now it's time to get out your yardstick and learn how to measure the quality of a real estate investment.

5

Measuring the Return on a Real Estate Investment

Ever since Neanderthal Man first sublet the summer cave, income-property owners have been devising methods of measuring the success of their investments. In this chapter, we're going to look at several of these methods and discuss their usefulness to modern-day investors. We'll start with some of the cash flow measurements that have their origins in the precomputer days and work our way along to the more sophisticated techniques, such as internal rate of return.

Payback Period, Cash-on-Cash Return, Gross Rent Multiplier, Debt Coverage Ratio

One of the oldest and simplest measures is the payback period. You can define this as the length of time required to recover your initial cash investment. Let's say you invest $100,000 in cash to purchase a $500,000 property. The balance, of course, is financed. The property generates a positive cash flow of $20,000 per year. Hence, the payback period is five years. To achieve a quick payback, your property must have a strong positive cash flow. The sooner you get your investment back, the sooner you can begin to "make" money. Sooner is better.

The payback period has been known colloquially as the "bingo year," presumably because that is what the savvy and sophisticated investor would exclaim upon seeing the return of the Prodigal Down Payment. In the preceding example, the investor would have described year 5 as his or her bingo year.

One weakness of this method is that it does not take into account the time value of money. It treats a dollar received at some future date as being just as valuable as a dollar received—or invested—today. Looking again at the preceding example, if the property had no cash flow at all for four years and then $100,000 in year 5, it would still represent a five-year payback. However, you would have missed the chance to collect and reinvest $20,000 per year for the first four years. Even if you had reinvested the early cash flows at money market rates, you would certainly have accumulated some interest by the end of year 5. One five-year payback of $100,000 is not necessarily as good as another.

A method that is similar to the payback period is the cash-on-cash return. With this approach, you look at the cash flow (usually before taxes) from a particular year of a property's operation—customarily the first year—and compare it with the cash you invested to purchase that property. You express the result as a percentage, so if you have a $10,000 cash flow this year from a property in which you initially invested $100,000 of your own cash, you would have a 10% cash-on-cash return.

Cash-on-Cash Return = Cash Flow before Taxes / Cash Investment

Cash-on-Cash Return = 10,000 / 100,000

Cash-on-Cash Return = 10%

The cash-on-cash return is perhaps even less illuminating than the payback period because it considers a property's performance over just a single year. Nonetheless, it has typically been a very popular measure, probably because it expresses its result as a simple rate of return. It is easy to look at such a number and say, "A rate of 10% is better than the rate I can get on a T-bill. I like that."

Both the payback period and the cash-on-cash return are entirely dependent on the property's cash flow, which is just one of the four ways you can make money with a real estate investment, as discussed in our Introduction. As such, these measurements can obscure the truth as easily as they can reveal it. On the face of it, cash flow is good. One way to enhance a property's cash flow for a particular year, however, might be to spend little or no money on maintaining that property. Deferring maintenance or improvements can prop up a sagging cash flow, at least for the short term, and give the appearance of a higher cash-on-cash return. The very actions that might increase the apparent return would, at the same time, make the property less attractive and ultimately less valuable.

Consider next a situation that is quite the opposite. Suppose that you can substantially increase a property's value in the long run, but at the expense of its cash flow in the short run. Examples should come to mind easily. A five-year program of repairs and capital improvements might decimate your cash flow, but it might also ultimately attract better tenants and produce a more robust income stream. In so doing, you increase the value of the property so that the real profit can be realized at a later time, perhaps when you sell.

The point here is obviously not to say that a strong cash flow is bad and a weak cash flow is good. You need to recognize that cash flow–based measures of investment quality look at only a part of the total investment picture. They can lead you astray if you don't take the time to look behind the numbers.

A cousin to the cash flow measures is the *gross rent multiplier* (GRM). GRM is a method of estimating or expressing a property's value as a multiple of its gross rental income.

Gross Rent Multiplier = Market Value / Gross Scheduled Income (annual)

By transposing this equation, we also get:

Market Value = Gross Rent Multiplier × Gross Scheduled Income (annual)

There is probably no more basic way to evaluate an income property, and yet this technique still has some usefulness. Most of us are familiar with the "comparable sales" approach that is used to estimate the value of a home. If your neighbors' homes are similar to yours in size and finish, and if several sold recently for $300,000 to $325,000, then yours should sell for a price in that same range. The GRM is a technique that looks at comparable income-producing properties and establishes a typical income multiplier. If other properties have sold recently for seven times gross income, then the subject property should also be worth about seven times its gross income.

This approach achieved its ascendancy in the precomputer (indeed, the precalculator) days for obvious reasons. As a potential buyer, you could stand on the sidewalk, gaze appreciatively at the property, multiply the rent by some whole number without even moving your lips, and determine immediately if the seller were anywhere close to serious.

This simplicity notwithstanding, GRM can be useful. It does overcome some of the hazards of the cash flow methods by making a partial end run around the operating expenses and capital improvement costs of the subject property. By using comparable sales and establishing a rent multiplier based on a number of other properties, GRM essentially establishes by default a typical level of annual expenses and improvements for this group of properties. If the subject property belongs in the group (i.e., if it is comparable to the others), then it should have comparable expenses. Hence, a seller could not distort your estimate of value by temporarily deferring maintenance. You might still undervalue a property, however, if its gross rent had not yet caught up to the seller's ambitious rehabilitation of the property.

An investment measure that remains widely used is the debt coverage ratio, aka debt service coverage ratio. This is the ratio between the annual net operating income and the annual debt service.

Debt Coverage Ratio = Net Operating Income / Annual Debt Service

A property with a 1.20 debt coverage ratio has income before debt service that is 1.20 times as much as the debt service—in other words, the property generates 20% more net income than it needs to make its mortgage payments.

> **Rule of Thumb:** Most lenders require a debt coverage ratio of at least 1.20 in order to finance an income property, and since the Great Recession, 1.25 or higher is not uncommon. This ratio is not going to tell you if you'll meet your own investment goals with this property, but it will tell the lender if you are likely to be able to meet the mortgage payments. A presentation that's designed to seek financing for an income property should always include the anticipated debt coverage ratio, preferably over a period of several years.

All the measures discussed here have at least the potential for shedding some light on the quality of our real estate investment, especially if we are comparing properties. None, however, succeeds in encompassing the whole investment, from acquisition to disposition. You need to consider not just the gross revenue and cash flows, but the timing of those income streams; and you certainly need to look at how the resale of your property will impact the overall success of your investment.

The proliferation of personal computers and of powerful software now makes it possible to create much more refined analyses that do indeed take into account issues such as resale and cash flow timing. You can even project varying holding periods, financing terms, and revenue streams, and you can test their impact on the overall success of your income-property investment. Let's look at some more powerful analytical measures, such as capitalization rate and discounted cash flow.

Capitalization Rate

We've already discussed "capitalization rate," or "cap rate," as it is usually called. To review, we define cap rate as the ratio between a property's net operating income (NOI) and its value.

Capitalization Rate = NOI / Value

You recall that a property's NOI is its gross scheduled income, less vacancy and credit loss, and less operating expenses.

Gross Scheduled Rent Income
less Vacancy & Credit Loss
less Operating Expenses
= Net Operating Income

Operating expenses include insurance, utilities, maintenance, and similar items, but they do not include mortgage payments, depreciation, capital expenditures, or income taxes. Hence, the NOI is the net income before debt service, capital costs, and income taxes.

Like GRM, cap rate is not a cash flow measure. You could mortgage the property up to the ridge beam and wipe out any hope of a positive cash flow. That malfeasance would have no effect at all on the property's NOI and hence none on its cap rate. Unlike GRM, however, cap rate is not strictly based on revenue. It is based rather on net operating income—that is, revenue after the deduction of operating expenses.

The benefit of using capitalization rate as a measure of a property's performance lies in part in the fact that nearly everyone else does. It is perhaps the easiest to calculate of the useful measures and is a good tool to compare a property's current performance with that of similar properties. Other investors, lenders, and brokers are probably going to know just what you mean when you say that a property "has a 12% cap." Since its use is widespread, data about prevailing cap rates are also readily available. Appraisers, brokers, and independent services can provide you with the typical cap rate for a particular type of property in a given location. The availability of that information can help you in determining if the property you are evaluating is an underachiever or overachiever compared with the market.

The downside to the capitalization rate, however, is the same as with most of the others we've considered so far. It looks at the property at a point in time (usually the current year) without regard to the property's expected performance over your entire holding period. It can certainly be useful to look at a single point in time—what's a reasonable estimate of value of the property today, and what is it likely to be worth in 10 years? But surely that doesn't give you a sense of the performance of the property over time. Investors buy the whole timeline. They commit a certain amount of cash to purchase the property on day 1, and they expect to receive periodic cash flows thereafter, including the proceeds of an ultimate resale.

Derived Capitalization Rate

It would not be unreasonable to ask, "Where do cap rates come from?" If the stork doesn't bring them, who does? The cap rate we have been talking about thus far is the rate that prevails in your particular marketplace; hence it is usually called the "market cap rate." You can dissect that rate, however, using an approach called "band of investment" or "derived cap rate." The derived cap rate breaks the calculation of the return into two components: financing and equity. The lender is getting a return on the financing; the investor is getting a return on the equity; the derived cap rate is the weighted average of the two.

A simple example should illustrate the process. Examine this calculation:

0.80×0.10785939	$= 0.086287512$	financing cap rate
0.20×0.12000000	$= 0.024000000$	equity cap rate
	$= 0.110287512$	derived cap rate

You are purchasing a property with 20% equity and 80% financing. You find that loans are available for 15 years at 7%. You start with the financing component, the so-called lender's cap rate. We need to reintroduce a term you saw in Chapter 3, "mortgage constant." The mortgage constant equals the payment amount on a loan of $1 at a given rate and term. If you use the Excel model called "4 Annuity Functions" in the mortgage calculations section of Chapter 3, you can calculate the monthly payment. (*Tip:* Use $1,000,000 as the amount so that you can display a meaningful number of digits in the payment. Then move the decimal point six places to the left. You should end up with 0.00898828.)

Since you are dealing with annual cap rates, you need to multiply the monthly mortgage constant by 12, getting an annual constant of 0.10785939 (rounding may affect this slightly). This is the lender's cap rate. Since the lender is contributing 80% of the money to this deal, multiply that by 0.80 to get the lender's portion of the derived cap rate.

What is the investor's cap rate? The classic approach is to decide on a "risk-adjusted safe rate." The logic here is that you take a safe rate such as the current T-bill and then bump it up to account for the risk and travails of being a real estate investor. (With a T-bill you always get paid and the Treasury Secretary never calls in the middle of the night to tell you the toilets are stopped up.) Multiply by 0.20 for the investor's portion of the derived cap rate.

But bump it up how high? You may detect a bit of circumlocution in our attempt to derive a cap rate that is more objective than the market cap rate, because ultimately you need to make a subjective judgment about how much of a risk adjustment you're going to make. Being an investor, and therefore a competitive creature, you are not going to settle for less than everyone else in your market is getting; and although you might want even more than that, wanting and expecting are two different things. It comes down to this: Your risk adjustment is typically market-driven, so you probably end up right back with something that is fairly close to the market cap rate.

Does this mean your entire derivation exercise was pointless? Not really, because you can run this process backward if you want to discern some useful information: namely, what kind of cash-on-cash return are investors in your market really getting? Consider the example above. If you know that the market cap rate is 11% and that the typical financing available is for 7%, 15 years with an 80% loan-to-value ratio, you can disassemble the weighted average to find out what the equity cap rate is. By doing so, you know that you should expect to achieve a 12% cash-on-cash return in your first year of ownership.

Discounted Cash Flow

Perhaps the simplest and most elegant definition of an investment is that it is the present worth of an anticipated future income stream. If you parse this definition, you reveal both the strengths and weaknesses of yet another measure, called *discounted cash flow analysis* (DCF):

- **Present worth** implies that there is a time value to money that you must take into account.

- **Anticipated** hints at an element of uncertainty. You are going to have to make projections regarding events (i.e., cash flows, resale) that have not yet occurred.
- **Future income stream** suggests that you will be looking at more than just a single point in time. You expect to experience not just one, but a series of cash flows whose timing and magnitude will affect the success of your investment.

Let's begin picking this definition apart by considering the time value of money, which we discussed in detail in Chapter 3. These concepts are critical to our understanding of investment analysis, so they are worth revisiting. According to the venerable "Show Me the Money" principle, you would prefer to have a dollar in the hand today, rather than the same dollar tomorrow or next year. The reason for your impatience is that the passage of time imposes what is called an "opportunity cost." If you receive the dollar today, you can invest it and earn some return during the next year. If you receive the dollar a year from now instead, that delay has cost you the opportunity to invest and hence has cost you the return which that opportunity represents.

Consider the difference between $1,000 received today and invested at 5% annual interest and the same $1,000 received not today, but at the end of some later year.

Pay Me Now		Pay Me Later	
Today	1,000	Today	0
By End of Year 1	1,050	Pay at End of Year 1	1,000
By End of Year 2	1,103	Pay at End of Year 2	1,000
By End of Year 3	1,158	Pay at End of Year 3	1,000
By End of Year 4	1,216	Pay at End of Year 4	1,000
By End of Year 5	1,276	Pay at End of Year 5	1,000

Clearly, the longer you have to wait to receive the money, the greater your opportunity cost. In this example, it costs you $50 to wait one year, but by the end of year 5, the cost of waiting has grown to $276. Now you know why banks charge interest on mortgages.

To understand the concept of present worth, or present value (PV) as it is commonly called, you just need to look at this chart from a slightly different perspective. Let's simplify it a bit for illustration.

Today	1,000
End of Year 5 (at 5%)	1,276

If 5% per year is what you can earn with your $1,000, then at the end of year 5, you will have $1,276. In other words, having $1,276 in five years is equivalent to having $1,000 today. So, the present worth—the value today—of $1,276, due in five years and discounted at 5% per year, is $1,000.

Of course, with real estate, you typically do more than just buy today and then sell at some later date to recover your initial equity plus profit. Stuff happens in between, and you usually call that stuff "cash flow." (At least that's what you call it when it's positive. When it's negative, your vocabulary may become more colorful.)

Returning to our definition, it is this "anticipated future income stream" that you will discount back to a PV. The income stream includes the cash flows that may occur each year, as well as the final cash flow, which is the sale of the property.

Cash Flows

Year 1	5,000
Year 2	6,000
Year 3	7,000
Year 4	8,000
Year 5	70,000 (cash flow plus resale)

Your objective is to discount these cash flows, which occur in different amounts and at different times, using an appropriate discount rate, back to a single PV. How do you do that?

Recall the example from Chapter 3, Figure 3.6. Following the same approach you saw then, you discount the year 1 cash flow ($5,000) for a period of one year, determining its PV. Then you discount the year 2 cash flow back two years, again determining its PV. You do the same for each of the cash flows, and when you're done, you have the PV of each of them. Finally, you add all the PVs together, and you have the present worth of the entire income stream.

If you take the cash flows shown above and discount them at 11%, you find that the PV of this income stream is $61,304.

One of the particular strengths of DCF is that it takes into account both the magnitude and the timing of your investment returns. Consider what happens if you change the timing of the cash flows in the previous example:

Cash Flows

Year 1	0
Year 2	1,000
Year 3	6,000
Year 4	13,000
Year 5	76,000 (cash flow plus resale)

The total of the cash flows is exactly the same as before, but their timing is different. The PV of the series of cash flows now drops to $58,865. Why? Because you have to wait longer to receive some of the money.

In order to use PV effectively, it is essential that you pick an appropriate discount rate. Remember our last example of the five cash flows? When you discounted them at 11%, you found them to be worth $58,865. If you were to take those same cash flows and discount them at 15%, their value would drop to $49,919.

How do you choose a discount rate? Recall that we said that discounting future cash flows compensates for the cost of a lost opportunity. By investing your money in this property, you don't have it available to invest somewhere else. The most suitable discount rate, therefore, is the one that best describes the lost opportunity. Your discount rate should be the rate of return that you could reasonably expect to achieve by investing the same amount of money in a similar investment posing a comparable risk. If other properties of this kind are typically returning 11%, then those properties are competing for your investment dollar, and 11% is an appropriate discount rate for you to use with this property as well.

In our definition, we stated that the discount rate should be applied to the income stream. What you mean by "income stream," however, may vary according to your purpose.

In the preceding examples, we've been using the term "cash flow" to describe the income stream. However, an appraiser will typically

define the income stream as the NOI for each year of the holding period, plus the eventual gross selling price (called the *reversion*) in the year
of resale. By using NOI and gross selling price, the appraiser is trying
to estimate the value of the property in terms of its ability to produce
income, independent of any financing or income tax considerations.

An investor may prefer to find the PV of the actual cash flows
instead, as we did in our examples. By this, we mean the cash flow after
taxes for each year of the holding period, plus the net sale proceeds
after taxes in the year of resale.

If you discount these cash flows, you are looking not at the value or
price of the overall property, but rather at the value of your initial cash
investment, your initial equity. What did you buy with the actual cash
you invested? You bought a series of after-tax cash flows occurring in
the future. If you discount those future cash flows, then you learn how
much they're worth today. You already know what you paid for them—
your cash investment—so now you'll know if you got more or less than
you paid for, or perhaps exactly the same.

The discounting of cash flows does take into consideration the
effects of leveraging the investment through mortgage financing. If you
discount the after-tax cash flows, then you can take into account the
investor's income tax expense or benefit as well. The more financing
you have, the less cash you must invest. At the same time, the more
financing, the less cash flow you are likely to have because of your
greater debt service.

DCF's PV calculation is a way for you to estimate the value of your
investment (i.e., the worth of the income stream). It takes into account
the time value of money, the occurrence of periodic cash flows, and the
ultimate resale of the property and—if you choose—it can also incor-
porate the effects of financing and taxation.

This is a substantial improvement over some of the crude investment evaluation techniques you looked at previously. However, it is not
a rate-of- return measure. As investors, we often feel more comfortable
with a measure that lets us compare one investment opportunity with
another. For that, we can estimate the *internal rate of return* of a series
of future cash flows.

Internal Rate of Return

If you have persevered to this point, then you are poised to master a concept that often seems mysterious to investors: *internal rate of return*.

Internal rate of return (IRR) holds a dubious distinction in the panoply of investment measures. It is the most widely used and oft-quoted rate of return for real estate, and at the same time, the least understood. The next time someone claps you on the back and proclaims a property's IRR, ask him or her, "Now just what exactly does that mean?" This writer will bet you a local suspension bridge (acquired recently in a friendly card game) that the answer, if any, will be unintelligible.

You will certainly reach an understanding of IRR more easily with a few small steps than with a giant leap. Lucky for you, the previous material provided you with just those steps.

Once again, let's back up just enough to get a running start. We defined an investment as an expected stream of income, and we defined the PV of that investment as the sum of the discounted values of each of the future cash flows. *To put it less technically:* Each year, the investment throws off some sort of cash flow—positive, you hope, but negative perhaps. In the year that you dispose of your investment property, you realize one extra cash flow—the proceeds of sale.

The longer you have to wait to collect your money, the less "PV" it has today. As you've seen repeatedly throughout this book, there is a time value to money.

Your real estate investment will produce cash flows periodically. For the sake of simplicity, you typically estimate these future cash flows on an annual basis. A cash flow you receive today is worth its face value, but you must discount each that you expect to receive later to its lower PV. Again, the longer you wait, the bigger the discount.

If you add up the PVs of each of the future cash flows, you arrive at the PV of the entire income stream; and since the income stream represents your investment, you now have the present worth of that investment.

Look at one more example. You purchase a building today, operate it for five years, and then resell it. Here are your actual cash flows:

Cash Flows (Undiscounted)

Year 1	1,000
Year 2	1,000
Year 3	1,000
Year 4	1,000
Year 5	1,000 plus 20,000 net sale proceeds

You also believe you should discount future cash flows by 11%. What that really means is that you think if you had this $25,000 in hand today, you could invest it for an average return of 11% per year over the next five years. You think this is true because you discover that other property investments of similar kind and risk are currently returning about 11% to their owners. You assume that for every year you don't have one of those cash flows in hand, you're going to lose a potential return of 11%, so that's how much of a discount you should apply to each.

The PV of each cash flow, discounted at 11%, looks like this:

Cash Flows (Discounted at 11%)

Year 1	900.90
Year 2	811.62
Year 3	731.19
Year 4	658.73
Year 5	593.45 plus 11,869.03 net sale proceeds

Add these all up, and you get not the $25,000 face value, but $15,564.92. That is the sum of the present worth of each of the expected future cash flows, including the resale. If you have made accurate projections of these cash flows and have selected an appropriate discount rate, then it is reasonable to say that the future economic benefit that you will derive from the property is worth about $15,565 today.

Does that mean the property itself is worth $15,565? If you pay all cash and have no other costs of acquisition (i.e., no attorney's fees, title search, recording fees, etc.), then this would indeed be the value of the property to you as an investor seeking an 11% return. But that's not how you usually buy property, so let's rephrase this statement: Given these cash flows occurring at these points in time, $15,565 is how much *cash* you, as an investor seeking an 11% return, would be willing to invest.

The sum of the discounted cash flows always represents the value of (i.e., what you're getting for) your cash outlay. Therefore, if you buy a property for all cash, then the sum of the discounted cash flows equals the value of the property, because that is how much cash you invest. If you finance the purchase, then the sum of the discounted cash flows represents the value of just your cash outlay.

Keep in mind, if you finance the property, you have less cash flow because you have to pay debt service; and you have less sale proceeds because you have to pay off the mortgage. It makes sense that when you discount these smaller cash flows, you get an amount that equates to your cash outlay, which itself is also less than the full property value in a leveraged investment.

At last, we get to the point. Up until now, you have assumed that you know or can project the future cash flows and the discount rate and that you will use that information to estimate the present worth of those cash flows. What if you already know the present worth of the future cash flows?

If you know the actual cash investment (the purchase price less financing and costs of acquisition), you have essentially declared, "If I make this deal on these terms, then the cash I must bring to the table is *by definition* the present value of the future cash flows." But at what discount rate?

Previously, you used the future cash flows and the discount rate to figure out the PV of your investment. Now, just as in eighth grade algebra (which this definitely is not), you're going to solve for a different variable: the discount rate. When you find it, you're going to call it the IRR.

Let's say this all together one more time:

If I know or can project the future cash flows and the proper discount rate, I can calculate the PV of my cash investment.

If I know or can project the future cash flows and the PV (i.e., the amount) of my cash investment, I can calculate the discount rate, which I will then call the IRR.

(*An aside:* Do not even think of taking a series of cash flows and a cash investment and attempting to figure an IRR manually. IRR must be figured using a binary search or "successive approximations" technique that will make you forget why you wanted to know the answer in the first place. There are other painless ways to solve for an IRR: Financial calculators can do this, and so can Microsoft Excel. We provide a basic

Excel model that you can download at http://www.realdata.com/book. You can also avail yourself of easy-to-use income-property analysis software, such as that provided by RealData.)

IRR is superior to most other measures of investment quality because it takes into account both the magnitude and the timing of every cash flow. A difficult concept to grasp at first, it is elegantly direct. Discount all future cash flows from the point in time when they occur back to the present using a single discount rate. When you find the unique rate that makes the sum of these discounted cash flows equal to the initial cash investment, you have found the IRR.

Let's use the data from the previous example to try some IRR computations. You can use an Excel model that applies the IRR function to a series of cash flows:

Initial Investment	0
Cash Flow, End of Year 1	0
Cash Flow, End of Year 2	0
Cash Flow, End of Year 3	0
Cash Flow, End of Year 4	0
Cash Flow, End of Year 5	0
Cash Flow, End of Year 6	0
Cash Flow, End of Year 7	0
Cash Flow, End of Year 8	0
Cash Flow, End of Year 9	0
Cash Flow, End of Year 10	0
Internal Rate of Return	n/a

(This model is available for you to download at http://www.realdata .com/book.) In each of the first four years you have a positive cash flow of $1,000.

In year 5, you have combined cash flow and sale proceeds of $21,000. Let's say that your initial cash investment is $15,565. Enter these amounts into the model:

Initial Investment	(15,565)
Cash Flow, End of Year 1	1,000
Cash Flow, End of Year 2	1,000
Cash Flow, End of Year 3	1,000

Cash Flow, End of Year 4	1,000
Cash Flow, End of Year 5	21,000
Cash Flow, End of Year 6	0
Cash Flow, End of Year 7	0
Cash Flow, End of Year 8	0
Cash Flow, End of Year 9	0
Cash Flow, End of Year 10	0
Internal Rate of Return	11.00%

Your IRR is exactly 11%. Should you be surprised? Not at all, because this computation is really the flip side of what you did in the previous PV example. There, you had the same cash flows for years 1 to 5, but you specified a known discount rate (11%) in order to compute the PV. Here, you specify the PV (how much cash you're going to invest) in order to compute the overall discount rate (the IRR).

It should be clear that the more you pay to get the cash flows, the lower your overall rate of return will be; and the less you pay for them, the higher your rate of return. Let's say that you pay only $14,000:

Initial Investment	(14,000)
Cash Flow, End of Year 1	1,000
Cash Flow, End of Year 2	1,000
Cash Flow, End of Year 3	1,000
Cash Flow, End of Year 4	1,000
Cash Flow, End of Year 5	21,000
Cash Flow, End of Year 6	0
Cash Flow, End of Year 7	0
Cash Flow, End of Year 8	0
Cash Flow, End of Year 9	0
Cash Flow, End of Year 10	0
Internal Rate of Return	13.67%

Now you're doing better—better in fact than the typical investor in your area, who you determined was getting 11%. What if you pay $17,000?

Initial Investment	(17,000)
Cash Flow, End of Year 1	1,000
Cash Flow, End of Year 2	1,000

Cash Flow, End of Year 3	1,000
Cash Flow, End of Year 4	1,000
Cash Flow, End of Year 5	21,000
Cash Flow, End of Year 6	0
Cash Flow, End of Year 7	0
Cash Flow, End of Year 8	0
Cash Flow, End of Year 9	0
Cash Flow, End of Year 10	0
Internal Rate of Return	8.84%

Obviously, this is much less appealing. You say to yourself, and probably to the seller, the broker, and everyone else within earshot, that if other properties are yielding 11%, you are not going to settle for 8.84%.

But wait, there's more to this story. You've been zoned in on this idea of holding the property for five years. What if you hold it for more than five years or for less? Now you'll need to come up with some additional forecasts about cash flow beyond five years and about the selling price in years other than 5. In real life, the following might not occur, but let's make these following assumptions, both to keep things simple and to illustrate an important point about IRR: Stick with the $17,000 cash investment that made you so cranky in the last example. Say also that the annual cash flow will always be $1,000 and the resale price will be $20,000, no matter when you sell. Doing so will allow you to isolate your attention on the subject of timing. Try selling the property two years earlier than before (i.e., end of year 3) and two years later (end of year 7).

The following is end of year 7:

Initial Investment	(17,000)
Cash Flow, End of Year 1	1,000
Cash Flow, End of Year 2	1,000
Cash Flow, End of Year 3	1,000
Cash Flow, End of Year 4	1,000
Cash Flow, End of Year 5	1,000
Cash Flow, End of Year 6	1,000
Cash Flow, End of Year 7	21,000
Cash Flow, End of Year 8	0

Cash Flow, End of Year 9	0
Cash Flow, End of Year 10	0
Internal Rate of Return	7.87%

Now end of year 3:

Initial Investment	(17,000)
Cash Flow, End of Year 1	1,000
Cash Flow, End of Year 2	1,000
Cash Flow, End of Year 3	21,000
Cash Flow, End of Year 4	0
Cash Flow, End of Year 5	0
Cash Flow, End of Year 6	0
Cash Flow, End of Year 7	0
Cash Flow, End of Year 8	0
Cash Flow, End of Year 9	0
Cash Flow, End of Year 10	0
Internal Rate of Return	11.15%

So what happened? Clearly, your cash flow is not an impressive number with this property; the resale is where the payoff occurs. If you postpone that resale by another two years out to year 7, then the proceeds represent even less to you in current dollars, and your IRR on this investment drops. On the other hand, if you can accelerate your receipt of the big payoff, then those proceeds are worth more to you in current dollars, and your IRR increases. In fact, it increases to about 11%, making this look like a tolerable deal if you don't hold beyond the three-year horizon.

What usually happens, of course, is that neither the cash flows nor the potential sale proceeds remain static. Cash flows may bounce around a bit (more repairs one year than another, for example), but in general, you expect the trend to be upward over time. And you certainly expect the potential cash proceeds from selling the property to grow over the years, as the value of the property increases because of increasing NOI and the mortgage balance goes down.

IRR packs more analytical power than most other measures of investment quality you have seen so far, primarily because of its sensitivity to both the timing and the magnitude of cash flows. Now is when you can really start having some fun with the numbers and using their power to guide you to good investment decisions. Using the cash flows and the potential resale proceeds, for example, you could figure the IRR if you held the property for one year and then sold it, or for two years or three and so on.

> **Rule of Thumb:** When you make your forecasts for a property, don't just run the numbers for a single holding period (for example, five years, as in our case study). Run as many different holding periods as you can, and then look to see if there is one year where the IRR peaks. If so, this is the year you should consider selling to maximize your return. If there is no definitive peak, but rather a period of years where the IRR is more or less the same, that means there is no optimum sale year, and you can sell whenever it suits you.

Let's say that you run a five-year forecast on an income property, including a possible sale of the property in each of those years, and you get the following IRRs:

	Year 1	Year 2	Year 3	Year 4	Year 5
Internal Rate of Return	11.15%	13.72%	15.88%	12.14%	11.02%

What you observe here is that the IRR peaks in the third year. In other words, if you operate the property as planned and sell it at the end of three years, again as planned, your rate of return for that period of time would be higher than the rate for any other holding period. In a situation like this, IRR is more valuable than a simple rate-of-return calculation. If the IRR peaks, it is identifying an optimum holding period. Investors who don't understand IRR often complain, "This makes no sense. My IRR peaks at the end of year 3. But my cash flow from operations is going up in years 4, 5, and beyond, and so is the resale value of the property. How can the IRR go down when everything else is going up?"

It can; it often does; and it shouldn't be ignored. Picture this: You buy a property and successfully turn it around. In the first three years of ownership, you upgrade it physically, improve its management, and bring its rent roll up dramatically. Once it is stabilized and running like a top with all leases at market rents, you continue to enhance the income, but at a more modest consumer-price-index rate of growth.

So why does the IRR go down after year 3? Remember that the IRR is sensitive to the timing and magnitude of cash flows. For the first three years, you moved the cash flow from operation and the potential cash proceeds from resale up at an impressive rate. In the fourth year, you moved them up again, but at a significantly lesser amount. Keep in mind that the big cash flow increases came early, so they were especially valuable—it's that time value of money again, where these cash flows are discounted less severely because they occur earlier. Not only are the later cash flow increases smaller, but they are going to be discounted over a greater number of years. If you hold the property for four years instead of three, that fourth year dilutes the overall rate of return because (a) it wasn't as strong as each of the first three, and (b) it had to be discounted even more because it occurred yet another year later.

None of the later years in this example can match the performance of the first three, so every additional year of holding the property decreases further the overall return. In this analysis, the IRR is capable of delivering a very powerful and perhaps surprising message: "Don't be fooled by the fact that you show cash flow increases every year. You made your biggest impact in the first three years. That's when you should consider cashing out and doing this all over again somewhere else."

Now that you've mastered cash flow and resale and IRR, you don't have to look just for an optimum holding period. What happens to your IRR if you take a bigger mortgage and use less cash? What happens if you do the opposite? What if you spend money for improvements that allow you to raise rents—will that boost your return or reduce it?

This sounds terrific; you've apparently found the perfect way to measure your investment's return. But wait—the standard implementation of IRR has a few warts. Sometimes its results are imperfect, sometimes even misleading. Let's turn next to the potential problems with IRR and to some potential solutions.

Financial Management Rate of Return and Modified Internal Rate of Return

As the last section concluded, you reached an epiphany of sorts. You turned discounted cash flow on its head, solving for the rate rather than the present value. That rate—the internal rate of return—looked like it provided an excellent measure of investment return and a promising way to compare alternative investments because it was sensitive to the interplay between the timing and the magnitude of your investment's cash flows.

At last, with IRR, you had a measure that was a considerable improvement over static metrics like cash-on-cash return and gross rent multiplier, and one that was probably more informative than net present value (NPV).

Like all good mystery writers, however, I try always to have one or two good chapters left in the hole, bringing you back for more. Yes, there is a bit more to the story.

IRR is great, and most investors are quite comfortable using it. But even the venerable IRR has its critics. What are the problems with IRR, and how might you tweak it to overcome those problems?

The Problems with IRR

Straight-up internal rate of return works well in many situations, but not quite all. In the typical investment, you expect to have a single negative cash flow on day 1 to acquire the investment, perhaps followed by a series of periodic positive cash flows. The last of these will be the proceeds of sale when you finally dispose of the investment. In such a scenario, IRR usually works well and is quite intuitive. Take this typical series of cash flows:

Initial Investment (aka Year 0)	(100,000)
Cash Flow, End of Year 1	9,000
Cash Flow, End of Year 2	10,000
Cash Flow, End of Year 3	11,000
Cash Flow, End of Year 4	12,000
Cash Flow, End of Year 5	130,000

Perform an IRR calculation here, and you'll get 13.36%.

Things get a little dicey when your cash flows lose their comfortable regularity. Particularly vexing is a situation where your investment timeline expects to encounter some negative cash flows. Perhaps you're projecting a significant increase in the interest rate on your financing; or you expect to have some major (but unfunded) repairs; or you want to play "what if . . . ?" to see what will happen if you lose an important tenant and cannot replace that tenant quickly. Any of these possibilities could throw your projected cash flow for a future year into the negative.

That's where the arcane math behind IRR throws you a curve. In general, if you have more than one change of sign in the series of cash flows (and you must include the initial investment as one of the cash flows), then you may encounter "nonunique" results. "Nonunique" is a polite way of saying the same set of facts can give you more than one answer, which clearly is not helpful.

Consider this example from the classic text *Mastering Investment Real Estate* (Messner, Schreiber, Lyon, and Ward, Realtors National Marketing Institute, 1982):

Year 0 Initial Investment	(25,000)
Year 1 Cash Flow	150,000
Year 2 Cash Flow	(275,000)
Year 3 Cash Flow & Resale	150,000

In this series of cash flows, the sign changes three times; therefore, there could be as many as three different internal rates of return, i.e., rates at which you could discount these cash flows so that their net present value would equal zero. Indeed, there are three such rates: 0%, 100%, and 200%, and they're all mathematically correct.

The IRR is of little value if it presents you with multiple solutions for the same set of data and invites you to pick the one you like.

If IRR's relationship with negative cash flows is occasionally dysfunctional, it doesn't get along as well as it should with positive cash flows either. Conventional wisdom has long held that IRR assumes that positive cash flows can be reinvested until the end of the holding period at the same rate as the IRR itself. You will, of course, reinvest positive cash flows at the best rate you can reasonably obtain, and that rate is likely to be closely tied to the size of the cash flow. If your cash flow is large, you may be able to reinvest it in another piece of real estate. If it is small, then passbook savings may be your only option. The more that the calculated IRR exceeds your actual reinvestment rate, the more likely it is that the IRR will overstate the property's return—often by just a little, but given the right set of figures, potentially by a lot. What's an investor to do?

In order to take this discussion to the next level, you'll need to add two new terms to your investment lexicon:

Safe rate (sometimes called the *finance rate*). This is the interest rate at which you put money aside, in a secure and reasonably liquid form, so that it can grow to meet the amount or amounts needed to cover future negative cash flows. The rate from a money market or short-term certificate of deposit might be an appropriate choice for the safe rate. In computing FMRR and MIRR, discussed below, the safe rate is used to discount negative cash flows back in time—to a previous positive cash flow in FMRR or to the time when you make your initial investment and acquire the property (year 0) in MIRR—effectively determining how much cash you would have to set aside at that given time so that the cash could grow in interest to be exactly what you need to absorb the negative cash flow when it occurs.

For example, if you predict a negative cash flow of $15,000 at the end of year 1 and could put cash aside in a secure and liquid form at a 4% safe rate when you make your initial investment, then the amount you would need to set aside is $14,423. Check the math:

14,423 × 0.04 = 577 (the interest you earn in one year)

14,423 + 577 = 15,000

Reinvestment rate (sometimes called the *risk rate*). This is the rate at which you assume you can reinvest all positive cash flows. As discussed above, the internal rate of return presumes that you can reinvest positive cash flows at the same rate that the property yields (i.e., at the IRR). Often this is not true, especially when cash flows are too small to reinvest in a comparable piece of real estate.

Financial Management Rate of Return

You can use modified versions of IRR to deal with the problems of nonunique results and reinvestment of positive cash flows. Back in the '70s (the 1970s, that is), when this writer was a young investor in bell-bottom pants, the technique was called *financial management rate of return* (FMRR).

FMRR eliminates negatives by first discounting them back at the safe rate to the nearest previous positive cash flow, then adding that discounted negative amount to the positive cash. If there are any negative amounts left over after doing this, those are discounted back to the time you make your initial investment (i.e., year 0), also at the safe rate, and added to the initial investment. The procedure then compounds the remaining positive cash flows forward to the end of the holding period at a rate that is realistic for those cash flows. It is up to you, the analyst, of course, to specify the safe and reinvestment rates.

This process leaves you with a revised string of cash flows on which you can perform a proper IRR, a series that begins with a negative amount when you make your initial cash investment, ends with a positive amount when you dispose of the property, and presents all zeros for the intermediate cash flows.

For example, say that you found these among your series of cash flows:

Year 3 Cash Flow	30,000
Year 4 Cash Flow	(20,000)

If your safe rate were 4%, you would discount the (20,000) year 4 cash flow back one year at that rate. The result would be (19,231). Now in year 3 you can combine the positive 30,000 with the negative (19,231) and at the same time eliminate the negative cash flow in year 4.

Year 3 Cash Flow	10,769
Year 4 Cash Flow	0

Modified Internal Rate of Return

At some point, perhaps in the mid-'80s, this writer observed that most investors and brokers were using a variation of this variation on IRR called *modified internal rate of return* (MIRR). I can only speculate about what caused this shift, but I have a theory. Microsoft published its Excel spreadsheet software with MIRR as a built-in function. MIRR is perhaps slightly less precise than FMRR, but I suspect that it demands less computing power to calculate. The difference with MIRR is that it discounts all negative cash flows to year 0 rather than trying to mix and match individual negatives with offsetting positives. The difference between it and FMRR is typically slight.

Consider these cash flows, once again based on an example in the text by Messner et al.:

Year 0 Initial Investment	(10,000)
Year 1 Cash Flow	(50,000)
Year 2 Cash Flow	(50,000)
Year 3 Cash Flow	30,000
Year 4 Cash Flow	(20,000)
Year 5 Cash Flow	30,000
Year 6 Cash Flow	250,000

If you use a safe rate of 5% to discount negative cash flows, use a reinvestment rate of 10% for positive cash flows, and perform the admittedly tedious task of figuring the FMRR, you will find that your FMRR equals 19.4%. Use Excel's MIRR function with the same safe and reinvestment choices, and the result is 18.0%. Probably close enough for government work.

It's worth noting, however, that if you were to use Excel's IRR function on these cash flows, using a "guess" rate of 20% to narrow the field of possible answers, you would get an IRR of 25.2% for these same cash flows. Clearly, the difference in this example between IRR and MIRR is quite meaningful. The MIRR yields a more conservative and probably more realistic measurement.

Capital Accumulation Comparison

While FMRR and, more practically, MIRR address the chief deficiencies of IRR as a measure of return, they can still come up a bit short when you want to compare mutually exclusive investment alternatives. The problem here is in accounting for both the duration and the scale of your competing options. Using MIRR to compare opportunities that require the same initial investment and that will be held for the same length of time seems reasonable enough. But what if the alternatives require different amounts of cash or presume different holding periods?

Let's say that you want to decide between two properties, one requiring a cash investment of $100,000, the other $60,000. Clearly, you must really have $100,000 in hand if you're considering both options. To make an "apples-to-apples" comparison, you should invest $100,000 no matter which property you choose. When considering the property that requires only $60,000, your analysis should involve both the return you expect to receive from the property and the return you expect from the remaining $40,000 cash that you were free to invest elsewhere.

Likewise, if you project that you will hold one property for four years but the other for five, you should look at the final proceeds from the four-year property and take into account the return you could earn with those proceeds if you invested them elsewhere for one more year. In other words, when comparing two investment alternatives, you should try to equalize the holding periods.

That brings us to capital accumulation, aka accumulation of wealth. Properly speaking, a capital accumulation (CpA) comparison is not a rate-of-return measurement. However, it is a way you might address the issue of choosing among mutually exclusive investments that may require different amounts of up-front cash and involve different holding periods. This method allows you to compare these investment alternatives not with a rate-of-return percentage but rather in terms of accumulated dollars, even if those dollars don't remain in the particular investment for the entire time.

Consider two mutually exclusive investment opportunities, Property A and Property B, with the following cash flows:

	Property A	Property B
Year 0 Initial Investment	(100,000)	(60,000)
Year 1 Cash Flow	25,000	20,000
Year 2 Cash Flow	15,000	20,000
Year 3 Cash Flow	(15,000)	(12,000)
Year 4 Cash Flow	225,000	12,000
Year 5 Cash Flow		150,000

To perform a capital accumulation comparison, you begin by eliminating the negative cash flows, as you saw in the FMRR example above. Let's say you choose a safe rate of 4%.

	Property A		Property B	
Year 0 Initial Investment	(100,000)		(60,000)	
Year 1 Cash Flow	25,000		20,000	
Year 2 Cash Flow	15,000	(14,423)	20,000	(11,538)
Year 3 Cash Flow	(15,000)	↑	(12,000)	↑
Year 4 Cash Flow	225,000		12,000	
Year 5 Cash Flow			150,000	

You have effectively eliminated the negative cash flows from year 3 and promoted them as discounted amounts, which you will absorb into year 2.

Next, you compound all positive cash flows to the end of your longest holding period, year 5. You decide on a reinvestment rate of 9%.

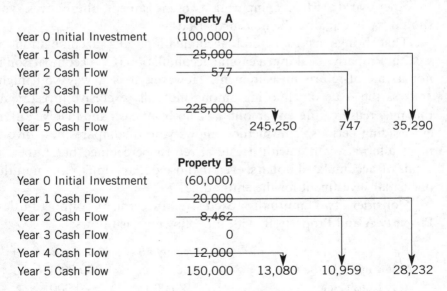

	Property A			
Year 0 Initial Investment	(100,000)			
Year 1 Cash Flow	25,000			
Year 2 Cash Flow	577			
Year 3 Cash Flow	0			
Year 4 Cash Flow	225,000			
Year 5 Cash Flow		245,250	747	35,290

	Property B			
Year 0 Initial Investment	(60,000)			
Year 1 Cash Flow	20,000			
Year 2 Cash Flow	8,462			
Year 3 Cash Flow	0			
Year 4 Cash Flow	12,000			
Year 5 Cash Flow	150,000	13,080	10,959	28,232

Note what you've done with Property A. Even though you expect to sell it at the end of year 4, you are comparing it with a property that you plan to sell at the end of year 5. To make a proper comparison, you must say to yourself, "I need to keep my money invested until the end of year 5, no matter which property I choose." To do that, you'll take your year 4 cash flow, which includes the sale proceeds, and invest it all for one more year at your reinvestment rate.

You have one last consideration to deal with: Clearly, you must be starting out with $100,000 cash in your pocket, or you wouldn't be considering the purchase of Property A. If you decide to buy Property B, then you'll have $40,000 left over to work with. To make a true comparison of these alternatives, you need to commit the same amount with either choice. You do that by assuming that you'll invest the remaining $40,000 for the five-year holding period at your reinvestment rate of 9%.

Your final series of cash flows, after discounting negatives and compounding positives, looks like this:

	Property A	Property B	
Year 0 Initial Investment	(100,000)	(60,000)	(40,000)
Year 1 Cash Flow	0	0	0
Year 2 Cash Flow	0	0	0

	Property A	Property B	
Year 3 Cash Flow	0	0	0
Year 4 Cash Flow	0	0	0
Year 5 Cash Flow	281,287	202,271	61,545
CpA	181,287		163,816
IRR	30.0%		33.7%
MIRR	24.8%		25.2%

Let's have an instant replay of what you did here, first using just Property A. If some of this is starting to sound familiar, you've probably noticed that this process of computing CpA looks a great deal like what you saw for FMRR above, except instead of looking for a rate of return, you're looking for a total accumulation of cash.

In the example, you first needed to eliminate the negative cash flow of $15,000 that occurred in year 3. You did that by discounting it back at 4% per year until its discounted amount could be absorbed by an earlier positive cash flow. In this case you had to go back only one year. Negative 15,000 discounted at 4% for one year is negative 14,423, which could be absorbed by year 2's positive 15,000, leaving a net for year 3 of the difference, 577.

(If you had some amount of negative cash flow that you could not absorb into positive cash flows, you would discount the negative cash back to year 0 and add it to the initial investment amount, again as described in FMRR.)

Next you compounded each of Property A's positive cash flows forward to year 5 at the reinvestment rate of 9%. Why five years when you expect to hold the property for just four? Because you're comparing Property A with an alternative and mutually exclusive investment that you would hold for five years. So to keep the alternatives in balance, you needed to keep your end of year 4 money in play at the reinvestment rate for the same amount of time as in Property B.

When you were done, your entire accumulation was a combined negative 100,000 and positive 281,287, or 181,287.

Property B worked the same way but required one additional step: equalizing your cash commitment by investing elsewhere the $40,000 that was not needed to purchase Property B. By investing that $40,000 at the reinvestment rate, you were able to compare two investment scenarios, each requiring $100,000 of cash.

As you can see, the total capital accumulation for Property A ($181,287) is greater than that for Property B ($163,816), so Property A is your preferred choice. Interestingly enough, if you were to do an IRR on the original cash flows, you would find that Property B's IRR, with 33.7%, is greater than Property A's 30.0%, while Property B's MIRR of 25.2% wins by a nose over Property A's 24.8%.

Why might that be so? The answer should lie in one or both of the "equalizing" factors: holding period or initial investment. Perhaps, in this example, $40,000 is working harder for you when invested in Property A than invested independently if you chose Property B.

You can use the capital accumulation comparison to weigh more than two alternatives, of course; and although our focus here is on real estate, there may come a time when you'd like to consider a non–real estate option (would that be an unreal opportunity?).

Let's expand the example above to include a third possible choice. Your best friend asks you to loan him $90,000 at 12% for six years so he can invest in a chinchilla ranch. You question the wisdom of his plan, but he's itching to invest, so you agree to consider the loan, subject to a capital accumulation comparison along with the two investment properties you are currently considering.

This gives you an opportunity to practice your CpA skills a bit more because you'll need to extend your horizon for all three investment options to six years to match the term of the loan.

You start by calculating the cash flows for the six years of the loan: A loan for $90,000 at 12% for 72 months requires a monthly payment of $1,759.52, or approximately $21,114 per year.

Your three investment options stack up like this:

	Property A	Property B	Loan
Year 0 Initial Investment	(100,000)	(60,000)	(90,000)
Year 1 Cash Flow	25,000	20,000	21,114
Year 2 Cash Flow	15,000	20,000	21,114
Year 3 Cash Flow	(15,000)	(12,000)	21,114
Year 4 Cash Flow	225,000	12,000	21,114
Year 5 Cash Flow		150,000	21,114
Year 6 Cash Flow			21,114

For Properties A and B, the discounting of the negative cash flows from year 3 will be exactly the same as in the original example; the addition of a sixth year has no impact here:

	Property A		Property B	
Year 0 Initial Investment	(100,000)		(60,000)	
Year 1 Cash Flow	25,000		20,000	
Year 2 Cash Flow	15,000	(14,423)	20,000	(11,538)
Year 3 Cash Flow	(15,000)	↑	(12,000)	↑
Year 4 Cash Flow	225,000		12,000	
Year 5 Cash Flow			150,000	
Year 6 Cash Flow				

However, the compounding of positive cash flows will be different from before because, in order to compare the cash flows for the properties with that for the six-year loan, you must treat each initial cash investment as if it were kept in play for six years.

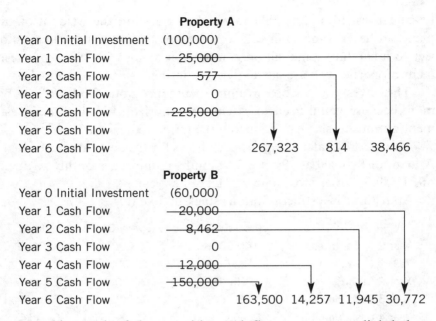

Note that each of these positive cash flows grows to a slightly larger amount than it did in the previous example, because each is being reinvested for an additional year.

Add it all up, and your capital accumulation if you hold these properties for six years instead of five looks like this:

	Property A	Property B	
Year 0 Initial Investment	(100,000)	(60,000)	(40,000)
Year 1 Cash Flow	0	0	0
Year 2 Cash Flow	0	0	0
Year 3 Cash Flow	0	0	0
Year 4 Cash Flow	0	0	0
Year 5 Cash Flow	0	0	0
Year 6 Cash Flow	306,603	220,474	67,084
CpA	206,603		187,558

Of the two real estate investments, Property A remains the preferred choice. Now you can see how you fare with the money you're lending, reinvesting the payments you receive (i.e., your positive cash flows) at 9%:

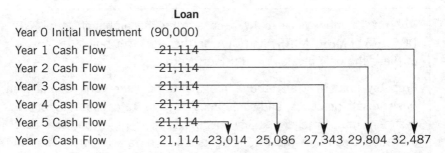

The five reinvested cash flows from years 1 through 5 combine with the year 6 amount to give you a total of $158,848 in the sixth year.

Remember that you used only $90,000 in making this loan, so you still have $10,000 left to invest. After you invest this extra cash for six years at the 9% reinvestment rate, your capital accumulation for this third option ends up as follows:

	Loan	
Year 0 Initial Investment	(90,000)	(10,000)
Year 1 Cash Flow	0	0
Year 2 Cash Flow	0	0
Year 3 Cash Flow	0	0
Year 4 Cash Flow	0	0
Year 5 Cash Flow	0	0
Year 6 Cash Flow	158,848	16,771
CpA		75,619

The CpA for this loan is clearly lower for either of the two real estate opportunities. You're going to have to find some way to tell your friend that you can't finance that chinchilla ranch.

You've come a long way from GRMs and payback periods. Now you understand how the key elements of a real estate investment interact. You understand the time value of money, the discounting of cash flows, the benefits and shortcomings of IRR, and even more advanced measures such as modified IRR and capital accumulation. Success comes to real estate investors who work the numbers to find and structure the best deals.

Rule of Thumb: We've really been stirring the alphabet soup—NPV, DCF, IRR, FMRR, MIRR, and CpA. Is there a silver bullet? Is any one of these the only measure you'll ever need?

Probably not. They all require judgments on your part—about cash flows, resale proceeds, and sometimes discount rate, safe rate, or reinvestment rate. In regard to any specific deal, you may be more confident about some of these judgments than you are about others, and that confidence—or lack of it—can influence how much you want to rely on any particular metric.

Perhaps you're evaluating a single property. Clearly, a capital accumulation comparison isn't necessary. Maybe you expect that property to enjoy robust positive cash flows. In that case, internal rate of return should do nicely. Or possibly the property will have some negative cash flows, and you would be best served by MIRR. The smart investor will understand all these techniques, consider them all, and use the one (or several) that seems best suited to the actual investment decision at hand. After all, you wouldn't keep just one kind of screwdriver or one size wrench in your basement toolbox. Do no less with your investments.

C H A P T E R 6

Case Studies: Apartment, Mixed-Use, and Triple-Net Lease

Different property types and diverse situations can conspire to present a variety of opportunities and challenges to the income-property investor. How do you sort all these out? Real-life experience always makes the best teacher, but you can also get a head start on the learning process with some guided practice using what we might call "unreal estate"—made-up case studies that allow you to work through common investment scenarios as if you were a participant in an actual transaction. Think of this as a kind of flight simulator for investors. You have already seen one such case in Chapter 4, and you've learned quite a bit about APOD forms, time value of money, net operating income, DCR, IRR, and more. Now let's work with a few additional case studies that not only can give you some further practice applying the concepts you've learned, but also can provide an introduction to some situations you haven't seen before.

Rule of Thumb: To get the most out of the examples in this chapter, we'll keep our attention on the before-tax cash flows, resale, and rates of return.

You had a healthy dose of tax calculations in the Chapter 4 case, along with a suggestion that you might be better served handing those off to your CPA while you keep your focus on the investment's metrics.

Note also that if you try working any of these examples independently and you find that you're off by a dollar or two here and there, please don't set fire to your calculator or to this book. Some computations may have extra decimals places lurking in the background, and different rounding methods can result in slightly different results.

Apartment Building Investment

For our first case, we're going to look at a property type that is fairly straightforward, at least in terms of its analysis: an apartment building. In this example, as well as in the other cases that follow, you need to step into the story, placing yourself in the deal as described.

You have already achieved substantial success in your career as the author of graphic science fiction novels and are now embarking on your new career as a real estate investor. Since this is your first venture, you feel more comfortable with the idea of owning and managing a residential property, so you have been looking exclusively at apartment buildings. A local agent has shown you a few properties, but none has excited your interest. However, there is a 16-unit building located near your home in a suburb of New York City that has caught your eye, and your attorney has told you that he has heard that the owner has an interest in selling. You decide to approach the owner directly.

The owner is indeed willing to discuss a possible sale, and so you begin your due diligence by asking him for a list of the current rents and the expenses for the past year. He provides the following:

4 studio apartments @ $1,000 per month
4 one-bedroom apartments @ $1,250 per month

4 two-bedroom apartments @ $1,500 per month
4 two-bedroom apartments, each with a second bath, @ $1,800 per month

Property taxes, $40,000 per year
Insurance, $15,000 per year
Water and sewer, $12,000 per year
Electricity for common area lighting, $2,800 per year

You confirm the rents by examining the leases, and you verify independently that the expenses are accurate as quoted.

You're able to observe that the building is brick, and the exterior appears to be in good condition. There is parking for 16 cars. You have $350,000 in cash available to invest, and your bank has said that the potential financing terms would be 80% loan-to-value, 1.20 minimum debt coverage ratio, 6.75% interest (fixed for 5 years and floating for the remaining 15 years of a 20-year term), with 1 point payable at the closing. Based on your research into recent sales and your interrogation of a local appraiser, you conclude that the current market capitalization rate for properties of this type in this neighborhood is about 9%.

You don't want to tip off that you're a beginner, and so you decide to play this really cool. Hence, you don't ask how much the owner wants for the property. You've been reading this really great book about real estate investing and financial measures, so you're confident you can do the math and come up with a price that makes sense for you.

Where to begin? Your first task is to start at the top and to compile the data about revenue, i.e., the gross scheduled income:

4 units @ 1,000 per month = 4 × 1,000 × 12 = 48,000
4 units @ 1,250 per month = 4 × 1,250 × 12 = 60,000
4 units @ 1,500 per month = 4 × 1,500 × 12 = 72,000
4 units @ 1,800 per month = 4 × 1,800 × 12 = 86,400
Gross Scheduled Income = 266,400

The seller has also provided you with information about operating expenses, so you decide that the correct approach is to take the revenue and expense data and build an Annual Property Operating Data (APOD) form. You saw such an APOD back in Chapter 2, so you have a good idea of what it should entail. Your summary looks like this:

Gross Income		266,400
less Operating Expenses		
Property Taxes	40,000	
Insurance	15,000	
Water and Sewer	12,000	
Electricity	2,800	
Total Expenses		69,800
Net Operating Income		196,600

As stated above, you've learned that the market capitalization rate for apartment buildings in this area is 9%. Armed with your income capitalization formula:

Value = Net Operating Income / Capitalization Rate

you proceed to do the math:

Value = 196,600 / 0.09

Value = 2,184,444

and conclude that the property is worth about $2.2 million.

You're ready to make an offer, right? Wrong. Really wrong.

Let's start by looking at that skeleton you called an APOD. You've made what is one of the most common mistakes committed by beginning (and sometimes even by more experienced) investors: You've focused on verifying and analyzing the information you've been provided, but you haven't thought about the information that might be missing. All the data you have in hand is indeed factually correct, but the story doesn't end there. You've made the erroneous and potentially damaging assumption that the seller or the seller's representative has told you everything you really need to know. As you will see in a moment, that can be an expensive mistake.

Let's go back and revisit the items typically listed on a generic version of an APOD form shown on the following page.

You will probably never encounter a property for which you will need to account for all the items on a laundry list such as this. However, with this apartment building, you have data for just the gross scheduled income and four operating expenses. There has to be more to the story than this.

INCOME
    Gross Scheduled Rent Income
    Other Income
TOTAL GROSS INCOME

VACANCY & CREDIT ALLOWANCE

GROSS OPERATING INCOME

EXPENSES
    Accounting
    Advertising
    Insurance (fire and liability)
    Janitorial Service
    Lawn/Snow
    Legal
    Licenses
    Miscellaneous
    Property Management
    Repairs and Maintenance
    Resident Superintendent
    Supplies
    Taxes
        Real Estate
        Personal Property
        Payroll
        Other
    Trash Removal
    Utilities
        Electricity
        Fuel Oi
        Gas
        Sewer and Water
        Telephone
        Other
TOTAL EXPENSES

NET OPERATING INCOME

Let's start again from the top. You accept the top-line revenue as correct, but do you really believe that you will never have a vacancy or a credit loss? Better if you assume at least a modest amount, say 3%.

Next look at the expenses. After you examine the previous figure and see that list of possible costs staring at you, you find it easier to put yourself inside the deal and imagine the realities of ownership. Some items now strike you as obvious:

- A 16-unit apartment building is certainly going to have a meaningful amount of repair and maintenance work every year.
- You'll surely need to hire someone to haul away the trash.
- The individual apartments, as in most such buildings, do not have separate water meters, so you'll be paying for water and sewer.

A few other items may not be so obvious, but they also require your consideration:

- Some tax accounting will be necessary, especially if, like many rental property owners, you hold title as an LLC and have to file a separate tax return.
- As the vacancy allowance implies, you're likely to have some turnover each year, so an advertising or commission expense is part of your cost of doing business.
- Apartment buildings like this one have hallways, and someone has to keep them clean; hence, janitorial service.
- Did you notice that the description said this property has 16 parking spaces and is in a suburb of New York? Think snow removal.
- There is the miscellaneous stuff that comes up whenever you own and maintain anything bigger than a breadbox: lightbulbs, furnace filters, floor mats, keys, whatever. Call them supplies.
- You hope all your legal work will be for the preparation of leases, but whatever the reason, you can probably count on some bills from your attorney each year.
- Speaking of legal work, you realize that you'll have closing costs associated with this purchase. These will include title search, title insurance, and attorney's fees. You'll plan on $10,000 to cover these costs.

It's a good thing you didn't try to make that $2.184 million offer. In addition to the 20% down payment and closing costs, you forgot that you needed to pay 1 point to close the loan. Your $350,000 would have fallen far short of what you would have needed.

One final item to think about is property management. Many owners of smaller properties ignore this cost because they handle the work themselves and have no out-of-pocket expenditure. From a budgeting perspective, that makes sense. However, right now, your purpose is to come up with a realistic number for net operating income in order to estimate the current value of the property. In that scenario, you should do what the typical appraiser would do, and that is to impute a cost for property management. Think of it this way: You may not be paying the money out to a third party (at least not at first), but your own time has a value, and that value should be included as part of the operating overhead for this investment.

It is common to pay professional property managers a percentage of collected rent, so for this example you'll assume that 5% of the gross operating income (GOI) is a fair amount to add to your APOD as the value of that service.

Now that you realize how much you don't know about this property, it's time to go back to the seller and demand more information. Much of what you need to see will be items that the seller has been paying and can account for by unveiling the property's books or tax returns. With some, like repairs and maintenance, you might be better off making your own estimates based on the actual condition of the property. As in the case you saw in Chapter 4, recent expenditures for repairs and maintenance may not always be a good indicator of the likely costs going forward.

Let's reconstruct this APOD now, based on the results of your enhanced due diligence:

INCOME	
Gross Scheduled Rent Income	266,400
TOTAL GROSS INCOME	266,400
VACANCY & CREDIT ALLOWANCE	7,992
GROSS OPERATING INCOME	258,408

EXPENSES

Accounting	2,000
Advertising	1,000
Insurance (fire and liability)	15,000
Janitorial Service	4,800
Lawn/Snow	2,400
Legal	4,000
Property Management	12,920
Repairs and Maintenance	15,000
Supplies	500
Taxes	
Real Estate	40,000
Trash Removal	10,400
Utilities	
Electricity	2,800
Sewer and Water	12,000
TOTAL EXPENSES	122,820
NET OPERATING INCOME	135,588

You are seeing a significantly lower NOI now that you have factored in a more realistic estimate of the costs of operating this property; and with that lower NOI will come a lower estimate of the current value:

Value = Net Operating Income / Capitalization Rate
Value = 135,588 / 0.09
Value = 1,506,533

That's a price difference of almost $700,000 compared with your original estimate, a serious amount by anyone's standards. In a real deal, the variance might not be quite so dramatic. For the purpose of driving home a point, we've introduced a considerable number of expense items that needed to be filled in, but even if there were only a few, the effect on your estimate of value could certainly be enough to make the difference between a successful investment and major disappointment.

You're justifiably pleased with yourself for having dodged this overpayment bullet, and you feel ready to move forward with a lower offer;

but ever the attentive student, you again recall the case study you read in Chapter 4, where you saw an analysis that looked forward into projections about future years. Why should you do that, when you've already identified the likely appraised value of the property today? That valuation is important, but it doesn't address another issue that should concern you: "I'm going to own this for more than an instant; how might this investment perform over time?"

You decide that your "Annual" Property Operating Data should, in fact, be a multiyear projection and should drive an estimate of future cash flows and potential resale.

(*An editorial note:* You would typically want your projection of long-term ownership to go out 10 or even 20 years. That would allow you to see the effects of matters like possible interest rate adjustments on your mortgage or the need for future capital improvements, and so you could test a variety of longer holding periods. To make the numbers in our examples large enough to see, however, we'll go out no more than five years. Much as John Hancock felt about King George III, we're hoping you won't need your glasses to read what we've written.)

In order to produce your multiyear APOD, you'll need to estimate how your rental revenue and operating expenses will change over time. To do this, you'll have to ratchet up your due-diligence activities once again, going beyond the property itself to look at the market wherein it sits. What has been the trend in this neighborhood for apartment rents? How have the bigger-ticket costs such as property taxes and insurance changed in recent years? After your research, you decide to project a 3% annual increase for both the income and expenses. The only exception is that you'll maintain the assumption that you'll spend 5% of GOI for property management.

Your extended APOD looks like this:

	Year 1	Year 2	Year 3	Year 4	Year 5
INCOME					
Gross Scheduled					
Rent Income	266,400	274,392	282,624	291,102	299,836
TOTAL GROSS INCOME	266,400	274,392	282,624	291,102	299,836

VACANCY & CREDIT ALLOWANCE	7,992	8,232	8,479	8,733	8,995
GROSS OPERATING INCOME	258,408	266,160	274,145	282,369	290,840
OPERATING EXPENSES					
Accounting	2,000	2,060	2,122	2,185	2,251
Advertising	1,000	1,030	1,061	1,093	1,126
Insurance (fire and liability)	15,000	15,450	15,914	16,391	16,883
Janitorial Service	4,800	4,944	5,092	5,245	5,402
Lawn/Snow	2,400	2,472	2,546	2,623	2,701
Legal	4,000	4,120	4,244	4,371	4,502
Property Management	12,920	13,308	13,707	14,118	14,542
Repairs and Maintenance	15,000	15,450	15,914	16,391	16,883
Supplies	500	515	530	546	563
Taxes					
Real Estate	40,000	41,200	42,436	43,709	45,020
Trash Removal	10,400	10,712	11,033	11,364	11,705
Utilities					
Electricity	2,800	2,884	2,971	3,060	3,151
Sewer and Water	12,000	12,360	12,731	13,113	13,506
TOTAL OPERATING EXPENSES	122,820	126,505	130,300	134,209	138,235
NET OPERATING INCOME	135,588	139,655	143,845	148,160	152,605

Your main reason for extending the APOD is to forecast your NOI into the future. Having done this, you can now also estimate a number of this property's key investment metrics, chief among them its cash flow. You saw more detailed examples of pro formas earlier in this book, but we'll keep this one simple enough to focus on the key points:

	Year 1	Year 2	Year 3	Year 4	Year 5
NET OPERATING INCOME	135,588	139,655	143,845	148,160	152,605
– Debt Service, 1st Mortgage	109,969	109,969	109,969	109,969	109,969
– Capital Additions	0	0	0	0	0
CASH FLOW BEFORE TAXES	25,619	29,686	33,876	38,191	42,636
Cash-on-Cash Return (CFBT / Cash Inv.)	7.92%	9.18%	10.48%	11.81%	13.19%
Capitalization Rate	9.00%	9.27%	9.55%	9.83%	10.13%
Debt Coverage Ratio	1.23	1.27	1.31	1.35	1.39

PROJECTED SELLING PRICE	1,506,500	1,551,700	1,598,300	1,646,200	1,695,600
– Costs of Sale	105,455	108,619	111,881	115,234	118,692
– 1st Mortgage Payoff	1,175,708	1,144,134	1,110,361	1,074,237	1,035,598
BEFORE-TAX SALE PROCEEDS	225,337	298,947	376,058	456,729	541,310
Internal Rate of Return, Before Tax	–22.39%	4.85%	13.83%	17.55%	19.25%

Let's pick this apart. The top line, net operating income, comes from the extended APOD you just completed. NOI—revenue minus vacancy minus operating expenses—accounts for most of your cash flow but not quite all. If you have a mortgage, you have to make the payments, called "debt service," out of that NOI, so they appear below the NOI line here. (Check out Calculation 28 in Part II for ways to figure the mortgage payment. Remember that you are dealing with annual amounts everywhere, so don't forget to multiply your monthly payment by 12 to get your annual debt service.)

Another item that was not part of the APOD is capital additions, or improvements to the property. Say, for example, that you had to replace the elevator in this building. That would not be an operating expense; it would have to be written off a little at a time over a number of years as a capital cost. Still, you would probably be paying for it all at once, so it would take an immediate bite out of your cash flow. You are not anticipating any such capital costs in this example, but if you did, you would want to be sure to subtract them here as part of your calculation of cash flow.

That projection of expected future cash flow is certainly one of the main reasons you're producing this pro forma. Your first concern when you look at your projections is, "Can I anticipate a positive cash flow?" You're relieved to see that the numbers are indeed strongly positive, which means you don't believe you'll have to reach into your own pocket to support this property.

	Year 1	Year 2	Year 3	Year 4	Year 5
CASH FLOW BEFORE TAXES	25,619	29,686	33,876	38,191	42,636

You know that you're expecting to buy the property at exactly the 9% market cap rate, but you're pleased to see that the relationship between your NOI and the original price gets stronger each subsequent year.

	Year 1	Year 2	Year 3	Year 4	Year 5
Capitalization Rate	9.00%	9.27%	9.55%	9.83%	10.13%

The *debt coverage ratio* (DCR) often doesn't get the amount of attention from investors that it deserves, but here again you're looking at positive news. Remember that the lender was requiring at least a 1.20 DCR in order to underwrite the mortgage. You clear that hurdle the first year, and your ratio gets stronger each subsequent year.

	Year 1	Year 2	Year 3	Year 4	Year 5
Debt Coverage Ratio	1.23	1.27	1.31	1.35	1.39

The next part of your abbreviated pro forma concerns the eventual resale of the property. As mentioned above, we're squeezing just five years of projections onto these pages, but your actual investment horizon may go out a good deal further than that. Nonetheless, you can still gather some useful insights even with this shorter forecast. Notice that your pro forma is "selling" the property every year. By using that approach, you're posing the question, "What is my overall return if I sell after one year, or after two years, or three, etc.?"

Before you look at the bottom line of this report, consider how you get there. First you need to make an estimate of the possible resale value in each of the future years. By now you're comfortable with the idea that capitalizing the NOI is a credible approach. You do need to ask yourself, however, "What cap rate should I use?" The easiest answer is that you could use the same cap rate at which you purchased the property—the so-called going-in cap rate—as a reasonable estimate of your exit cap rate.

	Year 1	Year 2	Year 3	Year 4	Year 5
PROJECTED SELLING PRICE	1,506,500	1,551,700	1,598,300	1,646,200	1,695,600

Next, you will need to recognize that you are unlikely to see a buyer parachute in, on cue, with cash in hand, when you are ready to sell. You will probably require the services of a broker and an attorney, and their fees are called "costs of sale." In this example, you will estimate 7% of the selling price to cover those costs.

	Year 1	Year 2	Year 3	Year 4	Year 5
– Costs of Sale	105,455	108,619	111,881	115,234	118,692

Since we're on the subject of transaction costs, it's important to recognize that your initial financial commitment includes more than just the down payment. The example stated that you needed to pay 1 point to the lender (1% of the amount of the mortgage). You probably need to obtain title insurance, as well as the assistance of a lawyer or title agent to close the purchase. Your initial investment in this deal must take these costs into account so that your return-on-investment calculations will be meaningful.

You now have a picture of the complete income stream, which includes the year-by-year cash flows and the final sale proceeds. From those, along with your initial cash investment, you can calculate the internal rate of return. (See Chapter 5 for more about IRR.) How does it look?

	Year 1	Year 2	Year 3	Year 4	Year 5
Internal Rate of Return, Before Tax	−22.39%	4.85%	13.83%	17.55%	19.25%

If you sell at the end of the first year, your return is negative. Is that a deal killer? Probably not. Keep in mind that the property has not had much of an opportunity to grow in value in just one year, and you will have to absorb both the costs of acquisition (closing fees, loan point) and the costs of resale before you have even had a chance to learn the correct zip code for this building. Too much overhead, too little time.

The second year is better, though not great. By the time you get to the third year, it's starting to look promising, and by the fourth you are seeing the kind of high-teens IRR that apartment investors tend to like.

Since you're a prudent investor, however, you won't settle for an analysis with just one pass. You will ask yourself, "Do I think there is any reason why the market in this location might get stronger or weaker in coming years?" Then you will rerun your projections with exit cap rates that are above and below the rate at which you bought the property. Are you still OK with the results?

If you must resell at a 9.5% cap rate:

	Year 1	Year 2	Year 3	Year 4	Year 5
Internal Rate of Return, Before Tax	−45.20%	−7.54%	6.68%	13.02%	16.17%

If you can resell at an 8.5% cap rate:

	Year 1	Year 2	Year 3	Year 4	Year 5
Internal Rate of Return, Before Tax	3.09%	17.12%	20.84%	22.03%	22.33%

Clearly, you'll sell for a higher price with the lower exit cap rate, and therefore your overall return will improve. The higher exit cap rate means you'll sell for a lower price and see a lower overall return. The numbers here suggest that the return should improve steadily, even with the high exit cap rate, if you are prepared to hang in for a longer time. No amount of math can make that personal decision for you, but your pro forma can at least give you a reasonable sense of the kind of returns you might achieve over a range of holding periods and exit cap rates.

> **Rule of Thumb:** Don't assume that the information provided by the seller or broker is complete, even if the figures you do receive are, themselves, accurate. An overestimation of revenue or an underestimation of expenses can result in a dramatic skewing of your opinion of a property's value.

> **Rule of Thumb:** There is a second moral to our story: It is wise not to wrap up your analysis of a property's suitability as an investment with just a value estimate based on capitalization of the NOI. That capitalization is a key step, but it looks at a property at a point in time. In all likelihood, you intend to own and operate that property well beyond that point in time, so you need to make projections about how it might perform over the long haul. What will the overall return look like over time if market cap rates change, if you have to lose rental income while you remodel some of the units, if your adjustable-rate mortgage spikes after the fifth year, if the roof needs replacing during your intended holding period? Such events can affect your long-term return. You need to factor in possibilities like these when you consider what purchase price makes good sense to you—not just what is the appraised value today, but what adjustment, if any, you need to make in your offering price to account for the possibility of future adverse circumstances.

Mixed-Use Property

Perhaps you're ready now to go outside your comfort zone and start dealing with commercial tenants. One way to make that transition is with a mixed-use property. As its name implies, this type combines both residential and nonresidential units. The retail uses in this example will give you an opportunity to learn about some important new topics. Here's the deal:

This building has two retail spaces on the ground level and 16 apartments on the four floors above. The total rentable area of the structure is 50,000 square feet.

Retail Tenants

A regional bank occupies 7,500 square feet and currently pays $30 per square foot per year. The bank is now in the third year of a 10-year lease ("now" = year 1 of your analysis); the rent will step up to $36 per square foot at the beginning of the fifth year of the lease. In addition to the base rent, the bank pays a pro rata share of property taxes in excess of $30,000 and of insurance expense in excess of $10,000. (*Note:* By "pro rata share" we mean a share based on the size of the bank's space compared with the total rentable area of the building.)

A restaurant occupies 2,500 square feet, paying $32 per square foot per year. This tenant is in the last year of a four-year lease and has an option to renew at $38 per square foot at the end of that term. The restaurant also pays a pro rata share of property taxes in excess of $30,000 and of insurance expense in excess of $10,000. As a restaurant, it is best known for its exceedingly small portions and its surly wait staff.

Residential Tenants

In the interests of simplicity—and so you don't have to compute yet another residential rent roll—we will take the same 16 apartment units from the last problem, lift them with a huge crane, and place them gently on top of those street-level retail units. Hence, you will have the same residential gross scheduled income of $266,400 in the first year and the same 3% annual rate of increase for subsequent years that you saw in the apartment case study.

Also from the previous case, you learned your lesson about relying on property data supplied by the seller, and so you have done your due diligence quite thoroughly this time. You expect the first-year operating expenses to look like this:

Accounting	4,000
Advertising	5,000
Electricity (common areas)	5,000
Insurance (fire and liability)	16,000
Janitorial Service	4,800
Lawn/Snow	2,000
Legal	5,000
Property Management	5% of Gross Operating Income
Repairs and Maintenance	22,000
Sewer and Water	14,000
Supplies	1,000
Taxes	
Real Estate	50,000
Trash Removal	24,000

You anticipate each of these expenses to rise at 3% annually, except for property management, which will always float at 5% of the gross operating income. You should recognize that you could forecast different rates of increase for different expenses if you find reason to believe that such would be appropriate. For example, your analysis of the market might lead you to expect steeper increases for property taxes and insurance or more modest hikes for some other expenses. In this case, however, your research has made you comfortable with an across-the-board 3%.

You've spoken to a lender and have found that financing is available at 80% loan to value for 20 years, with interest at 7% for the first five years. After that time, the rate will become adjustable. The loan requires a debt coverage ratio of at least 1.25 and payment of 1 point. You will also pay $12,000 in closing costs related to the purchase.

Your search of recent transactions shows that similar properties in this location have sold at a 9.5% capitalization rate.

The owner has listed the property for sale at $4.25 million.

As in the previous case, and as with any income-and-expense statement, you want to start at the top with the revenue. You are using the same rent roll as in the apartment case, so you know that the gross scheduled income from the residential units is $266,400 in the first year, increasing annually at 3%. Next you need to determine the revenue from the retail units. That may prove to be a bit trickier. Let's start with the base rent:

The bank occupies 7,500 square feet and pays $30 per square foot per year in the first year.

7,500 × 30.00 = 225,000

The bank is now in the third year of a 10-year lease, and its rent will step up to $36 per square foot at the beginning of the fifth year of the lease, i.e., two years from now.

7,500 × 36.00 = 270,000

Once again, for the sake of readability, we confine ourselves to a five-year projection:

	Year 1	Year 2	Year 3	Year 4	Year 5
Bank, Base Rent	225,000	225,000	270,000	270,000	270,000

The restaurant occupies 2,500 square feet and pays $32 per square foot per year in the first year.

2,500 × 32.00 = 80,000

If the restaurant exercises its option to renew at $38 per square foot next year, its rent will increase to $95,000.

2,500 × 38.00 = 95,000

	Year 1	Year 2	Year 3	Year 4	Year 5
Restaurant, Base Rent	80,000	95,000	95,000	95,000	95,000

So far, so simple; but recall that both of these retail tenants must also pay a pro rata share of property taxes in excess of $30,000 and of insurance expense in excess of $10,000. You have just struck a mother lode of new terminology and concepts, all having to do with commercial leasing—so what we have here is (by design) a teachable moment. Let's deal with the vocabulary first and then do the math.

The arrangement by which a commercial tenant pays all or part of certain operating expenses goes by any of several names, including expense recoveries, expense reimbursements, or pass-through expenses. These terms are synonymous, and they mean that some or all of a property's operating costs are going to be borne by the tenants. The details of each tenant's obligation to pay are defined in that tenant's lease. What expenses are typically "recoverable," i.e., passed on to the tenant? Property taxes and insurance are among the most customary. If a building has areas that are shared by all tenants or used by the public when they engage with tenants—areas such as lobbies, hallways, elevators, restrooms, parking lots—then the landlord may choose to pass on the cost of their upkeep in the form of "common area maintenance."

When you think about common area maintenance, you also have to keep in mind the notion of "rentable square area" (or rentable square feet). If the property's layout does, in fact, include common areas, then the leases may define each tenant's rentable area as including not just the space physically occupied by the tenant (its "usable area") but also a portion of the common area. The landlord is not being arbitrary in doing so. In order to be able to provide usable space for tenants in a shopping center, the owner may also have to provide lobbies, walkways, elevators, and restrooms. These common areas don't generate income to the owner, but they do spawn maintenance costs. (See Calculation 37 for more about building measurements.)

Rule of Thumb: As the landlord, you should never expect your tenants to pay a recoverable expense directly to the party to whom it is owed. You should pay the expense yourself and then bill the tenant for reimbursement. Why is this important? Just imagine these nightmare scenarios: Your tenant was obligated to pay the cost of fire and liability insurance but fails to do so in a timely manner. A fire or accident occurs. You may have no insurance when you need it most. Similarly, the tenant fails to pay the property tax as agreed. Who is going to face the penalty charges, the threat of a tax lien, and the bad publicity? You are. The proper way to handle expense recoveries is to specify in the lease that you will provide the tenant with an invoice and documentation of the amounts due on some specific schedule—monthly, quarterly, semiannually, annually—and that the failure to pay you, the landlord, as agreed will put the tenant in default of its lease.

The most common way of allocating recoverable expenses is as you've seen described in this problem, which is according to the tenant's pro rata share of total rentable space. In this case, the bank occupies 15% of the 50,000 square foot total, and the restaurant occupies 5%. However, the landlord and tenant can agree to any formula that suits them (provided, of course, that they do not agree to anything that is contrary to law). For example, the tenants could have agreed to reimburse based on their relative occupancy of just the commercial space (75% for the bank and 25% for the restaurant). The proportions are the same, but the actual dollar amounts reimbursed would be much greater if based like this, solely on the commercial space.

Likewise, the parties do not necessarily have to agree that the entire amount of an expense will be passed on to tenants. Recall that this case study says the tenants will pay a share of property taxes in excess of $30,000. That $30,000 actually has a name. It is called an "expense stop." An expense stop is an amount at which the parties have agreed that the landlord's obligation to pay a particular expense will stop and the tenants' obligation to reimburse will begin.

A common variation of this theme is the base-year expense stop. In that situation, the amount of the stop is not predetermined in the lease. The landlord agrees to pay the full amount of certain expenses in the first year (the "base year"). That amount becomes the base-year expense stop, and the tenant agrees to pay each year thereafter the excess over the base-year amount. It sounds reasonable enough, but tenants are sometimes reluctant to enter into this kind of arrangement. They may prefer an explicitly predefined expense stop, rather than a base-year stop, fearing that the landlord might juggle the timing of base-year expense payments so as to make the base-year stop artificially low.

It has taken us a while to get to the next calculation, but now we're ready. What is the amount of expense recovery that each tenant will pay?

The insurance expense for the first year is $16,000. That's $6,000 over the $10,000 expense stop for insurance, so each tenant must pay a percentage of that $6,000. The property tax expense for the first year is $50,000. That's $20,000 over the expense stop for taxes, so each tenant must pay a percentage of that 20,000.

Since the bank occupies 7,500 of the 50,000 total rentable square feet, it must pay 15% of the excess for each expense:

Bank

Insurance reimbursement	$(16{,}000 - 10{,}000) \times 0.15 = 900$
Property tax reimbursement	$(50{,}000 - 30{,}000) \times 0.15 = 3{,}000$
Total reimbursements	3,900

The restaurant occupies 2,500 square feet, or 5% of the space.

Restaurant

Insurance reimbursement	$(16{,}000 - 10{,}000) \times 0.05 = 300$
Property tax reimbursement	$(50{,}000 - 30{,}000) \times 0.05 = 1{,}000$
Total reimbursements	1,300

Total reimbursements from bank and restaurant, year 1	$5,200

That takes care of the first year, but you will not be able to estimate the recovery amounts for future years until you first estimate the expenses for those years. Sounds like a job for the extended APOD. Let's look at just the two expenses that are reimbursable. Each grows at 3% per year.

	Year 1	Year 2	Year 3	Year 4	Year 5
Insurance (fire and liability)	16,000	16,480	16,974	17,483	18,007
Taxes, Real Estate	50,000	51,500	53,045	54,636	56,275

For each subsequent year, you need to do the same as you just did for the first year: apply the recovery percentages (15% for the bank, 5% for the restaurant) to the insurance cost in excess of $10,000 and to the property tax in excess of $50,000. When you do so, you arrive at these totals:

	Year 1	Year 2	Year 3	Year 4	Year 5
Bank, Insurance Pass-Through	900	972	1,046	1,123	1,201
Bank, Tax Pass-Through	3,000	3,225	3,457	3,695	3,941
Bank Total	3,900	4,197	4,503	4,818	5,142
Restaurant, Insurance Pass-Through	300	324	349	374	400
Restaurant, Tax Pass-Through	1,000	1,075	1,152	1,232	1,314
Restaurant Total	1,300	1,399	1,501	1,606	1,714
Total Expense Recoveries	5,200	5,596	6,004	6,424	6,856

Note that the total amount passed through does not equal the total amount in excess of the "stop." That's because *only* the commercial tenants are paying a share—15% and 5%, respectively—of the recoverable expenses.

> **Rule of Thumb:** You realize that you have not dealt with expense recoveries before, and you are not entirely sure how to account for them. Should you treat them as negative expenses, i.e., as offsets to the cost of the expense items, or as income? The industry standard is to treat them as income. The proper and clearest method of presentation is to show, as an expense, the full amount that the owner is actually responsible for paying, and to show, as a separate revenue line, the amount that the tenant is obligated to pay to the landlord as "additional rent," which is the way such reimbursements are typically characterized in a commercial lease.

It's time to return to your extended APOD in earnest and to pull all this together:

	Year 1	Year 2	Year 3	Year 4	Year 5
INCOME					
Commercial Income					
Total Base Rent	305,000	320,000	365,000	365,000	365,000
Expense Recoveries	5,200	5,596	6,004	6,424	6,856
Total Commercial Income	310,200	325,596	371,004	371,424	371,856
Total Residential Income	266,400	274,392	282,624	291,103	299,836
TOTAL GROSS INCOME	576,600	599,988	653,628	662,527	671,692
VACANCY & CREDIT					
ALLOWANCE	17,298	18,000	19,609	19,876	20,151
GROSS OPERATING INCOME	559,302	581,988	634,019	642,651	651,541
OPERATING EXPENSES					
Accounting	4,000	4,120	4,244	4,371	4,502
Advertising	5,000	5,150	5,305	5,464	5,628
Insurance (fire and liability)	16,000	16,480	16,974	17,483	18,007
Janitorial Service	4,800	4,944	5,092	5,245	5,402
Lawn/Snow	2,000	2,060	2,122	2,186	2,252
Legal	5,000	5,150	5,305	5,464	5,628

Property Management	27,965	29,099	31,701	32,133	32,577
Repairs and Maintenance	22,000	22,660	23,340	24,040	24,761
Supplies	1,000	1,030	1,061	1,093	1,126
Taxes					
Real Estate	50,000	51,500	53,045	54,636	56,275
Trash Removal	24,000	24,720	25,462	26,226	27,013
Utilities					
Electricity	5,000	5,150	5,305	5,464	5,628
Sewer and Water	14,000	14,420	14,853	15,299	15,758
TOTAL OPERATING EXPENSES	180,765	186,483	193,809	199,104	204,557
NET OPERATING INCOME	378,537	395,505	440,210	443,547	446,984

Anything that can make your presentation clear and easy to understand is a good thing. Since this a mixed-use property, you decided that it would be useful to distinguish between the commercial and residential sources of revenue. Also, within the commercial, you distinguish between the base rent and the expense recovery revenue. Note that you have applied the vacancy and credit allowance to the total gross income, including the expense recoveries. If you lose the tenant, you will also lose the recovery. Likewise, you have applied the 5% property management fee to the total gross operating income, including the recoveries.

Now that you have your NOI, you can run your first test of this investment. The market cap rate is 9.5%, and the asking price is $4.25 million. Does that price sound right? You know the drill:

Value = Net Operating Income / Capitalization Rate

Value = 378,537 / 0.095

Value = 3,984,600

Given the benefit of rounding, it looks like this property might appraise closer to $4 million, not $4.25 million. You'll produce a pro forma assuming a $4 million purchase price. Since this is mixed-use property, you'll add some additional detail so that any reader of your report will have a clear understanding of the various sources of revenue:

	Year 1	Year 2	Year 3	Year 4	Year 5
INCOME					
Commercial Income					
Total Base Rent	305,000	320,000	365,000	365,000	365,000
Expense Recoveries	5,200	5,596	6,004	6,424	6,856
Total Commercial Income	310,200	325,596	371,004	371,424	371,856
Total Residential Income	266,400	274,392	282,624	291,103	299,836
TOTAL GROSS INCOME	576,600	599,988	653,628	662,527	671,692
– VACANCY & CREDIT ALLOWANCE	17,298	18,000	19,609	19,876	20,151
GROSS OPERATING INCOME	559,302	581,988	634,019	642,651	651,541
– OPERATING EXPENSES	180,765	186,483	193,809	199,104	204,557
NET OPERATING INCOME	378,537	395,505	440,210	443,547	446,984
– Debt Service, 1st Mortgage	297,715	297,715	297,715	297,715	297,715
– Capital Additions	0	0	0	0	0
CASH FLOW BEFORE TAXES	80,822	97,790	142,495	145,832	149,269
Cash-on-Cash Return (CFBT / Cash Inv.)	9.58%	11.59%	16.88%	17.28%	17.69%
Capitalization Rate	9.46%	9.89%	11.01%	11.09%	11.17%
Debt Coverage Ratio	1.27	1.33	1.48	1.49	1.50
PROJECTED SELLING PRICE	3,984,600	4,163,200	4,633,800	4,668,900	4,705,100
– Costs of Sale	278,922	291,424	324,366	326,823	329,357
– 1st Mortgage Payoff	3,123,874	3,042,244	2,954,713	2,860,855	2,760,212
BEFORE-TAX SALE PROCEEDS	581,804	829,532	1,354,721	1,481,222	1,615,531
Internal Rate of Return, Before Tax	–21.49%	9.72%	27.60%	25.94%	24.80%

How do these projections look to you? Your eyes move immediately to the cash flow row, and you're pleased to see that the amounts estimated there are healthy and growing. You check out the debt coverage ratio and can see that you've cleared the 1.25 hurdle required by your lender. As in the apartment example, your first-year IRR is negative, but by the third year it is quite strong and stays that way for the remainder of your forecast.

This appears to be a solid investment opportunity if purchased at $4 million. You are so pleased with yourself for finding it that you decide to celebrate by treating yourself to dinner at the restaurant on the ground floor. At some point about halfway through your entrée, reality comes crashing down on you. The only thing worse than the service in this place is the food. You look around and observe that there is only one other patron. You now realize that this business is terminal. It's hanging on by a pastry hook. It's not going to renew its lease next year; or if it does, it will surely go bankrupt before the lease runs out.

In other words, you need to make substantial revisions to the projections you just made about this property's future income stream. You have four issues to address:

1. Can you still get a rental rate of $38 per square foot, plus pass-throughs, with a new tenant? You decide yes, that is still a realistic rent.
2. It generally takes longer to find a tenant for retail space than for an apartment. You're going to assume six months of vacancy at the beginning of year 2.
3. You expect to need the services of a commercial leasing broker to find that new tenant. After a bit of give-and-take, you negotiate a commission rate of 4% of the total rent for the term of the lease.
4. It is unlikely that a new tenant will want to operate using the décor of a failed restaurant. You're probably going to need to make some sort of concession to the new tenant regarding fit-up of the space. The two most likely options are that you'll have to offer several months' free rent while the new tenant remodels or you'll have to give a tenant improvement (TI) allowance. You opt to give the tenant $20 per square foot toward improvements.

You decide, wisely, to skip dessert and proceed directly to your office to rebuild your pro forma. Year 2 is going to look much different now. With six months of vacancy, you will collect only half the base rent and half the expense reimbursements you had previously anticipated from the restaurant.

	Year 1	Year 2	Year 3	Year 4	Year 5
Restaurant, Base Rent	80,000	47,500	95,000	95,000	95,000
Restaurant, Pass-Through	1,300	700	1,501	1,606	1,714

You are also going to have to pay that leasing commission. Let's assume that you sign up the next tenant for five years at a flat $38 per square foot and that the commission is charged only on the base rent:

$38/sf per year × 2,500 sf × 5 years × 4% commission = $19,000

You also agreed to spot the new tenant $20 per square foot as a TI allowance:

2,500 sf × $20 = $50,000

Your pro forma now looks like this:

	Year 1	Year 2	Year 3	Year 4	Year 5
INCOME					
Commercial Income					
Total Base Rent	305,000	272,500	365,000	365,000	365,000
Expense Recoveries	5,200	4,896	6,004	6,424	6,856
Total Commercial Income	310,200	277,396	371,004	371,424	371,856
Total Residential Income	266,400	274,392	282,624	291,103	299,836
TOTAL GROSS INCOME	576,600	551,788	653,628	662,527	671,692
– VACANCY & CREDIT ALLOWANCE	17,298	16,554	19,609	19,876	20,151
GROSS OPERATING INCOME	559,302	535,234	634,019	642,651	651,541
– OPERATING EXPENSES	180,765	184,146	193,809	199,104	204,557
NET OPERATING INCOME	378,537	351,088	440,210	443,547	446,984
– Debt Service, 1st Mortgage	297,715	297,715	297,715	297,715	297,715
– Capital Additions	0	0	0	0	0
– Leasing Commissions	0	19,000	0	0	0
– Tenant Improvements	0	50,000	0	0	0
CASH FLOW BEFORE TAXES	80,822	–15,627	142,495	145,832	149,269
Cash-on-Cash Return (CFBT / Cash Inv.)	9.82%	–1.90%	17.31%	17.72%	18.13%

Capitalization Rate	9.46%	8.78%	11.01%	11.09%	11.17%
Debt Coverage Ratio	1.27	1.18	1.48	1.49	1.50
PROJECTED SELLING PRICE	3,984,600	3,695,700	4,633,800	4,668,900	4,705,100
– Costs of Sale	278,922	258,699	324,366	326,823	329,357
– 1st Mortgage Payoff	3,123,874	3,042,244	2,954,713	2,860,855	2,760,212
BEFORE-TAX SALE PROCEEDS	581,804	394,757	1,354,721	1,481,222	1,615,531
Internal Rate of Return, Before Tax	–21.49%	–28.02%	23.81%	22.95%	22.29%

Rule of Thumb: "Cap rate" is a metric that's attached to a point in time, and its meaning can get a bit fuzzy when you're talking about some time after your purchase of the property. When you think about cap rate as part of a transaction rather than part of an appraisal, you typically translate "value" to mean "purchase price," i.e., the actual rather than the potential price. If you puzzled over the calculation of the cap rate in year 2 of this example, it's because we added the tenant improvements to the purchase price before we divided it into the NOI. Think of it this way: You first bought the land and building as a capital asset; then you bought the capital improvements as an addition to that asset. Hence, the sum of the two becomes your total purchase price for the asset when you weigh it against the income it produces in a given year.

Your attention goes immediately to the cash flow line, where you look for the year 2 results. You are dismayed to see a negative $15,627. That's about $113,000 less than you were expecting if no vacancy had occurred. Of course, the reason you have a negative cash flow is that you are not only losing revenue from the vacant restaurant space, but also spending extra money for a leasing commission and tenant improvements. A negative cash flow really means that you have to make up the difference out of your own pocket. You look at your IRR and see that it too looks dismal in the second year. The good news is that it bounces back in year 3, assuming, of course, that you do indeed successfully re-lease the restaurant.

The likelihood of losing a tenant motivates you to test a lower price, $3.8 million; you rerun your numbers:

	Year 1	Year 2	Year 3	Year 4	Year 5
INCOME					
Commercial Income					
Total Base Rent	305,000	272,500	365,000	365,000	365,000
Expense Recoveries	5,200	4,896	6,004	6,424	6,856
Total Commercial Income	310,200	277,396	371,004	371,424	371,856
Total Residential Income	266,400	274,392	282,624	291,103	299,836
TOTAL GROSS INCOME	576,600	551,788	653,628	662,527	671,692
− VACANCY & CREDIT ALLOWANCE	17,298	16,554	19,609	19,876	20,151
GROSS OPERATING INCOME	559,302	535,234	634,019	642,651	651,541
− OPERATING EXPENSES	180,765	184,146	193,809	199,104	204,557
NET OPERATING INCOME	378,537	351,088	440,210	443,547	446,984
− Debt Service, 1st Mortgage	282,829	282,829	282,829	282,829	282,829
− Capital Additions	0	0	0	0	0
− Leasing Commissions	0	19,000	0	0	0
− Tenant Improvements	0	50,000	0	0	0
CASH FLOW BEFORE TAXES	95,708	−741	157,381	160,718	164,155
Cash-on-Cash Return (CFBT / Cash Inv.)	11.93%	−0.09%	19.61%	20.03%	20.46%
Capitalization Rate	9.96%	9.12%	11.43%	11.52%	11.61%
Debt Coverage Ratio	1.34	1.24	1.56	1.57	1.58
PROJECTED SELLING PRICE	3,984,600	3,695,700	4,633,800	4,668,900	4,705,100
− Costs of Sale	278,922	258,699	324,366	326,823	329,357
− 1st Mortgage Payoff	2,967,680	2,890,132	2,806,978	2,717,812	2,622,201
BEFORE-TAX SALE PROCEEDS	737,998	546,869	1,502,456	1,624,265	1,753,542
Internal Rate of Return, Before Tax	3.90%	−11.32%	31.49%	28.52%	26.69%

You find that the lower price means you can close the deal with a smaller mortgage, and the resulting lower debt service just about wipes out your negative cash flow. Now you're only $741 in the hole in year 2. You won't worry about the DCR of 1.24 in year 2. It's only 0.01 below the threshold; and, besides, you already have the mortgage by then. Your IRR in the second year looks a little less painful as well, coming in now at a still-negative −11.32%, while subsequent sale years remain strong in the mid-20s and as high as 31%. You decide that the potential for tenant loss means this property presents a higher risk than you originally thought, and so you will press your case for a price of $3.8 million.

> **Rule of Thumb:** When you pause to reflect on your analysis of this transaction, you realize that an estimate of value based solely on capitalizing the first year's net operating income would have missed the risk posed by the failing tenant. You might have been happy to go ahead at $4 million because that income capitalization process looks at the property at a point in time—namely, the present—and doesn't lead you to think about what might be lurking down the road. A better strategy is to combine that capitalization with the kind of multiyear pro forma we have been looking at here and also to remember to look beyond the numbers as presented and to seek out the story behind the story.

Triple-Net Lease

Now that you have some experience with commercial tenancies, perhaps you would like to look into a specialization: the *triple-net lease*, aka NNN. This scenario is a variation of what you saw with the retail portion of the mixed-use property.

What exactly is a triple-net lease? It is a lease where the tenant agrees to pay (in addition to its base rent) the net taxes, insurance, and maintenance costs. Those are the three "nets" in "triple net." The tenant will pay for all repairs and maintenance to its own space, and if that space is part of a multitenant property such as a shopping center, the tenant will also pay its pro rata share of common area maintenance. Utility costs are usually metered separately and paid directly by the tenant, so this lease structure effectively insulates the owner from virtually all the costs of operating the property.

Technically, any rental could be triple net, but owners use this type of lease most commonly with single-tenant, freestanding commercial properties. Let's take a look at an example:

You are considering the purchase of a single freestanding building occupied by a pharmacy. The building has 10,000 rentable square feet on one level. The pharmacy is part of a national chain. The parent company guarantees the lease, which is currently at $36 per square foot and has 13 years left to run. There is an escalation clause that increases the base rent 6% every three years. The next such escalation will occur three years from now, i.e., in year 4 of your analysis.

The tenant is responsible for all interior and exterior maintenance and repairs, snow removal, sewer and water charges, trash removal, and exterior lighting. The tenant will arrange for those services and utilities and pay the charges directly.

The tenant will reimburse you for 100% of the insurance premium and property taxes paid by you. The year 1 amounts are as follows, and you expect them to increase by 3% per year:

Insurance (fire and liability)	12,000
Property Taxes	55,000

You expect to pay $5,000 for accounting and bookkeeping services and will budget $2,000 per year for legal services. You assume that each of these costs will rise about 3% annually. The tenant is not responsible for these expenses.

You have $2 million in cash to invest and can obtain financing for 15 years at 5.0%, with a maximum 65% loan-to-value ratio. The lender requires a debt coverage ratio of at least 1.25 and payment of 1 point to obtain the loan. You will spend about $12,000 on legal costs to close the transaction.

Your search of recent transactions shows that other freestanding single-use properties in this area have sold recently at a 7% capitalization rate. The owner has listed the property for sale at $5.5 million.

You've gained enough experience analyzing income properties that you can get right down to business. You'll first build an extended APOD and then create a cash flow and resale pro forma.

The revenue portion of your APOD will display the base rent and expense reimbursements. The base will start at $36 per square foot per year times 10,000 square feet, or $360,000. This amount will continue until year 4, when a 6% step-up occurs, making the new base rent $381,600. The reimbursements will start off as the sum of the insurance and tax expenses ($12,000 and $55,000, respectively), with each increasing 3% per year. As a triple-net tenant, the pharmacy will pay directly for any repairs, maintenance, and utilities, so your projection of gross scheduled income looks like this:

	Year 1	Year 2	Year 3	Year 4	Year 5
Base Rent	360,000	360,000	360,000	381,600	381,600
Insurance Pass-Through	12,000	12,360	12,731	13,113	13,506
Tax Pass-Through	55,000	56,650	58,350	60,101	61,904
	427,000	429,010	431,081	454,814	457,010

Now you can build the rest of your APOD. You know that you have budgeted $5,000 for bookkeeping and accounting, as well as $2,000 for legal services, with each growing at 3% per year. However, you decide to plug in two more items because you know the bank's appraiser will get testy if they are omitted. You add a 2% allowance for vacancy and credit loss and put in an expense for property management equal to 3% of GOI. Since you have a high-quality tenant on a long-term lease, you don't really expect that you'll have to deal with either vacancy or management concerns; but you know your lender expects to see them in the appraisal, so you decide to include them in your analysis.

Your five-year APOD looks like this:

	Year 1	Year 2	Year 3	Year 4	Year 5
INCOME					
Commercial Income					
Total Base Rent	360,000	360,000	360,000	381,600	381,600
Expense Recoveries	67,000	69,010	71,081	73,214	75,410
Total Commercial Income	427,000	429,010	431,081	454,814	457,010
TOTAL GROSS INCOME	427,000	429,010	431,081	454,814	457,010
VACANCY & CREDIT ALLOWANCE	8,540	8,580	8,622	9,096	9,140
GROSS OPERATING INCOME	418,460	420,430	422,459	445,718	447,870
OPERATING EXPENSES					
Accounting	5,000	5,150	5,305	5,464	5,628
Insurance (fire and liability)	12,000	12,360	12,731	13,113	13,506
Legal	2,000	2,060	2,122	2,186	2,252
Property Management	12,554	12,613	12,674	13,372	13,436

Taxes

Real Estate	55,000	56,650	58,350	60,101	61,904
TOTAL OPERATING EXPENSES	86,554	88,833	91,182	94,236	96,726
NET OPERATING INCOME	331,906	331,597	331,277	351,482	351,144

You can divide the first-year NOI by the prevailing market cap rate of 7% to see how the lender's appraiser might value the property:

331,906 / 0.07 = 4,741,514   Rounded = $4.75 million

It comes as no surprise that the seller wants to get more than you would consider a fair price, but $750,000 seems like an awfully big spread. You decide to take your analysis to the next step and to build a pro forma based on your estimate of $4.75 million.

	Year 1	Year 2	Year 3	Year 4	Year 5
INCOME					
Commercial Income					
Total Base Rent	360,000	360,000	360,000	381,600	381,600
Expense Recoveries	67,000	69,010	71,081	73,214	75,410
Total Commercial Income	427,000	429,010	431,081	454,814	457,010
TOTAL GROSS INCOME	427,000	429,010	431,081	454,814	457,010
− VACANCY & CREDIT ALLOWANCE	8,540	8,580	8,622	9,096	9,140
GROSS OPERATING INCOME	418,460	420,430	422,459	445,718	447,870
− OPERATING EXPENSES	86,554	88,833	91,182	94,236	96,726
NET OPERATING INCOME	331,906	331,597	331,277	351,482	351,144
− Debt Service, 1st Mortgage	292,989	292,989	292,989	292,989	292,989
CASH FLOW BEFORE TAXES	38,917	38,608	38,288	58,493	58,155
Cash-on-Cash Return (CFBT / Cash Inv.)	2.28%	2.26%	2.25%	3.43%	3.41%
Capitalization Rate	6.99%	6.98%	6.97%	7.40%	7.39%
Debt Coverage Ratio	1.13	1.13	1.13	1.20	1.20
PROJECTED SELLING PRICE	4,741,500	4,737,100	4,732,500	5,021,200	5,016,300
− Costs of Sale	331,905	331,597	331,275	351,484	351,141
− 1st Mortgage Payoff	2,945,665	2,796,573	2,639,853	2,475,116	2,301,950
BEFORE-TAX SALE PROCEEDS	1,463,930	1,608,930	1,761,372	2,194,600	2,363,209
Internal Rate of Return, Before Tax	−11.88%	−0.56%	3.32%	8.81%	9.10%

As in the previous cases, your initial focus moves to the cash flow line. Here you see that the cash flow is positive, but the 2.28% cash-on-cash in the first year does not suggest a particularly robust return. The debt coverage ratio grabs your attention next, and you find that number especially disconcerting. At 1.13, it falls far short of the 1.25 that the lender requires. That means you are unlikely to secure the mortgage financing you plan to apply for: 65% of $4,750,000 ($3,087,500), 5% interest, 15-year term. You revisit this loan with your lender. Would the lender perhaps consider a longer term, thus reducing the debt service? No. How about a lower interest rate or simply a lower DCR requirement? No and no. Dead end. What else can you do?

You take a look at the amount of cash required to close the deal as you've structured it so far: 65% LTV equates to a 35% down payment of $1,662,500 and loan amount of $3,087,500. You have to pay 1 point to secure the loan, so that equals $30,875. Your closing costs are $12,000, so in total you need $1,705,375. You realize that you have $2 million available to invest. What if you put all of it into the deal? Then you would have a smaller mortgage and lower debt service—and even your one loan point will be slightly less. To clarify this in your own mind, you construct a simple "sources and uses of funds" table:

Sources		Uses	
Cash Investment	2,000,000	Purchase Price	4,750,000
1st Mortgage	2,789,899	Loan Point	27,899
		Closing Costs	12,000
	4,789,899		4,789,899

Next you rebuild your cash flow and resale pro forma to see if this larger down payment resolves your DCR concern:

	Year 1	Year 2	Year 3	Year 4	Year 5
INCOME					
Commercial Income					
Total Base Rent	360,000	360,000	360,000	381,600	381,600
Expense Recoveries	67,000	69,010	71,081	73,214	75,410
Total Commercial Income	427,000	429,010	431,081	454,814	457,010
TOTAL GROSS INCOME	427,000	429,010	431,081	454,814	457,010
– VACANCY & CREDIT ALLOWANCE	8,540	8,580	8,622	9,096	9,140

GROSS OPERATING INCOME	418,460	420,430	422,459	445,718	447,870
– OPERATING EXPENSES	86,554	88,833	91,182	94,236	96,726
NET OPERATING INCOME	331,906	331,597	331,277	351,482	351,144
– Debt Service, 1st Mortgage	264,748	264,748	264,748	264,748	264,748
CASH FLOW BEFORE TAXES	67,158	66,849	66,529	86,734	86,396
Cash-on-Cash Return (CFBT / Cash Inv.)	3.36%	3.34%	3.33%	4.34%	4.32%
Capitalization Rate	6.99%	6.98%	6.97%	7.40%	7.39%
Debt Coverage Ratio	1.25	1.25	1.25	1.33	1.33
PROJECTED SELLING PRICE	4,741,500	4,737,100	4,732,500	5,021,200	5,016,300
– Costs of Sale	331,905	331,597	331,275	351,484	351,141
– 1st Mortgage Payoff	2,661,735	2,527,014	2,385,401	2,236,542	2,080,067
BEFORE-TAX SALE PROCEEDS	1,747,860	1,878,489	2,015,824	2,433,174	2,585,092
Internal Rate of Return, Before Tax	–9.25%	0.32%	3.60%	8.34%	8.62%

You nailed it. Now the DCR is exactly 1.25 in the first year, as needed. (*True confession:* The author designed this story to have a happy ending, just in case the book is ever made into a movie.)

Now that you know the deal is possible, you want to decide if it's desirable. The cash flow is a little healthier because you have less debt to pay. Your IRR is pretty dismal until the first rent increase occurs in year 4, when it reaches a more promising 8.34%.

Really? Is 8.34% worthy of consideration after the higher IRRs you saw in the previous examples? It's time to recognize that not every investment is created equal and that reward is inextricably tied to risk. This triple-net lease investment differs from the apartment building and mixed-use property in several important ways:

- **Financial stability of the tenant.** Your tenant here is a national retailer and so presumably has deep pockets. That doesn't mean there is no possibility of its going broke tomorrow, but your chances of getting paid each month, in full and on time, are significantly better than they are with your zero-star restaurant in the mixed-use property—and probably better than with some apartment tenants. In short, the odds favor a satisfactory and uninterrupted revenue stream with the national tenant.

- **Length of lease.** Your national tenant has committed to a long-term lease, which should give you reasonable confidence about having an interrupted cash flow over an extended investment horizon. Local business tenants might favor a shorter term, such as five years, with an option to renew. Apartment tenants typically sign one- or two-year leases. Again, the nod for long-term rent stability goes to this national tenant.
- **Protection from uncertainty about expenses.** Your triple-net tenant is paying virtually all your current operating expenses. Even better is the fact that it is paying your future operating expenses, which insulates you from uncertainty about situations over which you have no control, such as rising property taxes or unusual and unplanned demands for maintenance. Here again, triple-net tenancy improves your odds for a stable cash flow.
- **Minimal management.** If the tenant is responsible for all repairs and maintenance, and the time between turnovers is measured in decades, then you should be able to enjoy a relatively low-impact management style. With apartments, someone may contact you in the middle of the night to tell you the heat isn't working, but that type of on-call oversight should not be necessary with a triple-net tenant.
- **Likelihood of lower return.** You may properly envision the conjoining of risk and reward as a law of nature. If this investment presents a lower risk than other property types, then you should expect that it will also offer a lower return. When you look at the internal rate of return in the figure above, you can see that it doesn't climb past much beyond half of what you've seen with the previous properties.

As you reflect on this IRR, you recall that it includes two assumptions that might be necessary for purposes of valuation but perhaps less critical for evaluation. You have assumed that there will be a vacancy and credit loss, as well as an expense for property management; but you also know that you wouldn't be buying this NNN property with its long-term lease to a national tenant if you thought there might be any real chance of encountering either vacancy or significant management costs. You decide to run your pro forma one last time to see the impact of removing these items.

	Year 1	Year 2	Year 3	Year 4	Year 5
INCOME					
Commercial Income					
Total Base Rent	360,000	360,000	360,000	381,600	381,600
Expense Recoveries	67,000	69,010	71,081	73,214	75,410
Total Commercial Income	427,000	429,010	431,081	454,814	457,010
TOTAL GROSS INCOME	427,000	429,010	431,081	454,814	457,010
– VACANCY & CREDIT ALLOWANCE	0	0	0	0	0
GROSS OPERATING INCOME	427,000	429,010	431,081	454,814	457,010
– OPERATING EXPENSES	74,000	76,220	78,508	80,864	83,290
NET OPERATING INCOME	353,000	352,790	352,573	373,950	373,720
– Debt Service, 1st Mortgage	264,748	264,748	264,748	264,748	264,748
CASH FLOW BEFORE TAXES	88,252	88,042	87,825	109,202	108,972
Cash-on-Cash Return (CFBT / Cash Inv.)	4.41%	4.40%	4.39%	5.46%	5.45%
Capitalization Rate	7.43%	7.43%	7.42%	7.87%	7.87%
Debt Coverage Ratio	1.33	1.33	1.33	1.41	1.41
PROJECTED SELLING PRICE	5,042,900	5,039,900	5,036,800	5,342,100	5,338,900
– Costs of Sale	353,003	352,793	352,576	373,947	373,723
– 1st Mortgage Payoff	2,661,735	2,527,014	2,385,401	2,236,542	2,080,067
BEFORE-TAX SALE PROCEEDS	2,028,162	2,160,093	2,298,823	2,731,611	2,885,110
Internal Rate of Return, Before Tax	5.82%	8.25%	8.96%	12.25%	11.76%

You remind yourself that you're stretching a bit beyond the limits of prudence by taking out vacancy and management—your wax wings might melt if you fly too close to the sun—but at the same time you're encouraged by the possibility of the improved return. You're now in the 8 to 9% range before the year 4 rent increase and into double digits afterward. Not bad for an investment with relatively low risk. You feel comfortable going forward if you can close the deal at this $4.75 million price.

Rule of Thumb: Who might prefer to purchase a triple-net lease property? You may have heard of "target-date mutual funds." These are funds that tilt away from aggressive (read: riskier) investments and toward a more conservative asset mix as the investor's retirement age approaches. The reasoning here is that the typical retiree will place greater importance on lack of volatility and preservation of capital and that the trade-off will be a lower return. The person who invests in a NNN property often subscribes to similar logic and is willing to accept a lower return in exchange for the certainty of uninterrupted cash flow with minimal hands-on management. Forward-thinking investors might consider purchasing such a property long before retirement so that they might then own it free and clear and achieve maximum cash flow when they need it most.

PART 2

THIRTY-SEVEN CALCULATIONS EVERY REAL ESTATE INVESTOR NEEDS TO KNOW

7

Calculation 1:
Simple Interest

What It Means

Simple interest is a method of computing interest where you apply the interest rate only to the original principal amount.

By contrast, with compound interest, you apply the interest rate to the original principal and also to all accumulated interest. You'll see that in the next section.

How to Calculate

You can calculate the simple interest earned or the total amount after interest using these formulas:

Interest = Principal × Rate × Time
Amount = Principal × [1 + (Rate × Time)]

Example

Let's assume that you have $1,000 that you can invest at 12% annual simple interest. In the first year, you earn 12% of $1,000, or $120. In the second year, you again earn 12% of $1,000, or $120. In the third year, you do the same, and so on.

Interest = 1,000 × 0.12 × 1 = $120

An important consideration here, as with all other interest calculations, is to be certain that you express both the interest rate and the number of periods in identical terms. In other words, the preceding example really says:

Interest = 1,000 × 12% (0.12) per year × 1 year = $120

You have to be sure that you express both the interest rate and the term in the same way, in this case as years. What if you were earning simple interest at the rate of 1% per month for one year instead? You have the following:

Interest = 1,000 × 1% (0.01) per month × 12 months = $120

Now you receive $10 per month (1,000 × 0.01) for 12 months.

Perhaps you want to calculate the amount you will have accumulated after a certain period of time. The formula reads like this:

Amount = Principal × [1 + (Rate × Time)]

Try it, using the same facts as in the original example. If you invest $1,000 at 12% simple interest, how much would you have after one year?

Amount = 1,000 × [1 + (0.12 × 1 year)]
Amount = 1,000 × (1 + 0.12)
Amount = 1,000 × 1.12 = $1,120

That makes perfect sense. If, as in the first example, you start with $1,000 and you earn $120 interest in one year, surely you'll end up with $1,120 at the end of that year.

Exercise your high school algebra and see how this works if you earn interest at the same rate for three years.

Amount = 1,000 × [1 + (0.12 × 3 years)]
Amount = 1,000 × (1 + 0.36)
Amount = 1,000 × 1.36 = $1,360

Again, this makes sense. You are earning simple (noncompounded) interest; if you earn $120 in one year, it's logical that you would earn $360 in three years.

Test Your Understanding

You invest $1,000 at an annual rate of 10% simple interest for 30 months. How much do you have in your account at the end of that time?

Answer

You need to use the following formula:

Amount = Principal × [1 + (Rate × Time)]

Remember to measure rate and time the same way. That means you need to express both the rate and time as monthly or as yearly. If you want to express the rate monthly, it would be 10/12% per month. That's a tough one to do in your head. It would be easier to express the time in years, since 30 months is exactly 2.5 years. Now it's easy:

Amount = Principal × [1 + (Rate × Time)]
Amount = 1,000 × [1 + (0.10 × 2.5)]
Amount = 1,000 × (1 + 0.25)
Amount = 1,000 × 1.250 = $1,250

Calculation 2: Compound Interest

What It Means

With *compound interest*, you apply the interest rate to the original principal and also to all accumulated interest. This is different from simple interest, where you apply the interest rate only to the original principal amount.

How to Calculate

You can calculate the compound interest earned or the total amount after interest using any of several methods.

1. You can make a timeline to track the progress of the compounding. Consider $1,000 invested at 5% per year compounded annually:

Year	Starting Balance	Interest	Ending Balance
1	1,000.00	50.00	1,050.00
2	1,050.00	52.50	1,102.50
3	1,102.50	55.13	1,157.63

and so on.

At the end of the first year, $1,000 grows by 5% to $1,050. Unlike with simple interest, the $50 earned in year 1 is added to the balance. The aggregated amount grows again by 5% in year 2, earning $52.50 and increasing the pot to $1,102.50. You do it all over again in year 3 or for as many years as you want.

As with all interest calculations, it is essential that you express both the interest rate and the number of periods in identical terms. In our example here, both the rate and the term are expressed in years. We could have used quarters, months, even days—as long as we used the same for rate as for term.

2. The formula for the amount to which principal will grow at compound interest over time reads as follows:

Amount (Future Value) = Principal × (1 + Periodic Rate) ^ Number of Periods

This formula is a little trickier than some others we've seen. Taking it in the proper order of operations, you should begin with 1 + the periodic rate and raise that sum to a power equal to the number of periods. When you have that result, you can multiply it by the principal to get the final amount.

For example, say that you put $1,000 into your bank, earning interest at 5% per year. How much will it be worth in two years?

Take 1 + the periodic rate and raise that sum to a power equal to the number of years.

(1 + 0.05) ^ 2
1.05 × 1.05 = 1.1025

Multiply that by the original principal:

1,000 × 1.1025 = 1,102.50

If you want to know the total amount of interest earned, subtract the principal you started with from the final amount; the difference is the interest.

Interest = 1,102.50 less 1,000 = 102.50

3. You can also use the table "Annual Compound Interest Factors" found at http://www.realdata.com/book. The following is a snippet of the table:

Annual Compound Interest Factors

Years	4.375%	4.500%	4.625%	4.750%	4.875%	5.000%	5.125%	5.250%
1	1.043750	1.045000	1.046250	1.047500	1.048750	1.050000	1.051250	1.525000
2	1.089414	1.092025	1.094639	1.097256	1.099877	1.102500	1.105127	1.107756
3	1.137076	1.141166	1.145266	1.149376	1.153496	1.157625	1.161764	1.165913
4	1.186823	1.192519	1.198235	1.203971	1.209728	1.215506	1.221305	1.227124
5	1.238747	1.246182	1.253653	1.261160	1.268703	1.276282	1.283897	1.291548
6	1.291294	1.302260	1.311634	1.321065	1.330552	1.340096	1.349696	1.359354
7	1.349508	1.360862	1.372298	1.383816	1.395416	1.407100	1.418868	1.430720
8	1.408549	1.422101	1.435766	1.449547	1.463443	1.477455	1.491585	1.505833
9	1.470173	1.486095	1.502171	1.518400	1.534786	1.551328	1.568029	1.584889
10	1.534493	1.552969	1.571646	1.590524	1.609607	1.628895	1.648390	1.668096

To use this table, look up the factor that corresponds to the rate of growth and the number of years that the principal will grow at that rate, compounded annually. Multiply the original principal by this factor to determine the amount to which it will grow over time (i.e., its future value).

Amount (Future Value) = Principal × Factor from Compound Interest Table

Notice that this looks very much like the formula in method #2 above. The difference is that the factor has replaced (1 + Periodic Rate) ^ Number of Periods, which means, of course, that the table factor represents the result you would find if you calculated (1 + Periodic Rate) ^ Number of Periods for any combination of rate and term.

4. You can also create a basic Excel formula to calculate growth at compounded interest. Open a blank Excel spreadsheet and use the "FV" function in any cell:

=FV(Periodic Rate,Number of Periods,,–Principal)

For example, to calculate the future value of $1,000 invested at 5% per year for two years, enter:

=FV(0.05,2,,–1000)

When you press the "Enter" key, you see that the future value is $1,102.50.

5. Finally, as in Part I, Chapter 3, you can download a premade Excel template (see http://www.realdata.com/book):

Present Value	Periodic Rate	No. of Periods	Future Value	
1,000.00	5.00%	2	$1,102.50	calculate future value

Example

Let's assume again that you have $1,000 that you can invest at a 12% annual rate, with interest compounded annually. You hold the investment for three years.

Use the formula in method #2 and start by finding 1 + the periodic rate:

(1 + 0.12), or 1.12

Next, take that sum and raise it to a power equal to the number of periods, in this case three, because you're looking for the total amount after three years.

1.12 × 1.12 × 1.12 = 1.404928

Then multiply that by the original principal to determine the final amount that $1,000 grows to at 12% per year, compounded annually, after three years:

1,000 × 1.404928 = $1,404.93 (rounded)

Is there another way you can perform this calculation to check your result? Yes, you can choose any of the other four methods shown in this chapter. Try one and see if you do indeed get the same answer.

Rule of Thumb: All else being constant, the more frequently interest is compounded, the more dollars of interest are earned.

A 6% savings account will earn more by the end of a given period of time with monthly compounding than it will with annual compounding. Most financial institutions will convey the benefits of more frequent compounding by telling you not only the interest rate but also the "APY," or annual percentage yield. In the case of your 6% account, monthly compounding generates an APY of 6.17%.

Test Your Understanding

You invest $2,000 at a rate of 8% compounded quarterly. How much do you have in your account at the end of one year? How much less would you have earned if the interest were compounded annually?

Answer

The table of compound interest factors is annual, so that won't help you with this quarterly compounding problem. You can, however, use any of the other methods of quarterly compounding. Let's try the formula first:

Amount = Principal × (1 + Periodic Rate) ^ Number of Periods

If the compounding occurs quarterly, then you need to express both the rate and number of periods in terms of quarters:

8% per year / 4 = 2% per quarter

Similarly, 1 year = 4 quarters. Start with 1 + the periodic rate and raise that sum to a power equal to the number of periods.

1 + 0.02 = 1.02
1.02 × 1.02 × 1.02 × 1.02 = 1.0824

You multiply this result by the principal to get the amount at the end of four quarters.

Amount = Principal × 1.0824
Amount = 2,000 × 1.0824 = $2,164.86

You can also obtain this result using a timeline chart like the one we used in our example. On this occasion, however, you must express the chunks of time as quarters instead of years.

Year	Starting Balance	Interest	Ending Balance
1	2,000.00	40.00	2,040.00
2	2,040.00	40.80	2,080.80
3	2,080.80	41.62	2,122.42
4	2,122.42	42.45	2,164.87

This method gives you a result that is one cent different from what you obtain with the formula. Why the difference? In your timeline, you rounded off the interest and balance to the nearest penny in each row. The cumulative effect of this rounding pushes your result to the extra cent. Try the calculations in the table without rounding. What's your final result?

If you compounded the interest on this account annually instead of quarterly, you would have earned interest just once by the end of the year. In effect, no compounding would have occurred because there would have been only one period. Your final account balance would have been 8% higher than the original principal amount, that is, 2,000 × 1.08, or $2,160, compared with $2,164.86 if the interest were compounded quarterly, a difference of $4.86.

9

Calculation 3: Rule of 72s

What It Means

Here is a great little parlor trick to calculate the approximate number of years for an investment to double in value at a particular rate of compound interest.

Simply take the rate of growth and divide it as a whole number into 72. Keep in mind that the answer is not precise; you would need to divide into 72.73 to nail the exact amount.

How to Calculate

Number of Years to Double in Value (approximate) = 72 / Rate of Growth

Example

You purchase a piece of property for $100,000 in an area where property values have grown at 8% annually. If they continue to grow at that rate, about how long will it take for the property to double in value?

Number of Years to Double in Value (approximate) = 72 / Rate of Growth
Number of Years to Double in Value (approximate) = 72 / 8
Number of Years to Double in Value (approximate) = 9 years

Test Your Understanding

You have owned a piece of property for six years. During that time, the rise in values has been steady, and the property has doubled in value. What is the approximate annual rate of appreciation that you have experienced?

Answer

Number of Years to Double in Value (approximate) = 72 / Rate of Growth

Transpose the formula to:

Rate of Growth = 72 / Number of Years to Double in Value (approximate)
Rate of Growth = 72 / 6
Rate of Growth = 12, or 12% per year

10

Calculation 4: Present Value of a Future Cash Flow

What It Means

By now, you're certainly familiar with the notion of an asset whose value increases over time because of the application of a compounding rate of growth. The most commonplace example is a savings account. You place a certain amount of money into the account; by the end of the first year, that money has grown because it has earned interest. By the end of the next year, that principal and interest combined earn more (compounded) interest, and so on. A similar process takes place when a piece of real estate appreciates in value over time.

When you find the *present value of a future cash flow*, you are running the compound interest process in reverse. You know, or at least believe, you can predict the value of the cash flow at a particular time in the future. You also know the rate of interest, which you now refer to as the "discount rate" because it's reducing, not increasing, the value of this asset. What you're trying to figure out is what this asset—this cash flow—is worth to you today.

Why do you want to know? Producing cash flows is a large part of what income properties do for you. They generate them each year as you operate the property, and with any luck, they produce one last big one when you sell the property. You want to know the total value of all those future cash flows in today's dollars. That's what your investment is worth at a given rate of return (i.e., discount rate).

In order to be able to calculate the present worth of a property's entire future income stream—a process called discounted cash flow analysis—you have to start by knowing how to discount a single cash flow to its present worth.

How to Calculate

The formula:

Present Value = Future Value / $[(1 + i)^n]$

(where i is the interest rate per period and n is the number of periods) is not impossible to solve manually, but doing so is difficult enough to encourage you to find another way.

You can use the Excel template for compound interest provided at http://www.realdata.com/book, where you simply fill in the three unknowns, and Excel calculates the present value.

Present Value	Periodic Rate	No. of Periods	Future Value
$0.00	0.00%	0	$0.00

You can also use the "Annual Present Value Factors" table provided at http://www.realdata.com/book. Use that table to look up the factor that corresponds to the annual discount rate and the number of years to discount. Multiply the future value by the factor to obtain its discounted present value. We'll use that table for our examples here.

Example

You believe that the sale of your property five years from now will produce cash proceeds of $200,000. If you discount that cash flow at 11% per year, what is its present value?

Go to the table and look up the factor where the column for 11% intersects the row for five years. You should find 0.593451.

Now, multiply the future value by this factor to calculate its present value:

Present Value = Factor from Table × Future Value
Present Value = 0.593451 × 200,000
Present Value = 118,690 (rounded)

> **Rule of Thumb:** Choosing an appropriate discount rate is probably the most difficult part of this process. Discounting the value of future cash flows is how you are compensated for having to wait to receive your money and for undertaking the risk of making the investment. How much you should be compensated—that is, how large the discount rate should be—ultimately comes down to a question of what else is competing for your investment dollar. Your discount rate should be the rate of return that you could reasonably expect to achieve by investing the same amount of money in a similar investment posing a comparable risk.

Test Your Understanding

You purchase a property that produces a first-year operating cash flow of $4,000. You sell the property at the end of that first year and receive sale proceeds of $180,000. Based on the performance of other properties in the area, you believe a discount rate of 10% is appropriate. What is the present value of the cash flows you received while owning this property?

Answer

A sidebar before solving this problem: This particular example highlights a convention that is used in most investment analyses, that of "annualizing" the information. In real life, you would not receive all your operating cash flow on the last day of the year so that you could neatly discount it all back as one number.

On the one hand, and especially because you're dealing with the time value of money, it would seem that playing fast and loose with the timing could distort the discount calculation. On the other hand, remember that all these numbers are based on forecasts and that the alternative to annualizing is for you to attempt to forecast the cash flows on a monthly (dare we say weekly?) basis. It's not unreasonable to assert that if you try to make 12 times as many estimates, you're unlikely to improve the overall accuracy of your projections. Indeed, the opposite is probably true. It's also true that an attempt to make monthly projections would be so time-consuming as to be self-defeating. Imagine a 10-year projection now requiring 120 estimates to determine the timing of revenue and expenses.

We'll observe the convention here and annualize the information. Now, on to the answer:

You have two cash flows that occur during your single year of ownership: $4,000 from the operation of the property and $180,000 from the sale. As explained above, you'll treat them both as occurring at the end of year 1 (EOY1).

This makes a total cash flow of $184,000 to be discounted over one year at 10%. Go to http://www.realdata.com/book and look up the factor for one year and 10%. You should find 0.909091.

Present Value = Factor from Table × Future Value

Present Value = 0.909091 × 184,000

Present Value = 167,273 (rounded)

You will obtain the same result with the Excel template. Note that you may find a difference of a few cents between the results you get by using the table and those from the Excel model. This is because the table goes out only six decimal places, leaving the possibility of a small error due to rounding.

11

Calculation 5: Gross Rent Multiplier

What It Means

The *gross rent multiplier* (GRM) is a simple method by which you can estimate the market value of an income property. The GRM is a market-driven measurement. You presume that, if buyers have recently been paying X times the gross income for properties in a certain location, then the market value of a property you are considering for purchase should work out to that same "X times" its gross income.

The advantage of the GRM is that it is so easy to calculate. You don't need a computer; you probably don't even need the back of an envelope, but rather can do the math in your head. The disadvantage is that nothing so basic is likely to be extraordinarily accurate or reliable. GRM ignores the time value of money, and it makes no differentiation between properties where tenants may pay all, some, or none of the operating expenses.

This measurement can serve as a useful precursor to a serious property analysis, however. For example, if you see that a property is offered for sale at a GRM significantly higher than what is typical in the market, you can expect that a detailed analysis is probably not going to make this investment look more appealing, except at a substantially lower price. You can then decide if you want to spend the time doing research and making projections in a case where the GRM warns you that the property is probably greatly overpriced.

How to Calculate

Gross Rent Multiplier = Market Value / Gross Scheduled Income (annual)

By transposing this equation, you also get:

Market Value = Gross Rent Multiplier × Gross Scheduled Income (annual)

Example

You find that five apartment buildings have sold in the past six months on the upper West Side of town. The sales data are shown below:

Property	Selling Price	Gross Income
1	680,000	97,000
2	1,127,500	165,800
3	950,000	128,000
4	1,385,500	227,400
5	800,000	115,000

The math is straightforward. For each property, you divide the selling price by the gross income to determine its GRM.

Property	Selling Price / Gross Income	GRM
1	680,000 / 97,000	7.010
2	1,127,500 / 165,800	6.800
3	950,000 / 128,000	7.422
4	1,385,500 / 227,400	6.093
5	800,000 / 115,000	6.957

> **Rule of Thumb:** Because the GRM is market-driven, there is no universally correct number—but there are reasonable limits. Realistically, you would probably be surprised (and suspicious) to see a GRM below 4 and aghast to see one higher than 10.

Test Your Understanding

1. What is the average GRM indicated by the preceding sales in the example?
2. If you are considering the purchase of a similar property, also on the upper West Side and with a gross rent of $150,000, what would be that property's value, as indicated by the neighborhood's average GRM? Round the answer to the nearest $5,000.
3. What range of possible values would these prior sales suggest? Again, round the answer to the nearest $5,000.

Answer

1. The average GRM for the area would equal the sum of the GRMs divided by 5.

   (7.010 + 6.800 + 7.422 + 6.093 + 6.957) / 5 = 34.282 / 5 = 6.8564

2. To find the value indicated by the average GRM, you multiply the gross rent by the GRM.

   150,000 × 6.8564 = $1,028,460, or $1,030,000 (rounded)

3. To find the range of value indicated by the GRMs in the sample, multiply the gross rent by the smallest and by the largest GRM in the sample.

   150,000 × 6.093 = $913,950
   150,000 × 7.422 = $1,113,300

   The GRMs of the sales in the area suggest a range of values between $915,000 and $1,110,000 after rounding.

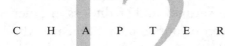

Calculation 6: Gross Scheduled Income (Potential Gross Income)

What It Means

The *gross scheduled income* (sometimes called *potential gross income*) is the annual income of a property if all rentable space were, in fact, rented and all rent collected. In short, it is the maximum potential income without regard to any possible vacancy or credit losses.

How to Calculate

What, on the surface, should be an unremarkable calculation, does provoke some debate among appraisers and analysts. Do you count occupied units at their actual rents or at their potential rents (which could be higher or even lower than actual if the market has changed)? Do you figure the value of vacant units at market rent, at a rental rate comparable to your own rented units, or at the rate that will minimize vacancy?

These questions are interesting but ultimately academic. Gross scheduled income is an estimate. In the next two chapters you'll be reminded that you need to subtract a vacancy and credit loss in order to convert your potential rent income into your actual rent income, the *gross operating income* (GOI). The GOI is real; it's what you really collect. So whatever approach you use to state the gross scheduled income, you'll then use the vacancy and credit loss to adjust it to the actual amount collected.

The author has a bias toward sticking as close to reality as possible—it's simpler, it's practical, and it's easier to defend when showing your numbers to most sellers, buyers, and lenders. Describing the property's "scheduled" rent in terms of the actual rent for occupied units and the potential rent for vacant units makes sense for your purposes as an investor. Hence the following formula:

Gross Scheduled Income (for a given year) =
Total rent payable for that year under existing contracts for occupied space
+ Total potential rent (at market rates) for vacant space

Example

You have a property with four rental units. Two units are occupied and leased at $20,000 per year. The third unit is occupied and rented at $22,000 per year. The fourth unit is vacant but has an annual rental value of $22,000. What is the property's gross scheduled income?

Gross Scheduled Income =

Unit #1	20,000 (actual)
Unit #2	20,000 (actual)
Unit #3	22,000 (actual)
Unit #4	22,000 (vacant, estimated)
Total	84,000

Test Your Understanding

You have a property with four units.

- Unit #1 rents for $1,000 per month and has a scheduled rent increase in month 7 to $1,200.
- Unit #2 rents for $1,200 per month.
- Unit #3 rents for $1,300 per month.
- Unit #4 rents for $1,000 per month, but will be vacant at the end of month 2. The market value of this unit when it becomes available will be $1,200 per month.

What is the property's gross scheduled income?

Answer

- Unit #1 will rent for six months at $1,000 and six months at $1,200.

  $(6 \times 1,000) + (6 \times 1,200) = 6,000 + 7,200 = 13,200$

- Unit #2 will rent for 12 months at $1,200.

  $12 \times 1,200 = 14,400$

- Unit #3 will rent for 12 months at $1,300.

  $12 \times 1,300 = 15,600$

- Unit #4 will rent for two months at $1,000; its potential rent for each of the next 10 months is $1,200.

  $(2 \times 1,000) + (10 \times 1,200) = 2,000 + 12,000 = 14,000$

You add the annual amounts for the four units to get the total for the property:

Gross Scheduled Income = 13,200 + 14,400 + 15,600 + 14,000 = 57,200

13

Calculation 7: Vacancy and Credit Loss

What It Means

Vacancy and credit loss is the potential rental income that is lost due to space that lies unoccupied or due to nonpayment of rent by tenants.

You'll use vacancy and credit loss to reduce the gross scheduled income (i.e., the property's total potential income) to give you the gross operating income (GOI), which is the amount of revenue you actually expect to collect.

This term is also called vacancy and credit allowance, reflecting its use as an estimate of future losses that may occur due to turnover and uncollectible rent.

A number of real-world factors can impact vacancy and credit loss. If the rents that you charge are less than what tenants must pay for comparable properties, then it's reasonable to assume that no one will ever leave to get a better deal elsewhere. If a particular location experiences a very high demand, vacancies may disappear until developers respond to that demand by building more space. If they build too much space, vacancy can swing in the opposite direction, as supply then exceeds demand. Difficult economic times can affect both vacancy and credit issues. Businesses may be reluctant to expand, thus reducing the absorption of available space. Tenants may run into cash flow difficulties and choose to pay their suppliers before they pay their landlords.

How to Calculate

You will typically estimate vacancy and credit loss as a percentage of gross scheduled income:

Vacancy and Credit Loss (in dollars) =
Gross Scheduled Income × estimated % Vacancy and Credit Loss

Example

Your property is fully occupied and has a gross scheduled income of $84,000. Next year you will be raising rents by 6% and estimate that you should allow for a 2% vacancy and credit loss. How many dollars of revenue do you estimate you will lose?

First, you must determine the correct gross scheduled income. If you expect 6% more than this year, take the current year's amount and multiply it by 1.06 (multiplying by 1 would give you the same as the current year; multiplying by 1.06 gives you 6/100, or 6% more):

Next Year's Gross Scheduled Income = 84,000 × 1.06 = 89,040

Second, calculate the vacancy and credit loss as a percentage of income:

Vacancy and Credit Loss = 89,040 × 0.02 = 1,781

Rule of Thumb: Almost every property experiences vacancy from time to time. If your property never has a vacancy, you probably are not charging high enough rents. (The alternative explanation is that you are a truly wonderful human being and your tenants don't want to move out and have you feel a sense of rejection. Please let me know what your partners say when you give them this explanation.)

When you seek financing for an income-producing property, the lender will almost certainly expect you to project some amount of vacancy and credit loss. It's better for you to do it rather than to ignore the issue and have the loan officer come up with a number. Your local market will probably dictate what's reasonable, but if you have no idea, then choose a percentage that's large enough to be visible but not so big as to throw your cash flow projections into free fall—perhaps 2 to 4%.

Test Your Understanding

1. You know that a property has a gross scheduled income of $100,000 and a GOI (i.e., income after vacancy and credit loss) of $97,500. What is the percentage of vacancy and credit loss?
2. If a property has a GOI of $76,000 after experiencing a 5% vacancy and credit loss, what must its gross scheduled income be?

Answer

1. First, figure out the dollar amount of loss. If you start with $100,000 and are left with $97,500, then your vacancy and credit loss is $2,500. You can now restate the question as, "2,500 is what percentage of 100,000?" or:

   2,500 = What percentage? × 100,000

   Transpose this to:

   2,500 / 100,000 = What percentage?
   0.025 = What percentage?
   0.025 is the decimal representation of 2.5%

2. You know that:

   Gross Scheduled Income
   less Vacancy and Credit Loss
   = Gross Operating Income

You also know that in this problem the vacancy loss is equal to 5% of the gross scheduled income, so the two expressions are interchangeable. And you know the GOI is $76,000. Restate the problem like this:

Gross Scheduled Income
less 5% of Gross Scheduled Income
= 76,000

Now things should fall into place:

95% of Gross Scheduled Income = 76,000
Gross Scheduled Income = 76,000 / 0.95 = 80,000

You can test to prove if this answer is correct. If the gross scheduled income is $80,000 and you lose 5% to vacancy and credit, are you left with $76,000 as the original problem says? Try it.

14

Calculation 8: Gross Operating Income (Effective Gross Income)

What It Means

The *gross operating income* (GOI) (also called *effective gross income*, or EGI) equals the property's annual gross scheduled income less vacancy and credit loss. GOI is not the property's potential income, but represents instead the actual income that you expect to collect.

If you've read the previous two chapters about gross scheduled income and vacancy and credit loss, then you should implicitly understand GOI; it is simply the difference between those two amounts. We won't belabor the term here but will just provide a quick review of the calculation. If you haven't done so already, you should read the previous two chapters.

How to Calculate

Gross Operating Income = Gross Scheduled Income less Vacancy
and Credit Loss

When you analyze a property's income and cash flow, you'll generally start from the top down, so it is useful to picture the calculation like this:

Gross Scheduled Income
less Vacancy and Credit Loss
= Gross Operating Income

Example

You have a property that is fully rented and takes in revenue of $5,000 per month. You expect a vacancy and credit loss of 3%. What is the GOI?

You first need to know the gross scheduled income. You have no vacant units to account for in calculating the gross scheduled income, so you can multiply the monthly income of $5,000 by 12 to find the annual amount:

Gross Scheduled Income = 12 × 5,000 = 60,000

Next, you need to figure the vacancy and credit loss, which in this case you estimate to be 3% of the gross.

Vacancy and Credit Loss = 60,000 × 0.03 = 1,800

Now you have a simple subtraction to perform:

Gross Scheduled Income	60,000
less Vacancy and Credit Loss	1,800
= Gross Operating Income	58,200

Test Your Understanding

You have a property with 12 units.

• Units #1 through #4 each rent for $1,400 per month.

- Unit #5 rents for $1,200 per month. In month 10, the rent will increase to $1,350.
- Units #6 though #9 each rent for $1,600 per month.
- Unit #10 is vacant. Its fair market value is $1,500 per month.
- Unit #11 rents for $1,600 per month but will be vacant at the end of month 9. The market value of this unit when it becomes available will be $1,600 per month.
- Unit #12 rents for $1,275 per month.

You estimate a vacancy and credit loss of 7%.

What is the property's GOI? Does the allowance for vacancy seem reasonable?

Answer

According to the formula, you must first determine the gross scheduled income and the vacancy loss. Then you can find the difference, which is the GOI.

Gross Scheduled Income
less Vacancy and Credit Loss
= Gross Operating Income

- Units #1 through #4 each rent for $1,400 per month, or $16,800 per year. There are four such units, so their combined rent is 4 × 16,800, or 67,200.
- Unit #5 will rent for nine months at $1,200 and for the last three months at $1,350: (9 × 1,200) + (3 × 1,350) = 14,850 for this unit.
- Units #6 through #9 each rent for $1,600 per month, or $19,200 per year. There are four such units, so their combined rent is 4 × 19,200, or 76,800.
- Unit #10 is vacant, but its market rent is $1,500 per month, or $18,000 per year. You expect to find a tenant at that rent by month 5.
- Unit #11 rents for $1,600 per month but will go vacant at the end of month 9. However, its market rent will still be $1,600, so this unit represents 12 × 1,600, or 19,200, in scheduled rent.
- Unit #12 rents for $1,275 per month, or $15,300 per year.

You now have the total scheduled rent for all the units and can add them up to get the gross scheduled income:

Units #1 through #4	67,200
Unit #5	14,850
Units #6 through #9	76,800
Unit #10	18,000
Unit #11	19,200
Unit #12	15,300
Gross Scheduled Income	211,350

Now figure the vacancy and credit loss:

Vacancy and Credit Loss (in dollars) =
Gross Scheduled Income × estimated % Vacancy and Credit Loss
Vacancy and Credit Loss = 211,350 × 0.07 = 14,795

The rest is just subtraction:

Gross Scheduled Income	211,350
less Vacancy and Credit Loss	14,795
= Gross Operating Income	196,555

Finally, does the vacancy and credit loss seem reasonable? In the previous chapter, we talked about vacancy and credit losses around 3 to 4%. Why should you be assuming 7% here? You can't ignore the facts that are in the example, and when you analyze a real property, you must not ignore its real circumstances. Unit #10 is vacant, and you expect it to remain so for four months, perhaps to undergo renovations. Whatever the reason, if you assume, as the example states, that it will be empty, then you'll lose $6,000 in rent for that period. Similarly, you expect to lose three months' rent from Unit #11, or $4,800. Combined, these predicted vacancies represent just over 5% of the gross scheduled income, so an allowance of 7% is indeed reasonable.

15

Calculation 9:
Net Operating
Income

What It Means

Net operating income (NOI) is a property's income after being reduced by vacancy and credit loss and all operating expenses. Mathematically, it is a property's gross operating income less the sum of all operating expenses.

NOI represents a property's profitability before consideration of taxes, financing, or recovery of capital. Perhaps easier is to think of it as the number of dollars a property returns in a given year if the property is purchased for all cash and if there is no consideration of income taxes or depreciation.

NOI is one of the most important calculations you'll make in regard to any real estate investment. If you revisit Part I, Chapters 2 through 5 of this book, you'll notice that NOI is at the center of almost every discussion. It represents an essential component of many of the chapters in Part II as well.

In order to calculate NOI correctly, you must be clear about what is and what is not an operating expense. An operating expense is one that is necessary for the maintenance of a piece of real property and ensures its continued ability to produce income. Loan payments, depreciation, and capital expenditures are not considered operating expenses.

How to Calculate

Net Operating Income = Gross Operating Income less Operating Expenses

You may prefer a "top-down" approach to this calculation, which is easier to visualize:

Gross Scheduled Income
less Vacancy and Credit Loss
= Gross Operating Income
less Operating Expenses
= Net Operating Income

It is quite common to use an Annual Property Operating Data (APOD) form to simplify the computation of NOI. That form includes all of the most common line-item expenses. You saw it in Chapter 2, but because it is so useful to the calculation of NOI, we'll repeat it on the following page for your convenience.

Example

You have a property with a scheduled gross income of $100,000, vacancy and credit loss of 3%, and total operating expenses of $35,000. What is this property's net operating income?

Begin with the gross scheduled income and use that to calculate the dollar amount of the vacancy and credit loss:

Vacancy and Credit Loss = 100,000 × 0.03 = 3,000

Now you can calculate the GOI:

Gross Scheduled Income	100,000
less Vacancy and Credit Loss	3,000
= Gross Operating Income	97,000

Annual Property Operating Data

Property Address:
Date:
Prepared by:

INCOME	$	%	Comments
Gross Scheduled Rent Income			
Other Income			
TOTAL GROSS INCOME			
VACANCY & CREDIT ALLOWANCE			
GROSS OPERATING INCOME			
EXPENSES			
Accounting			
Advertising			
Insurance (fire and liability)			
Janitorial Service			
Lawn/Snow			
Legal			
Licenses			
Miscellaneous			
Property Management			
Repairs and Maintenance			
Resident Superintendent			
Supplies			
Taxes			
Real Estate			
Personal Property			
Payroll			
Other			
Trash Removal			
Utilities			
Electricity			
Fuel Oil			
Gas			
Sewer and Water			
Telephone			
Other			
TOTAL EXPENSES			
NET OPERATING INCOME			

From this, subtract the operating expenses to determine the NOI:

Gross Operating Income   97,000
less Operating Expenses   35,000
= Net Operating Income   62,000

Rule of Thumb: Use this with caution! Chapters 4 and 5 describe in some detail how investors will often apply a capitalization rate to the NOI in order to estimate the value of a property. The choice of an appropriate cap rate is an issue that is very dependent on time and place—in other words, you should be using the rate that other similar properties are achieving in the same location and at the same time. I have seen cap rates as low as 4% and as high as 18%. Such extremes, of course, are not the rule. Historically, cap rates have tended to gravitate more around the 8 to 12% range.

What some investors will do—particularly if they don't have a computer, calculator, or back of an envelope handy—is to use 10% as an initial and informal screening technique. Why? Primarily because you can do the math in your head. To capitalize an NOI at 10%, you must divide it by 0.10, which is the same as simply adding a zero to it. So, if you were to apply a 10% cap rate to the NOI in the example above, you would presume that the property would be worth about $620,000.

This is not a technique on which you should ever base a decision to buy or sell. Some investors will use this to decide whether to spend their time (not their money) looking at a property proposal. If someone comes up to you at a business luncheon and tells you about a great property he has for sale with a $50,000 NOI for only a million bucks, you'll know it's time to step away from the jalapeño dip.

If you decide a proposal has some surface credibility, remember that the numbers can be manipulated to conceal as well as reveal. The relationship between the price and the NOI may look reasonable because the seller has applied some creativity to make the numbers come out right. Go back to Chapter 2 and review our discussion of reconstructing the owner's representations.

Test Your Understanding

A seller presents you with the following information about a property:

> Four units, all occupied; two rent for $1,000 per month, two rent for $1,200 per month
> Property taxes, $4,800
> Property insurance, $1,900
> Water, $1,800
> Sewer, $800
> Repairs, $2,900
> Advertising, $250
> Supplies, $475
> Lawn and Snow, $425
> Depreciation, $2,900

Assume that you are able to confirm that these amounts are accurate.

Answer

Follow the top-down approach:

> Gross Scheduled Income
> less Vacancy and Credit Loss
> = Gross Operating Income
> ---
> less Operating Expenses
> = Net Operating Income

1. To calculate the annual gross scheduled income, first find the monthly income:

    $(2 \times 1,000) + (2 \times 1,200) = 2,000 + 2,400 = 4,400$

    Multiply that by 12 to get the annual gross scheduled income of $52,800.
2. The seller has not volunteered any information about vacancy or credit loss other than to tell you that the property is now fully occupied. Use a nominal amount, 2%, as an allowance:

Vacancy and Credit Loss = 52,800 × 0.02 = 1,056

3. Sum the operating expenses. You've satisfied yourself that the figures the seller has given you are accurate. However, note that she included depreciation, which is not an operating expense. Add up all the others for a total of $13,350.

Gross Scheduled Income	52,800
less Vacancy and Credit Loss	1,056
= Gross Operating Income	51,744
less Operating Expenses	13,350
= Net Operating Income	38,394

16

Calculation 10:
Capitalization Rate

What It Means

Capitalization rate (or *cap rate*, as it is more commonly called) is the rate at which you discount future income to determine its present value. For a related measure, see also net income multiplier (Part II, Calculation 11).

In practice, you will typically use cap rate to express the relationship between a property's value and its net operating income (NOI) for the current or coming year.

You can use the cap rate formula, discussed below, to serve three useful purposes:

1. Obviously, you can use it to calculate a property's cap rate. You'll want to do so when you know its NOI and what is presumably its value—probably a seller's asking price. What you're really doing in this situation is finding out if the property exhibits a cap rate that's in line with other similar properties in the area if you purchase it at the asking price.
2. If you know what is an appropriate cap rate for this type of property in this area, then you can transpose the formula to calculate a

reasonable estimate of value. In other words, forget about the seller's asking price; given the NOI and the prevailing cap rate, what should it be worth?

3. Finally, you can transpose it yet again to calculate the NOI. For example, if you know the prevailing cap rate and the seller's asking price, what NOI should you expect to hear when you call the listing broker?

How to Calculate

Mathematically, a property's simple or market capitalization rate is the ratio between its NOI and its value:

Capitalization Rate = Net Operating Income / Value

As discussed above, you can transpose the formula to solve for any of the variables:

Value = Net Operating Income / Capitalization Rate

and

Net Operating Income = Value × Capitalization Rate

Example

1. A property has an NOI of $30,000. If you buy it for $250,000, you'll be purchasing it at what cap rate?

Capitalization Rate = Net Operating Income / Value
Capitalization Rate = 30,000 / 250,000 = 0.12, or 12%

2. The prevailing cap rate for small office buildings in your city is 11%. You own a building with a current NOI of $66,000. What is a reasonable estimate of its value?

Value = Net Operating Income / Capitalization Rate
Value = 66,000 / 0.11
Value = 600,000

3. You see another small office building advertised for sale at $900,000. When you obtain the owner's statement of income and expenses and then reconstruct that statement to your satisfaction, what NOI would you expect to find?

Net Operating Income = Value × Capitalization Rate

Since this is the same type of property in the same location, you would use the same 11% cap rate.

Net Operating Income = 900,000 × 0.11
Net Operating Income = 99,000

Rule of Thumb: It's important to have accurate information about cap rates in your market area. Without that information, you can't determine if a property you're considering is providing a competitive return. You can seek such information from brokers, appraisers, and Internet resources. As of this writing, http://www.realtyrates.com is available as an excellent source.

If you're trapped in an elevator between floors, your cell phone battery is dead, and you must make a calculation before being rescued, use a cap rate in the range of 10 to 12%. After you are pulled to safety, make a few phone calls or do some Internet research to get a more exact rate.

Test Your Understanding

You are considering the purchase of a particular property. You receive the following information from the seller:

Gross operating income for the past 12 months	$122,000
Projected gross operating income for the next 12 months	$127,000
Operating expenses for the past 12 months	$46,000

You examine the source information (leases, expense records, etc.) and are satisfied that the owner's representations are accurate and reasonable.

The prevailing cap rate for properties of this type in your area is 11.5%. Using income capitalization as your method of estimating value, answer the following:

1. The seller bases his asking price on the following: Next year's gross operating income (GOI), last year's operating expenses, and a cap rate of 11%. To this he adds 10% extra for negotiating room. What is his asking price?
2. If you were to look at the property using this year's GOI and operating expenses, what cap rate would the property yield at the full asking price?
3. What do you believe is a fair price to pay for this property?
4. Why do you think the seller chose to use next year's GOI and a cap rate 0.5% lower than the market rate?

Answer

1. You must first calculate the NOI. Recall from the chapter on NOI:

Gross Operating Income
less Operating Expenses
= Net Operating Income

Remember that the seller has chosen to use next year's NOI.

Gross Operating Income	127,000
less Operating Expenses	46,000
= Net Operating Income	81,000

The seller now ascribes a value to the property using one of the transposed versions of the cap rate formula. Recall that he chooses to use a rate of 11%:

Present Value = Net Operating Income / Capitalization Rate
Present Value = 81,000 / 0.11
Present Value = 736,364

To this amount he adds 10% negotiating room:

736,364 × 1.10 = 810,000

The seller sets an asking price of $810,000.

2. Now you want to look at the property using this year's GOI and operating expenses:

Gross Operating Income	122,000
less Operating Expenses	46,000
= Net Operating Income	76,000

The question asks you to calculate the cap rate using this NOI and the seller's asking price; you need another version of the formula:

Capitalization Rate = Net Operating Income / Present Value
Capitalization Rate = 76,000 / 810,000
Capitalization Rate = 9.39%

3. To estimate what you believe will be a fair price for the property using income capitalization, you must decide what you will use for the cap rate and for the NOI.

The choice of cap rate is easy. You've already determined that 11.5% is the rate other properties of this type in this location are achieving. There is no reason to use the seller's choice of 11.0%. Go with 11.5%.

In this example, you've been given the GOI for both the past 12 months and the next 12. Which do you use in order to calculate the NOI? If you're the buyer, your likely attitude is that the property's performance in the future is not certain and that you shouldn't be paying for it as if it were. Further, that uncertain future also represents a degree of risk that you are taking off the shoulders of the seller and placing on yourself. You don't intend to pay for the privilege of relieving the seller of risk. Hence, you'll pay for what has occurred, not for what might occur. To put this less operatically, you'll use the GOI from the past 12 months:

Gross Operating Income	122,000
less Operating Expenses	46,000
= Net Operating Income	76,000

Now you calculate the present value:

Present Value = Net Operating Income / Capitalization Rate
Present Value = 76,000 / 0.115
Present Value = 660,870

4. The seller chose to use next year's GOI because it is higher. Since you're estimating the value by capitalizing the income, the higher the income, the higher the value. His rationale is that you are buying the income stream that begins when you take ownership, so the price should be based on that income. Notice that while he remembered to assert that the income would rise next year, he neglected to mention anything about the operating expenses and assumed instead that they would remain constant.

The choice of the lower cap rate also nudges the estimate of value upward. Given a constant NOI, the lower the cap rate, the higher the value. Compare the seller's suggested 81,000 NOI at his 11% and at the market's 11.5%:

Present Value at 11% Cap Rate = 81,000 / 0.11 = 736,364
Present Value at 11.5% Cap Rate = 81,000 / 0.115 = 704,348

A 1/2% difference in the cap rate doesn't sound like much, but the seller is trying to play the old salami game here. One slice at a time, and pretty soon he's got the whole salami. By using next year's GOI (just $5,000 more), last year's operating expenses, and a cap rate 0.5% below market—all seemingly small items—the seller was able to come up with an estimate of value, before negotiating room, of:

$736,364, $75,000 higher than yours

Clearly, there is no substitute for doing your own number crunching.

17

Calculation 11: Net Income Multiplier

What It Means

Net income multiplier (NIM) is the reciprocal of the capitalization rate.

As with cap rate, you use this to express the relationship between a property's value and its net operating income (NOI) for the current or coming year. NIM represents the amount that a typical investor would pay for each dollar of NOI.

Everything that was true about income capitalization as discussed in the previous chapter on capitalization rate is true about its cousin, NIM. Since you often want to use capitalization to estimate the value of a property, NIM provides a useful shortcut—the sort of thing for which the back of an envelope actually can be useful.

First, you establish what the prevailing cap rate is for similar income properties in your area. Second, you find the reciprocal of that rate. The result is the NIM. Finally, when you see the NOI of a prospective investment, you multiply the NOI by the NIM to get a quick reading of the property's value.

How to Calculate

To calculate the NIM, take the prevailing, market-driven cap rate and find its reciprocal:

Net Income Multiplier = 1 / Capitalization Rate

To use the NIM to estimate a property's value, multiply by the NOI:

Present Value = Net Income Multiplier × Net Operating Income

Example

Investors in your area are generally buying small apartment buildings at an 11.5% capitalization rate. What NIM does that represent?

Net Income Multiplier = 1 / Capitalization Rate
Net Income Multiplier = 1 / 0.115
Net Income Multiplier = 8.6957 (round to 8.7)

Rule of Thumb: The usefulness of the NIM depends on the accuracy of your information about cap rates in your area, so do your homework first. Garbage in, garbage out, as the computer folks say.

Also remember that NIM, like cap rate, gross rent multiplier, and several other measures, looks at an income property at a point in time. These measures provide a valuable insight, but you should remember that other measures, such as discounted cash flow and internal rate of return, provide another perspective by considering the potential income stream over time.

Test Your Understanding

1. You are considering the purchase of a particular property. The seller gives you the following information, which you judge to be accurate:

Gross Operating Income $160,000
Operating Expenses $72,000

The prevailing cap rate for properties of this type in your area is 11%.

Using the NIM, what is a reasonable estimate of value for this property?

2. You own an income property that throws off an NOI of $24,000. The prevailing cap rate in this location is 12%. What NIM corresponds to this rate?

You are approached by Walter, who is interested in purchasing the property. Walter, as a charter member of the Inept Order of the Uninformed, has taken a vow of ignorance. He offers to purchase your building for $280,000. Should you accept his offer? If Walter knew how to calculate a cap rate, what rate would his offer represent?

Answer

1. First you must calculate the NOI:

Gross Operating Income	160,000
less Operating Expenses	72,000
= Net Operating Income	88,000

Next, you need to determine the NIM:

Net Income Multiplier = 1 / Capitalization Rate
Net Income Multiplier = 1 / 0.11
Net Income Multiplier = 9.09

Finally, use the NIM to estimate the value of the property:

Present Value = Net Income Multiplier × Net Operating Income
Present Value = 9.09 × 88,000
Present Value = 800,000

2. First calculate the NIM:

Net Income Multiplier = 1 / Capitalization Rate
Net Income Multiplier = 1 / 0.12
Net Income Multiplier = 8.333 (round to 8.3)

The NOI and prevailing market cap rate indicate a value of $200,000. Assuming that (a) Walter has not asked you to take back the financing personally, (b) you believe he is capable of obtaining the necessary financing on his own, (c) there are no valuable minerals under the surface, and (d) the property is not located in the middle of a proposed sports complex or casino, then you will be pleased to accept his offer.

You do not want to hold the mortgage because, at this inflated price, Walter may have difficulty servicing the debt with the current revenue. A third-party lender would show no less reluctance to underwrite the loan unless Walter makes a substantial down payment (and thus takes out a relatively small loan). For more information on these topics, see the chapters on debt coverage ratio (Part II, Calculation 23) and loan-to-value ratio (Part II, Calculation 26).

His offer represents a cap rate of 8.57%, substantially less than what he should be able to achieve in this market.

18

Calculation 12: Taxable Income

What It Means

A property's *taxable income* is exactly what its name suggests: the amount on which you must pay federal income tax. Perhaps it would be more helpful to identify what taxable income is not: It's not your total rental income, not your income after operating expenses (i.e., NOI), and not your cash flow.

Taxable income in regard to real estate, like taxable income in the rest of your life, is whatever the tax code says it is. Fortunately, for purposes of this discussion, while there have been minor tweaks from time to time, the definition as it applies to real estate has remained basically constant. It's reasonable to believe that what you learn here will still be useful after the ink is dry.

Like cash flow, taxable income does begin with the property's revenue minus operating expenses, what you have come to know as the net operating income (NOI). From that point—and unlike cash flow—the NOI is then reduced, not by everything you spend, but rather by everything the current tax code allows you to deduct. For example, you cannot deduct your entire mortgage payment, but you can generally deduct the entire interest portion. If you revisit the discussion in Part I,

Chapter 4, you'll recall that you can also deduct depreciation and amortization. When you buy an investment property, you can't just take its purchase price as a tax deduction. You can, however, take the portion of the purchase price that represents the buildings (not the land) and write that portion off over what the tax code prescribes as its "useful life." This write-off is called depreciation. If you make an addition or capital improvement to the property, that too is written off through depreciation and not as a one-year tax deduction.

Another item that must be deducted over time instead of when it is actually spent is the premium you pay for obtaining a mortgage, called "points." If you get a 240-month mortgage, you will generally deduct the loan points over that period. Similarly, closing costs such as legal fees to acquire an investment property must also be written off over time, usually the same number of years as the property's useful life. You'll refer to the process of taking a partial annual tax deduction for an item that cannot be expensed in a single year as "amortization."

Finally, keep in mind that you must also count as taxable income any interest earned on property bank accounts or mortgage escrow accounts.

How to Calculate

Top-down calculation:

    Net Operating Income
    less Mortgage Interest
    less Depreciation, Real Property
    less Depreciation, Capital Additions
    less Amortization, Points and Closing Costs
    plus Interest Earned
    = Taxable Income

Let's look at the component parts. As you've seen before, NOI equals gross scheduled income, less vacancy and credit loss, less operating expenses. It's your collected income less operating expenses.

Unless you have an interest-only loan, your mortgage payments are made up of both interest and principal. Only the interest portion is deductible.

You can claim depreciation deductions based on the purchase price of the buildings and on the cost of capital improvements. The cost of new improvements is certainly unambiguous, but allocating the property's purchase price between land and buildings requires a judgment call on your part. The most common and defensible approach is to use the proportions that you find in your assessments for local property tax. If the town or city assesses your property's land at $25,000 and its buildings at $75,000, then regardless of what you paid for the property, you should be able to assume that 75% of the purchase price went to pay for the buildings.

The useful life of the buildings is specified in the tax code. As of this writing, you depreciate residential property over 27.5 years and nonresidential over 39 years. Also in the current law is the "half-month convention," which says that you can take only one-half month of depreciation in the month that you place a property into service and one-half in the month you dispose of it.

By current rules, you must amortize closing costs associated with the acquisition of an investment property over the same useful life that you use for depreciation purposes. You normally do this by adding the amount of the closing costs to the property's depreciable basis.

The rules regarding depreciation may change at any time the Congress feels like giving more or less benefit to real estate investors.

Capital additions (additions having a useful life of more than one year or improvements that are likely to prolong the life of the property) are treated the same as the main property. You typically depreciate them over the same useful life, starting when they are placed in service. The half-month convention applies to these as well.

You will amortize loan points over the number of months of the loan term. It is not unusual for a commercial mortgage to have its payment based on a relatively long term, such as 180 to 240 months, while at the same time requiring a "balloon payment" (i.e., a payoff of the outstanding balance at a much earlier date). In such a case, the balloon payment marks the term of the loan for purposes of amortizing the points. For example, say that you have a loan whose monthly payment is based on 240 months; but the loan also requires that you pay it off in full at the end of 60 months. You can amortize any loan points over the 60 months.

The last of the components is interest income. This is usually not included as part of the NOI because it does not derive from the operation of the property. Nonetheless, if you have property bank accounts or mortgage escrow accounts that pay you interest, you must add that to your property's taxable income.

Example

You purchase a small apartment building on January 1 for $280,000. You take out a 20-year $200,000 mortgage and pay 2 points to obtain the loan. Based on your municipal tax assessments, you judge that 75% of the property's value is in its buildings and 25% in the land. Your annual NOI is $30,000, and mortgage interest for the year is $20,500. Your checking account and mortgage escrow account combine to pay you $85 in interest for the year. You make no capital additions to the property. What do you estimate as your taxable income?

Let's begin with our top-down calculation model and fill in the items that are specified outright in the example:

Net Operating Income	30,000
less Mortgage Interest	20,500
less Depreciation, Real Property	
less Depreciation, Capital Additions	0
less Amortization, Points	
plus Interest Earned	85
= Taxable Income	?

Just two rows require some side calculations.

The first row we look at is Depreciation, Real Property. Before you can calculate the amount of depreciation allowed, you must first figure out how much of this property is depreciable. According to your local tax assessor, 75% of the value of this parcel lies in its buildings. Since only buildings can be depreciated, it is fair to say that 75% of the purchase price, or $210,000, represents the depreciable basis.

The example states that this is an apartment building, so clearly it is a residential property. That means you must depreciate it over 27.5

years. Dividing $210,000 by 27.5 years gives you approximately $7,636 per year as your depreciation deduction.

But wait, there's more. You bought this property on January 1, so you'll have to knock off one-half month of depreciation to satisfy the half-month convention. If the annual depreciation is $7,636, then the monthly depreciation is 1/12 of that amount, or $636. One-half month is $318; you reduce your annual depreciation by $318. For the first year, you can deduct $7,318 in depreciation. You can fill in one more row:

Net Operating Income	30,000
less Mortgage Interest	20,500
less Depreciation, Real Property	7,318
less Depreciation, Capital Additions	0
less Amortization, Points	
plus Interest Earned	85
= Taxable Income	?

That leaves amortization of points. As with depreciation, you need to start by figuring out the total amount; then you calculate how much of that you can deduct this year.

By definition, a point is 1% of the amount of the mortgage. You had 2 points on a $200,000 mortgage, and so 2% of 200,000 is 4,000. You can amortize the points over the term of the loan, which in this case is 20 years: 4,000 divided by 20 gives you an annual deduction of $200 for amortization of points. You can fill in the last number and make your taxable income calculation:

Net Operating Income	30,000
less Mortgage Interest	20,500
less Depreciation, Real Property	7,318
less Depreciation, Capital Additions	0
less Amortization, Point	200
plus Interest Earned	85
= Taxable Income	2,067

You can use the worksheet on the next page to estimate a property's taxable income. As with a similar form provided for cash flow, we included the most common expense items, so that you can use the form to work your way from the very top to the bottom.

Taxable Income

Date:

Prepared by:

INCOME	
Gross Scheduled Rent Income	
Other Income	
TOTAL GROSS INCOME	
VACANCY & CREDIT ALLOWANCE	
GROSS OPERATING INCOME	
EXPENSES	
Insurance (fire and liability)	
Property Taxes	
Repairs and Maintenance	
Supplies and Miscellaneous	
Utilities	
Other	
TOTAL EXPENSES	
NET OPERATING INCOME	
Less Interest, First Mortgage	
Less Interest, Second Mortgage	
Less Depreciation, Real Property	
Less Depreciation, Capital Additions	
Less Amortization, Points	
Plus Interest Earned	
TAXABLE INCOME	

Rule of Thumb: Don't be surprised to find that your taxable income is often less than your cash flow before taxes. Keep in mind that you have depreciation deductions that reduce your taxable income without reducing your cash flow.

All coins have a flip side, however. If you hold a property long enough, you'll exhaust your depreciation deduction. There is no way to start it over again, except if the property is sold to a new owner. That buyer can begin depreciating all over again based on his or her purchase price. I can hear what you're thinking, and you can forget it. Don't try to sell it back to yourself; it won't work.

Another situation you should be aware of occurs when your mortgage becomes "seasoned." This term does not mean that you can treat it like firewood and toss it into the flames. It means that you have progressed well into the full term of the loan so that a larger portion of each payment is applied to the principal. As you know, in an amortized loan with level payments, the earliest payments have the greatest proportion of interest and the smallest of principal. With each payment you make, you reduce the principal balance slightly, so that the next payment requires a little less interest, leaving a bit more available to apply to principal. Eventually, you're paying more principal than interest.

As we discussed in the Introduction, this amortization of your mortgage, paid for essentially by your tenants, is one of the four basic returns that you enjoy as a real estate investor. It can also be the source of some surprise if you're not paying attention. During the first year (or even several years, depending on the length of the loan), your debt service may be nearly all interest and therefore nearly all deductible.

It can be easy to get too comfortable with that idea. Imagine yourself the buyer of a small commercial property. You take out a 10- or 15-year mortgage. You also structure your commercial leases to give your tenants five years with an option for five more. Basically, your rent increases keep pace with the rise in your operating expenses, so you have a nice, level NOI over 10 years.

Your initial cash flow looks good, and all is right with the world. Perhaps halfway into that 5- or 10-year mortgage, you begin to notice that while your annual debt service remains constant, you have much more non-deductible principal and much less deductible interest. On the one hand, you know that is a good thing because your tenants are paying off the mortgage. On the other hand, your taxable income (and therefore your tax liability) is going up because you're paying less interest while at the same time your cash flow before taxes stays the same because your debt service remains constant.

This is not tragic. It's not even really unfair; a third party is relieving you of your mortgage debt, and that benefit is causing you some tax liability. What's critical is for you to recognize that you need to run your numbers and financial forecasts so that you can anticipate a situation like this. If you do anticipate that it will happen, you could structure your leases more aggressively or perhaps plan to refinance in order to extract some cash—paid for, of course, with deductible interest.

Test Your Understanding

You purchase a small strip shopping center on January 1 for $800,000. Consider the following facts about the purchase and the first year of operation:

1. The tax assessment for the entire property is $500,000, of which $150,000 represents assessed value of the land.
2. You take out a $500,000 mortgage at 8% for 20 years. The annual debt service is $50,186, of which $10,568 is principal. You pay 2 points to obtain the loan.
3. The center has 8,000 rentable square feet, and you charge $15 per square foot per year as rent.
4. You allow 2% for vacancy and credit loss.
5. You experience the following operating expenses:
   a. Property Taxes, $22,000

    b. Insurance, $6,000

    c. Repairs and Maintenance, $9,000

    d. Water, $7,000

    e. Sewer, $3,000

    f. Miscellaneous, $3,000

6. You replace the center's facade at a cost of $50,000 and place this in service in July.

7. Your property checking account earns $90 over the course of the year.

What is the property's taxable income for the year?

Answer

You don't have the NOI as a given here, so you'll need to start at the very top of the food chain with the gross scheduled income. Let's use the form shown earlier.

The property has 8,000 rentable square feet offered at $15 per square foot; therefore, the gross scheduled income is 8,000 × 15, or $120,000. Your allowance for vacancy and credit loss is 2% of that amount, or $2,400. The difference between these two amounts is your gross operating income:

INCOME	
Gross Scheduled Rent Income	120,000
Other Income	
TOTAL GROSS INCOME	120,000
VACANCY & CREDIT ALLOWANCE	2,400
GROSS OPERATING INCOME	117,600

From here, subtract the operating expenses to derive the NOI:

EXPENSES	
Insurance (fire and liability)	6,000
Property Taxes	22,000
Repairs and Maintenance	9,000
Supplies and Miscellaneous	3,000

Utilities	10,000
Other	
TOTAL EXPENSES	50,000
NET OPERATING INCOME	67,600

Next is the interest expense on your mortgage. You know that the annual debt service is $50,186, of which $10,568 is principal. The remainder, $39,618, is the interest for the current year.

less Interest, 1st Mortgage	39,618

Now you have to calculate the depreciation for the real property. As in the earlier example, you must first figure out the depreciable basis of the building. The tax assessment for the entire parcel is $500,000, of which $150,000 is land. That means the difference, $350,000, must be the tax assessment for the building. You can reasonably assert that 70% (350,000 divided by 500,000) of the value of this property lies in the building. If you purchased the building for $800,000, then 70% of that amount, $560,000, is the depreciable basis of the building.

You know you can't write the whole amount off in one year. How many years must you use as this property's useful life? It is not residential, so you must depreciate it over 39 years. Take the $560,000 depreciable basis of the building and divide it by 39 years to get the annual amount of $14,359.

As in the preceding example, you can't deduct the entire $14,359 because you purchased the property and placed it in service this year; you must reduce it by an amount equal to one-half month of depreciation. You can divide the full year amount by 12 and then by 2, or you can save a step and divide by 24 to determine the amount of depreciation you must give up: 14,359 / 24 = 598. For the first full year of ownership, you can take a full year of depreciation (14,359) less one-half month (598), or $13,761.

less Depreciation, Real Property	13,761

You made a capital addition to the property when you put on a new facade. The value of the addition is what you paid for it, $50,000, and its useful life is the same as what you use for the main property, 39 years. If you were able to take a full year of depreciation for this addition, that deduction would equal the cost divided by the useful life: 50,000 / 39, or $1,282. However, you need to take note not only of the half-month convention here, but also of the fact that you didn't place this improvement into service until July. In this case, you're entitled to take one-half month of depreciation for the month placed in service (July) and a full month for each of August through December. In other words, you can take 5.5 months of depreciation. If the annual depreciation is $1,202, then one month is worth $106.83 and 5.5 months are worth $588.

less Depreciation, Capital Additions   588

You took out a $500,000 mortgage for 20 years. The 2 points you paid to get this loan represent 2% of the loan amount, or $10,000. You must write this amount off over the 20-year term of the loan at $500 per year.

less Amortization, Points   500

Finally, you earned interest on your property bank account:

plus Interest Earned   90

You can now complete the form and find that your taxable income is $13,223.

INCOME	
Gross Scheduled Rent Income	120,000
Other Income	
TOTAL GROSS INCOME	120,000
VACANCY & CREDIT ALLOWANCE	2,400
GROSS OPERATING INCOME	117,600
EXPENSES	
Insurance (fire and liability)	6,000
Property Taxes	22,000
Repairs and Maintenance	9,000
Supplies and Miscellaneous	3,000
Utilities	10,000
Other	
TOTAL EXPENSES	50,000
NET OPERATING INCOME	67,600
Less Interest, First Mortgage	39,618
Less Interest, Second Mortgage	
Less Depreciation, Real Property	13,761
Less Depreciation, Capital Additions	588
Less Amortization, Points	500
Plus Interest Earned	90
TAXABLE INCOME	13,223

19

Calculation 13: Cash Flow

What It Means

Cash flow is all of a property's cash inflows less all of its cash outflows during a given period of time. Inflows are counted whether or not they must be included as taxable income, and outflows are counted regardless of deductibility. For example, cash flow is affected by the entire amount of a mortgage payment, even though only the interest portion is deductible. Cash flow is not affected by a depreciation deduction, which is not a cash item.

When you speak about cash flow, you usually mean *cash flow before taxes* (CFBT), which does not take into account the property's impact on the owner's income tax liability. *Cash flow after taxes* (CFAT) is the CFBT less any tax liability that arises from the operation of the property.

As discussed in Chapter 4, you can think of cash flow as the equivalent of the property's checkbook. It accounts for all the money that flows in and all that flows out. Inflows can include rent, loan proceeds, and interest on bank accounts. Outflows can include debt payments, operating expenses, and capital additions.

How to Calculate

Top-down calculation:

> Net Operating Income
> less Debt Service
> less Capital Additions
> plus Loan Proceeds
> plus Interest Earned
> = Cash Flow Before Taxes

Also:

> Cash Flow Before Taxes
> less Income Tax Liability
> = Cash Flow After Taxes

Let's look at the components of these formulas. We've discussed net operating income throughout this book. It equals gross scheduled income, less vacancy and credit loss, less operating expenses. If you don't recall those topics, please review them now.

Debt service is the total loan payment, including both interest and principal. If you are talking about a property's cash flow for a period of a year, then you must take into account the total of all loan payments for the year as part of that cash flow. The acronym ADS is commonly used to refer to annual debt service.

Capital additions are additions having a useful life of more than one year or improvements that are likely to prolong the life of the property. A capital addition is different from a repair, which maintains rather than increases the life of a property.

Regarding loan proceeds, this item does not refer to the original mortgage loan you took to purchase the property. Instead, it refers to the proceeds of financing you might obtain at a later date. For example, you might decide to build a second floor for office space above your strip shopping center. You also choose to refinance or take out a second mortgage to obtain most or all of the funds for construction. The cost of building the second floor would be a capital addition, reducing your cash flow, while the proceeds of the loan would increase your cash flow.

Example

You have a property that generates a net operating income of $30,000 annually. The monthly mortgage payment for this property is $2,175. Your checking account and mortgage escrow account combine to pay you $85 in interest for the year. What is your CFBT? The property's income also creates a tax liability of $540. What is your CFAT?

If your monthly mortgage payment is $2,175, you need to calculate your annual debt service:

Annual Debt Service = 2,175 × 12 = 26,100

The rest is straightforward:

Net Operating Income	30,000
less Debt Service	26,100
less Capital Additions	0
plus Loan Proceeds	0
plus Interest Earned	85
= Cash Flow Before Taxes	3,985
less Tax Liability	540
= Cash Flow After Taxes	3,445

The following table is a worksheet you can use to calculate a property's cash flow. Although line-item operating expenses are usually included only on the Annual Property Operating Data form (Chapter 3), we've included the most common expense items here (as well as a catch-all "other") so that you can use the form to work your way from the very beginning to the end, from gross scheduled income to CFAT.

Rule of Thumb: You're more likely to encounter surprise expenses than surprise income, so be realistic when forecasting the cash flow from a property you plan to buy. Do you expect the cash flow to be small or nonexistent? If so, the reality may well prove to be that you'll actually have a negative cash flow. This means you would need to inject your own personal funds at some point to pay the bills. Don't wait until this happens to decide if you can handle it. You can still do well, ultimately, with a property that has an occasional negative cash flow—but only if you know that you'll have the funds on hand to ride out those bumps.

Cash Flow

Date:	
Prepared by:	
INCOME	
Gross Scheduled Rent Income	
Other Income	
TOTAL GROSS INCOME	
VACANCY & CREDIT ALLOWANCE	
GROSS OPERATING INCOME	
EXPENSES	
Insurance (fire and liability)	
Property Taxes	
Repairs and Maintenance	
Supplies and Miscellaneous	
Utilities	
Other	
TOTAL EXPENSES	
NET OPERATING INCOME	
Less Annual Debt Service, First Mortgage	
Less Annual Debt Service, Second Mortgage	
Less Capital Additions	
Plus Loan Proceeds	
Plus Interest Earned	
CASH FLOW BEFORE TAXES	
Less Income Tax Liability	
CASH FLOW AFTER TAXES	

Test Your Understanding

You have a property with six tenants, each of whom pays $1,500 per month. You estimate a vacancy and credit loss of 2%. The property has operating expenses of $42,000 per year and a first mortgage payment of $3,400 per month. In month 6, you add a garage to the property at a cost of $30,000. Starting in month 7, you rent the garage at $120 per month. You take a $30,000 second mortgage to cover the cost of construction. Your monthly payment on this loan is $700, and it begins in month 7. Your bank pays you interest of $125. You also win the lottery for $40,000,000. What is your property's CFBT?

Answer

Listen carefully: You did *not* win the lottery. You never do. Like the rest of us, you still check discreetly between the sofa cushions for lost change. Managing your cash flow is essential, so pay attention.

This problem doesn't specify the net operating income, so you'll have to figure it out. Start by calculating your gross scheduled income. You have six tenants at $1,500 per month for 12 months. You also have a garage that you rent at $120 per month for six months.

Gross Scheduled Income = (6 × 1,500 × 12) + (120 × 6)
Gross Scheduled Income = (108,000) + (720) = 108,720

You estimate a vacancy and credit loss of 2%:

Vacancy and Credit Loss = 108,720 × 0.02 = 2,174

Now you have what you need to figure the net operating income:

Gross Scheduled Income	108,720
less Vacancy and Credit Loss	2,174
= Gross Operating Income	106,546
less Operating Expenses	42,000
= Net Operating Income	64,546

In order to continue, you must calculate the annual debt service. Your first mortgage has a monthly payment of $3,400, and you are making these payments for the entire year. Your new second mortgage calls for a monthly payment of $700 and begins in month 7, so you will have six payments.

Annual Debt Service = (3,400 × 12) + (700 × 6)
Annual Debt Service = (40,800) + (4,200) = 45,000

Now you can complete the cash flow calculation:

Net Operating Income	64,546
less Debt Service	45,000
less Capital Additions	30,000
plus Loan Proceeds	30,000
plus Interest Earned	125
= Cash Flow Before Taxes	19,671

20

Calculation 14: Cash-on-Cash Return

What It Means

The *cash-on-cash return* (also called the *equity dividend rate*) is the ratio between the property's cash flow in a particular year (usually before taxes) and the amount of the initial capital investment. It is expressed as a percentage.

Although you can calculate the cash-on-cash return based on projections for any future year, investors tend to look at this measurement as it relates to the expected cash flow in the first year of ownership. Since this calculation doesn't take into account any time value of money, it probably does make sense to measure the cash flow that occurs soonest after you make the investment.

The cash-on-cash return is not a particularly powerful tool, but it has always been popular as a "quick read" on an income property, probably because it allows an easy comparison to other types of investment. For example, you can say, "This property will give me a 6% cash return on my investment in the first year. If I invest in a CD instead, I'll get only 2%."

How to Calculate

Cash-on-Cash Return = Annual Cash Flow / Cash Invested

Example

You purchase property with a down payment of $20,000. In the first full year of operation, the property shows a net operating income of $14,000. Your monthly mortgage payment is $1,000. You have no other items that affect your cash flow for that year. What is your cash-on-cash return for year 1?

First, you need to figure out your cash flow. Do you recall how to do that?

Net Operating Income
less Debt Service
less Capital Additions
plus Loan Proceeds
plus Interest Earned
= Cash Flow Before Taxes

You have only two items in this example that you need to consider: NOI and debt service. Your NOI is given as $14,000. Your debt service is the monthly mortgage payment times 12 ($1,000 \times 12 = 12,000$). Your cash flow, therefore, is:

Net Operating Income	14,000
less Debt Service	12,000
= Cash Flow Before Taxes	2,000

Now you have the two items you need to calculate the cash-on-cash return:

Cash-on-Cash Return = Annual Cash Flow / Cash Invested
Cash-on-Cash Return = 2,000 / 20,000
Cash-on-Cash Return = 10%

> **Rule of Thumb:** Once upon a time, buyers of income property paid a great deal of attention to the cash-on-cash return. It's easy to calculate and, as mentioned above, allows a quick comparison to an alternative such as a CD or T-bill rate.
>
> You need to know about cash-on-cash because sooner or later someone offering you a property is going to quote this statistic as if you should be impressed. Cash flow is a good thing, and if the property actually has it, fine. Just don't forget the other, better ways of taking the pulse of an income-property investment, as discussed throughout this book.
>
> Don't forget, too, that someday you'll be selling a property and may encounter a buyer who thinks that the cash-on-cash return is really important. If it's important to your buyer, it's important to you. It always pays to know your stuff—knowing how to show this basic investment measure may be just what you need to do to close the deal.

Test Your Understanding

A property is fully rented and has four tenants each paying $1,000 per month. Operating expenses are $20,000. Your monthly mortgage payment is $1,800. Assume an allowance for vacancy and credit loss of 2%

1. You purchase the property with a $50,000 down payment. What is your cash-on-cash return?
2. The seller takes back a second mortgage for the entire $50,000 down payment. Debt service on this second mortgage equals $453 per month. Now what is your cash-on-cash return?

Answer

1. First calculate your cash flow. Since this problem doesn't tell you the NOI, start from the top down. The gross scheduled income is provided by four units at $1,000 for 12 months, or $48,000. You expect to lose 2% of that to vacancy and credit, or $960:

Gross Scheduled Income	48,000
less Vacancy and Credit Loss	960
= Gross Operating Income	47,040
less Operating Expenses	20,000
= Net Operating Income	27,040

The monthly mortgage payment is $1,800, so your annual debt service is $21,600. Subtract the debt service to calculate the cash flow:

Net Operating Income	27,040
less Debt Service	21,600
= Cash Flow Before Taxes	5,440

Finally, the cash-on-cash:

Cash-on-Cash Return = Annual Cash Flow / Cash Invested
Cash-on-Cash Return = 5,440 / 50,000
Cash-on-Cash Return = 10.88%

2. Two items change in this second scenario. One is the addition of a second mortgage whose debt service affects your cash flow:

Net Operating Income	27,040
less Debt Service, 1st Mortgage	21,600
less Debt Service, 2nd Mortgage	5,436
= Cash Flow Before Taxes	4

The second item to change is the amount of cash invested, which is now zero.

Cash-on-Cash Return = Annual Cash Flow / Cash Invested

Something is wrong with this picture. Anything divided by 0 equals infinity. Our cash flow doesn't matter; even if it were one penny, we would have the same infinite cash-on-cash return.

What's this all about? You have an income-property investment with no cash invested. Why can't you figure out this rate of return— or any other, for that matter?

You can't calculate the return because there is no such thing as a zero-cash-down investment. If you invest nothing, then you have no investment. You have nothing at risk. You could rephrase question #2 to ask, "What's the return on my investment if I make no investment?"

Rule of Thumb: Transactions with no money down do occur, although this writer suspects that successful deals of this kind are probably far less common than the purveyors of get-rich-quick tapes and seminars would have you believe. There are some practical considerations that argue against the likelihood of success:

1. To finance 100% of an income-property purchase means you're going to have more debt service than a typical buyer. This in turn means that you have a much greater likelihood of experiencing negative cash flow. Instead of reaching into your pocket one time to ante up the down payment, you may be reaching in every month to make up the difference between cash inflow and cash outflow.
2. The cost of this additional financing is likely to be high. Loaning the "down payment" component is a high-risk proposition. A third-party lender would expect a high rate and a short repayment term, both of which would be likely to suck the life out of your cash flow.
3. Why would a seller take back all the secondary financing if you don't put in your own cash? Maybe the property is difficult to sell; that won't change after you buy it, except that now it will be your problem. Maybe the seller has convinced you to agree to an inflated price, so the proceeds from the secondary financing are just gravy. Study this book and that won't happen to you.

If all the stars are lined up just right, a no-money-down deal can work out beneficially, but don't expect that to happen routinely.

21

Calculation 15: Sale Proceeds

What It Means

When you sell your investment property, you hope to leave the closing with a check in your pocket. The money you take home is called *sale proceeds*. To be more precise, it is called *before-tax sale proceeds* because Uncle Sam is waiting outside for his cut.

Most of our discussion in this book has focused on purchasing and operating an income-producing property, but for many investors, it is the sale of the property that makes the greatest impact. If all has gone according to plan, you are probably recovering your original investment plus the property's appreciation in value, plus the paydown (amortization) of your mortgage. When it does come time to settle up on your taxes, much of your profit from this venture may be taxed at capital gain rates, lower than the rate on ordinary income.

How to Calculate

Keep in mind that when you forecast the future sale of your investment property, your purpose is not to fulfill your childhood dream of mastering double-entry bookkeeping. Rather, it is to complete the final projections you need in order to judge the overall success of your investment. For simplicity, it's customary to make these projections in full-year increments. In real life, you may sell your property on November 7, and the attorney who closes this transaction will have to make adjustments for midmonth loan payoffs, per diem interest due, property taxes paid in advance, rent collected in advance, and security deposits, to name the most common. For your purposes, and for those of most investors, it is just as useful and far less complicated to assume that in whatever year you sell, you will do so just before the stroke of midnight on December 31. Please do not wear funny hats or bring noisemakers to the closing.

Given that you decide to forecast an end-of-year sale, the calculation becomes straightforward:

Selling Price
less Costs of Sale
less Mortgage Payoff
= Sale Proceeds Before Taxes
less Tax on Sale
= Sale Proceeds After Taxes

In Chapter 4 and in the chapters on capitalization rate and on net income multiplier, we've discussed how to estimate value by capitalizing net operating income. You can put that technique to work here to estimate the value of your property in the future.

You will then estimate the costs of sale. These costs usually include legal fees and brokerage commissions. Most investors estimate costs of sale as a percentage of the selling price.

Mortgage payoff amounts can be calculated in a number of ways (see Part I, Chapter 3, and Part II, Calculation 29). You can use one of the Excel models shown in Chapter 3, or you can download the RealData Calculator from http://www.realdata.com.

For more information on the calculation of the tax liability, see Part I, Chapter 4, and also gain on sale in Part II, Calculation 35.

You can use the following form to help you calculate sale proceeds.

Sale Proceeds	
Date:	
Prepared by:	
SELLING PRICE	
Less Costs of Sale	
Less First Mortgage Payoff	
Less Second Mortgage Payoff	
BEFORE-TAX SALE PROCEEDS	
Less Total Federal Tax on Sale	
AFTER-TAX SALE PROCEEDS	

Example

You estimate that you will sell your property for $500,000. You also estimate that you will pay 5% of the selling price for the services of a broker and 2% for an attorney. At the time of sale, you'll have a first mortgage with an outstanding balance of $200,000. What are your before-tax sale proceeds?

If you pay 5% to a broker and 2% to an attorney, your total costs of sale will be 7% of the selling price.

Costs of Sale = 500,000 × 0.07 = 35,000

Now you can take the formula or the preceding form and fill in the values:

Selling Price	500,000
less Costs of Sale	35,000
less Mortgage Payoff	200,000
= Sale Proceeds Before Taxes	265,000

> **Rule of Thumb:** Whenever you obtain a mortgage loan, print out an amortization schedule for that loan. It used to be necessary to order (and pay for) a schedule from a financial services provider. Use the free RealData Calculator program or download a basic Excel template we provide for readers of this book. You can also create such a schedule online with your web browser at http://www.realdata.com.
>
> Not only will an amortization schedule allow you to keep track of the outstanding balance of your mortgage loan, but it will also let you monitor the amount of interest paid and verify the information you receive from your bank on IRS form 1098 at the end of the year.

Test Your Understanding

You would like to forecast the proceeds of selling your property five years from now. You project that it will have an annual NOI of $50,000 at that time. Investment properties in your area have been achieving a cap rate of 11.5%. This rate has been steady for several years, and you believe it will hold. You expect to pay a 4% commission to a broker to sell the property and 2% for legal expenses to close the deal. You have a mortgage, and according to your amortization schedule, you will owe $212,000 when you sell.

What do you estimate will be your before-tax sale proceeds?

Answer

You have a few preliminary calculations to make before you "fill in the blanks." First, what will the property be worth when you sell? Recall this formula from our chapter on capitalization rates:

Value = Net Operating Income / Capitalization Rate

You have what you believe are reasonable estimates of the NOI and cap rate, so you can use those to predict the property's value at the time of sale:

Value = 50,000 / 0.115
Value = 434,783 (round to 435,000)

> **Rule of Thumb:** This is a good place to pause for a reality check. Don't forget that you are making forecasts and projections, polite terms for predicting the future. You can take the position that it is possible to make a reasonable estimate of your property's value in the future, but reasonable doesn't mean to the last dollar. Whenever you're running the numbers for the purpose of presentation to a third party, like a lender, round off your estimate of resale value to the nearest thousand at the very least, perhaps to the nearest 5,000 or 10,000, depending on the magnitude of the number. It demonstrates that you recognize this to be an estimate of value.

You also need to calculate your expected costs of sale, 4% for the broker and 2% for the attorney:

Costs of Sale = 435,000 × 0.06 = 26,100

This time, let's use the sample form provided earlier:

SELLING PRICE	435,000
less Costs of Sale	26,100
less 1st Mortgage Payoff	212,000
less 2nd Mortgage Payoff	0
BEFORE-TAX SALE PROCEEDS	196,900
less Total Federal Tax on Sale	
AFTER-TAX SALE PROCEEDS	196,900

You estimate before-tax sale proceeds of $196,900.

22

Calculation 16: Discounted Cash Flow

What It Means

In a previous chapter, you saw how to find the present value of a single future cash flow. Doing so allowed you to know the worth of that cash flow in current dollars.

The typical investment property generates more than one cash flow over time. You hope that it will generate positive cash from operations each year, and you certainly expect to end up with cash to take home from the eventual sale of the property. You consider these sale proceeds to be a cash flow also.

Collectively, your investment's cash flows represent its entire income stream. When you discount each of these cash flows back to its present value and then add those PVs up, the sum represents the present value of the entire income stream. We call this process of finding the present worth of the whole income stream *discounted cash flow*.

Why do you discount the cash flows individually instead of as a lump sum? As you've seen many times in our earlier discussions, the answer lies in the time value of money. These cash flows occur at different times. The longer you have to wait for a particular return, the more severely it has to be discounted and the less it is worth. A dollar received in 10 years is far less valuable than a dollar received in one year. You find the PV of each cash flow according to the length of time you must wait for it.

How to Calculate

Once again you can use a simple Excel template provided at http://www.realdata.com/book, where you just fill in the cash flows and the discount rate and Excel calculates the present value of each cash flow and displays the total:

		PV@ 11%
Cash Flow, End of Year 1	1,000	901
Cash Flow, End of Year 2	1,000	812
Cash Flow, End of Year 3	1,000	731
Cash Flow, End of Year 4	1,000	659
Cash Flow, End of Year 5	21,000	12,462
Cash Flow, End of Year 6	0	0
Cash Flow, End of Year 7	0	0
Cash Flow, End of Year 8	0	0
Cash Flow, End of Year 9	0	0
Cash Flow, End of Year 10	0	0
TOTAL PV		15,565

Earlier you saw how to calculate PV using the "Annual Present Value Factors" table. To calculate the discounted cash flow, you just compute several PVs and add them up. You use the table to complete the examples here. You can also use the following form to facilitate your calculations:

	Factor from PV Table		
	@	%	PV
Cash Flow, End of Year 1			
Cash Flow, End of Year 2			
Cash Flow, End of Year 3			

Cash Flow, End of Year 4 _____

Cash Flow, End of Year 5 _____

Cash Flow, End of Year 6 _____

Cash Flow, End of Year 7 _____

Cash Flow, End of Year 8 _____

Cash Flow, End of Year 9 _____

Cash Flow, End of Year 10 _____

TOTAL PV _____

Example

You operate a property and forecast that you will have the following cash flows:

Year 1	$1,000
Year 2	$1,200
Year 3	$1,550
Year 4	$1,975
Year 5	$2,350

You also estimate that the sale of your property five years from now will produce cash proceeds of $200,000. If you discount these cash flows at 10.5% per year, what is the present value of the entire income stream?

Start by entering the cash flows into the following form. Note that your cash flow for year 5 includes both the cash from operation and the cash from resale of the property:

		Factor from PV Table @ 10.5 %	PV
Cash Flow, End of Year 1	1,000		
Cash Flow, End of Year 2	1,200		
Cash Flow, End of Year 3	1,550		
Cash Flow, End of Year 4	1,975		
Cash Flow, End of Year 5	202,350		
Cash Flow, End of Year 6			

Cash Flow, End of Year 7
Cash Flow, End of Year 8
Cash Flow, End of Year 9
Cash Flow, End of Year 10

TOTAL PV

Go to the table and look up the factor where the column for 10.5% intersects the row for year 1. You should find 0.9049771. Do the same for years 2 through 5 and fill in the PV factors on the form:

		Factor from PV Table		
		@	10.5 %	PV
Cash Flow, End of Year 1	1,000	0.904977		
Cash Flow, End of Year 2	1,200	0.818984		
Cash Flow, End of Year 3	1,550	0.741162		
Cash Flow, End of Year 4	1,975	0.670735		
Cash Flow, End of Year 5	202,350	0.607000		
Cash Flow, End of Year 6				
Cash Flow, End of Year 7				
Cash Flow, End of Year 8				
Cash Flow, End of Year 9				
Cash Flow, End of Year 10				

TOTAL PV

Finally, multiply each cash flow by its factor to find its present value and then total all the PVs (Figure 22.4). Round your total to the nearest dollar:

		Factor from PV Table		
		@	10.5 %	PV
Cash Flow, End of Year 1	1,000	0.904977	904.98	
Cash Flow, End of Year 2	1,200	0.818984	982.78	
Cash Flow, End of Year 3	1,550	0.741162	1,148.80	
Cash Flow, End of Year 4	1,975	0.670735	1,324.70	
Cash Flow, End of Year 5	202,350	0.607000	122,826.43	
Cash Flow, End of Year 6				
Cash Flow, End of Year 7				
Cash Flow, End of Year 8				

Cash Flow, End of Year 9
Cash Flow, End of Year 10

	TOTAL PV	127,188

> **Rule of Thumb:** The sum of the discounted cash flows always represents the value of (i.e., what you're getting for) your cash outlay at a given rate of return. So your bottom line here is not the value of the property (unless you pay all cash), but rather the value of your cash investment. If your cash investment were less than $127,188, you would really be earning more than 10.5%. If your cash investment were more than $127,188, your real return would be less than the 10.5% you expected.

Test Your Understanding

You operate a property and forecast that you will have the following cash flows:

Year 1	$3,000
Year 2	$3,600
Year 3	$4,250
Year 4	$5,150
Year 5	$5,900
Year 6	$7,000
Year 7	$8,350

You also estimate that you will sell the property at the end of year 7 for $750,000. You expect your costs of sale to be 7%. At the time of sale, your mortgage will have an unpaid balance of $395,000. If you discount all cash flows at 10.0% per year, what is the present value of the entire income stream?

Answer

Before you can plug all the cash flows into the form, you need to calculate your final cash flow, the proceeds of sale. Recall the formula from the chapter on this subject:

Selling Price
less Costs of Sale
less Mortgage Payoff
= Sale Proceeds Before Taxes

Your costs of sale are 7% of the selling price, or $52,500.

Selling Price	750,000
less Costs of Sale	52,500
less Mortgage Payoff	395,000
= Sale Proceeds Before Taxes	302,500

You need to make one more calculation before you use the DCF form. The cash flow for year 7 is the combination of the cash flow from operation and the sale proceeds. Hence, the total cash flow for that year equals $8,350 plus $302,500, or $310,850.

Now on to the last form. Enter the cash flows; look up and enter the PV factors at 10.0% for years 1 through 7; multiply each cash flow by its factor; and, finally, add up the PVs to get the discounted cash flow of the entire income stream:

		Factor from PV Table @ 10.0 %	PV
Cash Flow, End of Year 1	3,000	0.909091	2,727.27
Cash Flow, End of Year 2	3,600	0.826446	2,975.21
Cash Flow, End of Year 3	4,250	0.751315	3,193.09
Cash Flow, End of Year 4	5,150	0.683013	3,517.52
Cash Flow, End of Year 5	5,900	0.620921	3,663.44
Cash Flow, End of Year 6	7,000	0.564474	3,951.32
Cash Flow, End of Year 7	310,850	0.513158	159,515.16
Cash Flow, End of Year 8			
Cash Flow, End of Year 9			
Cash Flow, End of Year 10			
		TOTAL PV	179,543

23

Calculation 17:
Net Present Value

What It Means

If you followed our earlier discussions of present value and discounted cash flow, then you need to take only a small step to understand *net present value* (NPV). Recall that you performed a discounted cash flow analysis to find the present worth of all the property's future cash flows at a given discount rate.

Let's say that you require a 10.5% rate of return on your investment. When you discount all the expected future cash flows back at that rate, the PV that you find as your answer is the amount of cash you need to invest at 10.5% to achieve those future cash flows—with exactly the same timing and amount that you predicted.

The discounted cash flow analysis tells you what the future cash flows are worth at a given rate of return, but that isn't necessarily how much you are going to pay for them. This is where NPV comes in. NPV is the difference between the PV of all future cash flows and the amount of cash you invest to purchase those cash flows. That's why it's called "net" present value.

If you invest exactly what the future cash flows are worth at a given discount rate (rate of return), then your investment is earning exactly that rate. If the PV of the cash flows is greater than the amount of your investment, you have a positive NPV, which is another way of saying that you're really doing better than the specified rate of return because you're getting more than you expected from your investment. If the PV of the cash flows is less than the amount of your investment, you have a negative NPV. That means that you're not doing as well as the specified rate of return.

A term closely related to NPV is profitability index. Be sure to read the chapter on that topic after you complete this one.

How to Calculate

Again, you can use the Excel template we provide at http://www .realdata.com/book. Just fill in the initial investment, the cash flows, and the discount rate, and Excel calculates the PV of each cash flow and displays the NPV:

Discount Rate	11.50%
Initial Investment	120,000
Cash Flow #1	9,000
Cash Flow #2	11,000
Cash Flow #3	12,750
Cash Flow #4	13,250
Cash Flow #5	165,000
Cash Flow #6	
Cash Flow #7	
Cash Flow #8	
Cash Flow #9	
Cash Flow #10	
Net Present Value	10,434

You can also use the form provided in Calculation 16, "Discounted Cash Flow," to find the PV of all the future cash flows and then apply the following formula:

Net Present Value = Present Value of all Future Cash Flows
less Initial Cash Investment

We'll use the form and the formula in the example that follows.

Example

You expect to purchase a property using a $75,000 cash investment, and you forecast that you will have the following cash flows:

Year 1	$700
Year 2	$900
Year 3	$1,150
Year 4	$1,375
Year 5	$1,500

You also estimate that the sale of your property five years from now will produce cash proceeds of $125,000. You believe your investment capital should achieve an 11.5% per annual return, so you choose to discount all future cash flows at that rate. What is the NPV of this income stream?

Use the discounted cash flow form to calculate the PV and then subtract your cash investment to compute the NPV. As you did in the chapter "Discounted Cash Flow," fill in the cash flows and present value factors. Remember that the cash flow for year 5 is the sum of that year's operating cash and sale proceeds.

		Factor from PV Table @ 11.5%	PV
Cash Flow, End of Year 1	700	0.896861	
Cash Flow, End of Year 2	900	0.804360	
Cash Flow, End of Year 3	1,150	0.721399	
Cash Flow, End of Year 4	1,375	0.646994	
Cash Flow, End of Year 5	126,500	0.580264	
Cash Flow, End of Year 6			
Cash Flow, End of Year 7			

Cash Flow, End of Year 8
Cash Flow, End of Year 9
Cash Flow, End of Year 10

Total PV:

Next, multiply each cash flow by its factor to find its PV and then total all the PVs. Round your total to the nearest dollar:

		Factor from PV Table @ 11.5%	PV
Cash Flow, End of Year 1	700	0.896861	627.80
Cash Flow, End of Year 2	900	0.804360	723.92
Cash Flow, End of Year 3	1,150	0.721399	829.61
Cash Flow, End of Year 4	1,375	0.646994	889.62
Cash Flow, End of Year 5	126,500	0.580264	73,403.40
Cash Flow, End of Year 6			
Cash Flow, End of Year 7			
Cash Flow, End of Year 8			
Cash Flow, End of Year 9			
Cash Flow, End of Year 10			
		Total PV:	76,474

Now apply the formula:

Net Present Value = Present Value of all Future Cash Flows
    less Initial Cash Investment
Net Present Value = 76,474 − 75,000
Net Present Value = 1,474

Rule of Thumb: An NPV of zero means you have achieved exactly your rate-of-return goal. A positive NPV means you've exceeded that goal. A negative NPV means you failed to reach the goal.

Test Your Understanding

You expect to purchase a property with $100,000 in cash and to operate it as follows:

	First Year
Net Operating Income	48,000
Debt Service	39,000

Years 2 and 3

- Net operating income increases by 3% each year.
- Debt service remains constant.
- You plan no capital additions.
- You earn no interest on your bank account.
- You expect to sell the property at the end of three years for $475,000.
- You'll spend 6% for costs of sale.
- At the end of three years, your mortgage balance will be $340,000.
- You believe your investment capital should achieve an 11.5% annual return.

What is the NPV of this investment?

Answer

First you need to calculate the cash flow for each year. Recall the formula:

Net Operating Income
less Debt Service
less Capital Additions
plus Loan Proceeds
plus Interest Earned
= Cash Flow Before Taxes

You have no capital additions, new loans, or interest earned, so your first-year cash flow is:

Net Operating Income	48,000
less Debt Service	39,000
= Cash Flow Before Taxes	9,000

In years 2 and 3, your net operating income will increase 3%:

48,000 × 1.03 = 49,440 less 39,000 Debt Service = 10,440 Cash Flow (Year 2)

49,440 × 1.03 = 50,923 less 39,000 Debt Service = 11,923 Cash Flow (Year 3)

You will sell for $475,000 less 6% costs of sale and $340,000 mortgage balance:

Selling Price	475,000
less Costs of Sale	28,500
less Mortgage Payoff	340,000
= Sale Proceeds Before Taxes	106,500

Your total year 3 cash flow from operation and resale is 11,923 plus 106,500, or $118,423.

You now have enough information to use the discounted cash flow form:

		Factor from PV Table @ 11.5%	PV
Cash Flow, End of Year 1	9,000	0.896861	8,071.75
Cash Flow, End of Year 2	10,440	0.804360	8,397.51
Cash Flow, End of Year 3	118,423	0.721399	85,430.21
Cash Flow, End of Year 4			
Cash Flow, End of Year 5			
Cash Flow, End of Year 6			
Cash Flow, End of Year 7			
Cash Flow, End of Year 8			
Cash Flow, End of Year 9			
Cash Flow, End of Year 10			
		Total PV:	101,899

One final step is necessary. You must find the difference between the PV of the future cash flows and your actual cash investment:

Net Present Value = Present Value of all Future Cash Flows
    less Initial Cash Investment
Net Present Value = 101,899 – 100,000
Net Present Value = 1,899

Your NPV is slightly positive, which means that you expect to achieve slightly better than the 11.5% rate of return that you specified as your requirement.

24

Calculation 18: Profitability Index

What It Means

Profitability index closely follows net present value (NPV) as a method of measuring investment return. With NPV, you take the present value (PV) of all future cash flows and subtract the amount of your initial investment. If the difference is zero or a positive number, then you have equaled or exceeded your required rate of return, indicated by the discount rate.

With profitability index, instead of finding the difference between PV and initial investment, you find the ratio. If the present worth of the cash flows equals your cash investment exactly, then the index will be 1.0.

On the surface, it would appear that this index is just another way of expressing the same result. In one sense, that's true because both the NPV and the profitability index weigh PV against initial investment. The index, however, offers an advantage if you want to compare two opportunities that require different initial investments. Because the index is a ratio, it is not sensitive to the amount of the investment. It tells you the proportion of dollars returned to dollars invested, rather than the amount.

How to Calculate

Profitability Index = Present Value of all Future Cash Flows / Initial Cash
Investment

Example

Consider the example shown in the chapter "Net Present Value." You
expected to purchase a property using a $75,000 cash investment. Your
forecast of cash flows yielded a PV of future cash flows of $76,474 and
an NPV of $1,474. Using that same data, what is the profitability index?

Profitability Index = 76,474 / 75,000
Profitability Index = 1.01965

> **Rule of Thumb:** A profitability index of 1.0 means you have exactly
> achieved your rate-of-return goal. An index greater than 1.0 means
> you've exceeded that goal. An index less than 1.0 means you failed to
> reach the goal.

Test Your Understanding

You are considering two pieces of property as investments. One property requires a cash investment of $125,000. You estimate the PV of all
its futures cash flows at $135,000.

The second property requires a cash investment of $75,000. Using
the same discount rate, you estimate the PV of its cash flows at $84,000.

What is the NPV of each? According to the profitability index,
which property appears to be more profitable?

Answer

To calculate the NPV, find the difference between the PV of the cash
flows and the initial investment:

Net Present Value = Present Value of all Future Cash Flows less Initial Cash
   Investment

Net Present Value (Property 1) = 135,000 − 125,000 = 10,000

Net Present Value (Property 2) = 84,000 − 75,000 = 9,000

To calculate the profitability index, divide the PV by the initial investment:

Profitability Index = Present Value of all Future Cash Flows / Initial Cash
   Investment

Profitability Index (Property 1) = 135,000 / 125,000 = 1.08

Profitability Index (Property 2) = 84,000 / 75,000 = 1.12

Property 1 has the greater NPV, but Property 2 appears more profitable; the value of its cash flows is greater in proportion to the size of the investment required to earn them.

25

Calculation 19: Internal Rate of Return

What It Means

Internal rate of return (IRR) is probably the rate-of-return measurement most widely used by real estate professionals. It allows you to take into account both the timing and the magnitude of cash flows produced by your income-property investment.

It's not a silver bullet; no approach to investment decision making is. And by no means should you use it to the exclusion of other measurements discussed in this book. Those others run a range from the simplistic to sophisticated, but virtually all of them can help fill in the whole picture. A property's operating expense ratios, for example, may not give you enough information by themselves to guide you to a purchase decision, but they still may tell you something you absolutely need to know.

If you read Chapter 5 or if you have taken this series of short, calculation-based chapters in sequence, then you know that you can apply a particular discount rate—your required rate of return—to a series of future cash flows to determine what that income stream is worth today. If you rearrange that process, you can recharacterize the present value (PV) as your known present cost (i.e., the amount of cash you have to invest in order to make this purchase) and treat the discount rate (the rate of return) as your unknown.

In discounted cash flow, you estimated the future cash flows and the proper discount rate and then used that information to calculate the PV of your cash investment.

Now, if you forecast the future cash flows and the PV (i.e., the amount) of your actual cash investment, you can calculate the discount rate, which you call the internal rate of return.

How to Calculate

If you try to figure an IRR manually, you'll spend a great deal of time. The process is an iterative, successive-approximations technique (math-speak for trial and error) that starts with a guess and narrows its way to a conclusion. Instead, use the Microsoft Excel template that you can download at http://www.realdata.com/book.

Initial Investment	0
Cash Flow, End of Year 1	0
Cash Flow, End of Year 2	0
Cash Flow, End of Year 3	0
Cash Flow, End of Year 4	0
Cash Flow, End of Year 5	0
Cash Flow, End of Year 6	0
Cash Flow, End of Year 7	0
Cash Flow, End of Year 8	0
Cash Flow, End of Year 9	0
Cash Flow, End of Year 10	0
Internal Rate of Return	n/a

Example

You're considering the purchase of a property that requires a $100,000 cash investment. You forecast the following annual cash flows:

Year 1	$100
Year 2	$0
Year 3	$825
Year 4	$1,275
Year 5	$2,000
Year 6	$2,750
Year 7	$3,900
Year 8	$5,280
Year 9	$6,150
Year 10	$7,000

You expect to receive sale proceeds of $225,000 at the end of year 10. What is this investment's IRR?

Enter the data into the Excel model as shown (remember that the cash flow for year 10 must include the sale proceeds):

Initial Investment	(100,000)
Cash Flow, End of Year 1	100
Cash Flow, End of Year 2	0
Cash Flow, End of Year 3	825
Cash Flow, End of Year 4	1,275
Cash Flow, End of Year 5	2,000
Cash Flow, End of Year 6	2,750
Cash Flow, End of Year 7	3,900
Cash Flow, End of Year 8	5,280
Cash Flow, End of Year 9	6,150
Cash Flow, End of Year 10	232,000
Internal Rate of Return	10.10%

Rule of Thumb: If you project that you will have negative cash flows in the future, then it may not be possible to solve for an IRR. The solution to this problem is a technique called modified internal rate of return (MIRR), which is a topic that is a bit more abstract than we want to cover here. For the stout of heart, go back to Chapter 5, where you can review MIRR and related topics.

For those readers who have taken our discussion of the time value of money to heart, you realize that the money you set aside on day 1 would be able to earn some interest while it waits to be used, so you actually could get away with putting aside somewhat less than the total amount needed to cover the future negative cash flows. This is one of the factors that MIRR would take into account and is why this shortcut is less than precise.

Test Your Understanding

Using the Excel model and data from the preceding example, answer the following:

1. What happens to the IRR if you maintain the same cash flows and same proceeds, but can purchase the property with a cash investment that is $10,000 less?
2. What happens to the IRR if you invest the original $100,000, but sell at the end of year 7 and receive proceeds of $205,000?
3. If you received no cash flows from operating the property, but only the sale proceeds at the end of year 10, what would the IRR be on your $100,000 investment?

Answer

1.

Initial Investment	(90,000)
Cash Flow, End of Year 1	100
Cash Flow, End of Year 2	0
Cash Flow, End of Year 3	825
Cash Flow, End of Year 4	1,275
Cash Flow, End of Year 5	2,000
Cash Flow, End of Year 6	2,750
Cash Flow, End of Year 7	3,900
Cash Flow, End of Year 8	5,280

Cash Flow, End of Year 9	6,150
Cash Flow, End of Year 10	232,000
Internal Rate of Return	11.31%

2.

Initial Investment	(100,000)
Cash Flow, End of Year 1	100
Cash Flow, End of Year 2	0
Cash Flow, End of Year 3	825
Cash Flow, End of Year 4	1,275
Cash Flow, End of Year 5	2,000
Cash Flow, End of Year 6	2,750
Cash Flow, End of Year 7	208,900
Cash Flow, End of Year 8	0
Cash Flow, End of Year 9	0
Cash Flow, End of Year 10	0
Internal Rate of Return	11.76%

3.

Initial Investment	(100,000)
Cash Flow, End of Year 1	0
Cash Flow, End of Year 2	0
Cash Flow, End of Year 3	0
Cash Flow, End of Year 4	0
Cash Flow, End of Year 5	0
Cash Flow, End of Year 6	0
Cash Flow, End of Year 7	0
Cash Flow, End of Year 8	0
Cash Flow, End of Year 9	0
Cash Flow, End of Year 10	225,000
Internal Rate of Return	8.45%

26

Calculation 20: Price, Income, and Expenses per Unit

What It Means

Like several other measurements we've discussed, these are not offered for their sophistication or insight. Some investors and brokers still use these, and for that reason, it's essential that you know what they mean.

And they mean exactly what they say. Take a property's price, gross scheduled income, or total operating expenses and divide that amount by the number of rental units. For example, if a building has 20 rental units and is offered at $400,000, then its price is $20,000 per unit.

Those who use this technique usually do so only with residential properties (i.e., apartment complexes) because the units in such properties tend to be more uniform in their ability to generate revenue. You commonly rent commercial property by the square foot, and so "per-unit" specifications are generally meaningless. Consider a shopping center with two anchor tenants and 50 smaller tenants. To describe the center as 52 units conveys no useful information.

How to Calculate

Price per unit = price / number of rental units
Income per unit = Gross Scheduled Income / number of rental units
Expenses per unit = Operating Expenses / number of rental units

Example

A building contains 30 apartments each rented at $1,000 per month. Its annual operating expenses are $210,000. The building is offered for sale at $1.5 million. What are its price, income, and expenses per unit?

Price per unit = price / number of rental units
Price per unit = 1,500,000 / 30
Price per unit = 50,000

Thirty rental units at $1,000 per month times 12 months yields a gross scheduled income of $360,000.

Income per unit = Gross Scheduled Income / number of rental units
Income per unit = 360,000 / 30
Income per unit = 12,000
Expenses per unit = Operating Expenses / number of rental units
Expenses per unit = 210,000 / 30
Expenses per unit = 7,000

Rule of Thumb: If you have information on a fair number of apartment buildings in a particular location, then you may be able to develop some benchmarks for these measurements. If so, you might use those benchmarks to decide if a property merits a serious look. If you don't have the data to develop such benchmarks, then just be aware that these measures have been around for a long time and are still taken seriously by some owners and brokers.

Test Your Understanding

Building A has 20 apartments. Half are rented at $1,000 per month, the rest at $1,200 per month. The buildings next door and across the street are each for sale at $30,000 per unit. Based on these buildings, what would you expect the owner of Building A to ask for her property?

Answer

If you apply the price-per-unit approach, then Building A has 20 units, and the other properties have established a pattern of asking $30,000 per unit. On that basis, you would expect the owner of Building A to ask 20 times 30,000, or $600,000. Note that the apartments' income plays no role in setting this asking price.

27

Calculation 21: Price, Income, and Expenses per Square Foot

In the previous chapter, you looked at price, income, and operating expenses per rental unit—measurements that merit your attention primarily because you are likely to encounter property owners and brokers who use these terms from time to time. It is more common, however, and generally more useful to think of commercial property in terms of its square footage.

What It Means

You can consider price, income, and expenses as they relate to a property's square footage. This relationship is meaningful because you typically rent commercial property by the square foot and because the square foot, unlike a unit, has a more or less constant dimension. If you review the chapter "Building Measurements," you'll see that not all square feet are created equal; but they are certainly more equal than the rental units in a shopping center, which may have a flower shop tucked in between two megastore anchor tenants.

How to Calculate

The only issue in what is otherwise a series of routine calculations concerns the definition of "square footage." Buyers, sellers, and brokers will toss around statements such as, "I bought that building for $150 per square foot," as a form of shorthand insider-speak, allowing them to make quick property comparisons. What they mean by "square foot" is often set by the practice in a local market. As a rule, the term usually denotes either gross building area (GBA) or the net rentable area (the usable square footage plus an allocation of common area). Hence, in the following formulas, use whichever form of square footage is common in your market.

Price per square foot = Price / Gross Building Area or Net Rentable Area

Income per square foot = Gross Scheduled Income / Gross Building Area
  or Net Rentable Area

Expenses per square foot = Operating Expenses / Gross Building Area
  or Net Rentable Area

Example

A small office building has a GBA of 8,000 square feet. Its gross scheduled income is $128,000 per year, and its operating expenses are $56,000. The building is offered for sale at $720,000. This market uses GBA as the basis of comparison. What are its price, income, and expenses per square foot?

Price per square foot = Price / Gross Building Area

Price per square foot = 720,000 / 8,000

Price per square foot = $90 per square foot

Income per square foot = Gross Scheduled Income / Gross Building Area

Income per square foot = 128,000 / 8,000

Income per square foot = $16 per square foot

Expenses per square foot = Operating Expenses / Gross Building Area

Expenses per square foot = 56,000 / 8,000

Expenses per square foot = $7

> **Rule of Thumb:** These three measurements can be useful in much the same way as the gross rent multiplier, discussed in an earlier chapter. They are a type of market data, not a return-on-investment analysis. They're useful because they can give you a sense of how well the property fits with others in the marketplace. Use them for that purpose, but don't use them to decide whether to buy or sell or for how much.

Test Your Understanding

A commercial property has a GBA of 10,000 square feet. It contains seven office suites, each with 1,250 usable square feet. Four of the offices rent for $16 per square foot, and three rent for $18 per square foot. Fifty percent of the common area is allocated to the tenants as part of the definition of their rentable square footage (RSF). (Refer to the chapter "Building Measurements" if you need to review these terms.) Operating expenses are $50,000.

1. If other properties like this one are listed for sale at about $110 per square foot of GBA, what might you expect the asking price of this property to be?
2. What is the RSF of each of the suites?
3. What is the annual dollar amount of rent for the suites rented at $16 per square foot? At $18 per square foot?
4. What is the income per square foot of the net rentable area?
5. What are the operating expenses per square foot of GBA?

Answer

1. Price per square foot = Price / Gross Building Area, so transpose this formula:

   Price = Price per square foot × Gross Building Area
   Price = 110 × 10,000
   Price = $1,100,000

2. Fifty percent of the common area is being added to the usable square footage to define the RSF. The common area is the difference between the GBA and total space that is usable by the tenants. Hence, calculate the common space as follows:

Common Area = 10,000 − (1,250 × 7)
Common Area = 10,000 − 8,750 = 1,250 square feet

According to the lease definition of RSF for this property, the total RSF will equal the usable square footage plus 50% of the common area.

Total Rentable Square Feet (this Property) = 8,750 + 625
Total Rentable Square Feet (this Property) = 9,375

There are seven suites of identical size, so:

Rentable Square Footage (each unit) = 9,375 / 7 = 1,339 RSF

3. Each suite will pay rent based on 1,339 RSF.

Annual Rent = Rate × RSF
Annual Rent = 16 × 1,339 = $21,424
Annual Rent = 18 × 1,339 = $24,102

4. The net rentable area is the total of the tenants' RSF, calculated above as 9,375 square feet.

   You must calculate the gross scheduled income. There are four units at $16 per square foot and three units at $18 per square foot. Using the information from answer #3, you have:

4 units @ 21,424 = 85,696
3 units @ 24,102 = 72,306
Total Rent = 158,002
Income per square foot = Gross Scheduled Income / Net Rentable Area
Income per square foot = 158,002 / 9,375
Income per square foot = $16.85

5. Expenses per square foot = Operating Expenses / Gross Building Area
Expenses per square foot = 50,000 / 10,000
Expenses per square foot = $5.00

28

Calculation 22: Operating Expense Ratio

What It Means

Operating expense ratio is the ratio of individual operating expenses or of total operating expenses to the gross operating income (GOI).

Recall that the GOI is the revenue after vacancy and credit loss. Think of GOI not as the amount that you ought to collect, but rather the amount that you really do collect. In that context, operating expense ratios tell you how the money you spend to operate the building relates to the money you receive.

This topic was described in great detail in Part I, Chapter 2, so we certainly won't repeat it all here. You can use a property's expense ratios to decide if the operation of a particular investment opportunity appears typical, based on your knowledge of other similar properties. These ratios can also alert you to possible problem areas, in regard both to how the property has been run and to how accurate are the seller's representations.

How to Calculate

You can apply this formula to an individual operating expense and to the total of all expenses:

Operating Expense Ratio = Operating Expense / Gross Operating Income

You can use the Annual Property Operating Data (APOD) form in Part I, Chapter 2, as a convenient worksheet for calculating these ratios. The Excel version, downloadable from http://www.realdata.com/book, will calculate the ratios automatically as you enter income and expenses.

Example

Your property has a GOI of $70,000 and operating expenses as follows:

Insurance (fire and liability)	7,000
Property Taxes	12,500
Repairs and Maintenance	8,500
Supplies and Miscellaneous	2,000
Utilities	4,500
Other	1,000

What is the operating expense ratio for each and for the total?

We'll use a condensed snippet of the APOD form for our example here.

GROSS OPERATING INCOME	70,000	
EXPENSES		
Insurance (fire and liability)	7,000	10.00%
Property Taxes	12,500	17.86%
Repairs and Maintenance	8,500	12.14%
Supplies and Miscellaneous	2,000	2.86%
Utilities	4,500	6.43%
Other	1,000	1.43%
TOTAL EXPENSES	35,500	50.71%

Divide each expense by the GOI to obtain its operating expense ratio.

> **Rule of Thumb:** It's important to look at the individual ratios, not just the ratio for total expenses. As you saw in Part I, Chapter 2, the total could appear entirely plausible while some of the individual items raise red flags.

Test Your Understanding

Your building has a gross scheduled income of $82,000. You estimate vacancy and credit loss of 4%. Your operating expenses for the year are as follows:

Insurance (fire and liability)	4,000
Property Taxes	9,620
Repairs and Maintenance	12,500
Supplies and Miscellaneous	3,800
Utilities	6,600
Other	3,400

What is the operating expense ratio for each and for the total? What is the percentage of GOI to gross scheduled income?

Answer

You'll need to start by calculating the vacancy and credit loss, which at 4% of the gross scheduled income equals 3,280. From there, you can once again use the APOD form, shown here condensed for our example:

INCOME		
Gross Scheduled Rent Income	82,000	100.00%
Other Income	0	0.00%
TOTAL GROSS INCOME	82,000	100.00%
VACANCY & CREDIT ALLOWANCE	3,280	4.00%
GROSS OPERATING INCOME	78,720	96.00%
EXPENSES		
Insurance (fire and liability)	4,000	5.08%

Property Taxes	9,620	12.22%
Repairs and Maintenance	12,500	15.88%
Supplies and Miscellaneous	3,800	4.83%
Utilities	6,600	8.38%
Other	3,400	4.32%
TOTAL EXPENSES	39,920	50.71%

Once you've determined the GOI, you divide each operating expense by that amount to calculate its operating expense ratio. Notice that the ratio for total expenses is exactly the same here as it was in the example further above. At the same time, the individual ratios are far different. As we stressed in Part I, Chapter 2, if these were presumably similar properties, you would definitely want to investigate the reasons for these differences.

Finally, the problem asks about the percentage of GOI to gross scheduled income. Of course, you could answer this question by dividing the GOI into the gross scheduled income. However, if you understand the meaning of GOI, then you know that you don't have to do that. You're told that the vacancy loss is 4% of the scheduled income. By definition, the GOI is what's left: 96%.

29

Calculation 23: Debt Coverage Ratio

What It Means

Debt coverage ratio (DCR) is the ratio between the property's net operating income (NOI) for the year and the annual debt service (ADS).

If your NOI and ADS are exactly the same (say $10,000), then the ratio is 10,000 divided by 10,000, or exactly 1.00. A DCR of 1.00 implies that you have exactly enough net income from the property to make your mortgage payments, not a nickel more or less. If your DCR is less than 1.00, it means the property does not generate enough income to pay the mortgage. If your DCR is greater than 1.00, then the property does generate enough, with some left over.

As you might expect, one person with reason to look at the DCR carefully is the mortgage lender. When you try to finance a property, that lender will examine the DCR to see if the property can expect to generate enough cash to cover its mortgage payments. You can be certain that "just enough" (i.e., 1.00) is not good enough. The lender wants to be sure that there is a margin for error, so both the current DCR and its future projections must be higher than 1.00.

How to Calculate

Debt Coverage Ratio = Annual Net Operating Income / Annual Debt Service

For a given year, first calculate the NOI and the ADS; then divide the former by the latter.

Each of these two components is discussed in greater detail elsewhere in the book, so we'll review them very briefly here:

1. Net Operating Income = Gross Scheduled Income, less Vacancy and Credit Loss, less Operating Expenses
   a. Your gross scheduled income is the total rent you expect to receive if all units are occupied and all tenants pay as agreed.
   b. This expectation may be reduced by the vacancy and credit loss, a loss of income that can occur if one or more units are unoccupied for a period of time or if some tenants simply fail to pay.
   c. Operating expenses can include items such as taxes, insurance, maintenance, supplies, trash removal, advertising, etc. Mortgage payments, interest, and depreciation are not operating expenses.
2. Annual Debt Service = Monthly Mortgage Payment × 12

   ADS is the total of mortgage payments for the year. If you make monthly mortgage payments, then the ADS equals that monthly payment times 12.

Example

You're considering the purchase of a four-unit apartment building. Each apartment rents for $800 per month. During the year recently ended, one unit was vacant for two months, but all the others were occupied continuously. All tenants paid their rents on time.

The property's operating expenses for the year were as follows: taxes, $6,000; insurance, $1,400; maintenance and repairs, $1,200; supplies, $400; and water, $600.

You are applying for a mortgage so that you can purchase the property. The monthly mortgage payment of principal and interest will be $2,000.

What is the DCR?

First, calculate the NOI.

Gross Scheduled Income = 4 units × $800 per month × 12 months = $38,400
Vacancy and Credit Loss = 800 × 2 months = $1,600
Operating Expenses = 6,000 + 1,400 + 1,200 + 400 + 600 = $9,600

The NOI calculation looks like this:

Gross Scheduled Income	38,400
less Vacancy and Credit Loss	1,600
less Operating Expenses	9,600
= Net Operating Income	$27,200

Second, figure the ADS:

Annual Debt Service = 2,000 monthly payment × 12 = $24,000

Finally, calculate the DCR:

Debt Coverage Ratio = 27,200 (NOI) / 24,000 (ADS) = 1.13

Rule of Thumb: Most lenders look for a DCR of at least 1.20, often even more. A property with a 1.20 DCR has income before debt service that is 1.20 times as much as the debt service—in other words, the property generates 20% more net income than it needs to make its mortgage payments.

You can be certain that the lender will examine the property's DCR carefully. You should do the same before you make an attempt to secure financing.

Test Your Understanding

In the example above, the DCR is not high enough to satisfy most lenders. What NOI would be necessary to achieve a satisfactory DCR? Is there a way you might make your case to the lender, suggesting that the property would indeed meet the debt coverage requirements?

Answer

If:

Debt Coverage Ratio = Annual Net Operating Income / Annual Debt Service

then you can transpose the formula to read:

Debt Coverage Ratio × Annual Debt Service = Annual Net Operating Income

In that case, if you're seeking a DCR of 1.20,

1.20 × 24,000 = Annual Net Operating Income
$28,800 = Annual Net Operating Income

With ADS of $24,000, you would need an NOI of $28,800 to achieve a DCR of 1.20.

Now, what do you say to the lender that doesn't like your original numbers? Remember that you are using last year's property history—a year in which one of the apartments was vacant for two months. As you prepare to purchase the property, you have no vacant units. Instead, the property is fully occupied with good, never-delinquent tenants. You might argue that, in the coming year, you can reasonably expect not to incur the $1,600 vacancy loss. Eliminating that loss would raise your NOI from $27,200 to $28,800, exactly what you need to achieve the lender's required DCR.

30

Calculation 24:
Break-Even Ratio

What It Means

You should know about the *break-even ratio* (BER, also sometimes called the *default ratio*) because it is a benchmark often used by lenders when underwriting commercial mortgages. Its purpose is to estimate how vulnerable a property is to defaulting on its debt should rental income decline. There is an old saying that when your outgo exceeds your income, your upkeep will be your downfall. Essentially, the lender is trying to gauge the proportion between your outgo and your income, so as not to share in that downfall.

You should review debt coverage ratio (another major benchmark favored by lenders) in the previous chapter and loan-to-value ratio in Part II, Calculation 26.

How to Calculate

Break-Even Ratio = (Debt Service + Operating Expenses) / Gross Operating
Income

Example

You expect first-year operating expenses of $22,000 and annual debt service of $24,000. If your gross operating income is $57,500, what is your property's BER?

Break-Even Ratio = (Debt Service + Operating Expenses) / Gross Operating
     Income
Break-Even Ratio = (24,000 + 22,000) / 57,500
Break-Even Ratio = 80%

Rule of Thumb: Most lenders look for a BER of 85% or less. If occupancy rates in a particular market are exceptionally low (meaning that the certainty of your revenue stream is especially dicey), lenders may require a BER that is several percentage points less than the average occupancy rate.

Test Your Understanding

1. Your property has 12 units that rent for $1,200 each. Your vacancy and credit loss is 7%; operating expenses average $6,700 per month; debt service is $5,350 per month. What is the property's BER? Will it satisfy the typical lender described in the Rule of Thumb above?
2. You have a property with debt service of $2,500 per month. Annual operating expenses are $28,000. What GOI must you have in order to satisfy your lender's requirement for a BER of 85%?

Answer

1. You need to start by calculating the GOI.

Gross Scheduled Income
less Vacancy and Credit Loss
= Gross Operating Income

You have 12 units at $1,200 for 12 months, so gross scheduled income and vacancy at 7% are as follows:

Gross Scheduled Income = 12 × 1,200 × 12 = 172,800
Vacancy and Credit = 172,800 × 0.07 = 12,096

Now you calculate the GOI:

Gross Scheduled Income	172,800
less Vacancy and Credit Loss	12,096
= Gross Operating Income	160,704

To figure the BER, you'll need to convert operating expenses and debt service to annual amounts:

Operating Expenses = 6,700 × 12 = 80,400
Annual Debt Service = 5,350 × 12 = 64,200

Finally, apply the BER formula:

Break-Even Ratio = (Debt Service + Operating Expenses) / Gross Operating
    Income
Break-Even Ratio = (64,200 + 80,400) / 160,704
Break-Even Ratio = 90%

The lender described in the Rule of Thumb will probably have doubts about this property's ability to meet its obligations should it face an increase in vacancy.

2. Start by applying Algebra 101 to transpose the formula:

Gross Operating Income = (Debt Service + Operating Expenses) / Break-Even
    Ratio
Gross Operating Income = [(2,500 × 12) + 28,000] / 0.85
Gross Operating Income = 58,000 / 0.85
Gross Operating Income = 68,235

31

Calculation 25: Return on Equity

What It Means

There are two ways of approaching the topic of *return on equity* (ROE) as it applies to real estate investments. In each of them, "return" has the same meaning: cash flow after taxes (CFAT). What differs is the meaning of "equity." In the traditional method, the equity is your initial cash investment. In the alternative technique, it is your initial cash plus the additional equity that has built up due to amortization of the mortgage and to increase in the value of the property.

The ROE is expressed as a percentage and typically is calculated for the first year only.

How to Calculate

First method:

Return on Equity = Cash Flow after Taxes / Initial Cash Investment

Second method:

Return on Equity = Cash Flow after Taxes / (Resale Value less Mortgage Balance)

Example

First method:

You purchase a property with $100,000 cash down. In the first year, your CFAT is $9,000. What is your ROE?

Return on Equity = Cash Flow after Taxes / Initial Cash Investment
Return on Equity = 9,000 / 100,000
Return on Equity = 9%

Second method:

You purchase a property with $100,000 cash down and have the same $9,000 cash flow. At the end of the first year, the property has a value of $408,000 and a mortgage balance of $298,000. What is the ROE with this method?

Return on Equity = Cash Flow after Taxes / (Resale Value less Mortgage Balance)
Return on Equity = 9,000 / (408,000 − 298,000)
Return on Equity = 9,000 / (110,000)
Return on Equity = 8.2%

Rule of Thumb: Although the conventional practice is to calculate ROE for the first year only, you may find that if you use the second approach described above, you can uncover an interesting and valuable nugget of information. Consider this situation: You make projections about the performance of your property going out 5 or 10 years. That means you have a predicted selling price for each of those years and you have the loan balances; hence, you have what, according to the second method, is your potential equity for each of those years. You also forecast your CFAT, so you can make the calculation of CFAT / equity to get the ROE for each of those years. When you do so, it's quite possible that you'll notice your ROE starts going down at some point, even though the value of the property and the CFAT continue to go up.

How can this happen? It occurs if the equity is increasing at a rate that is faster than the cash flow. Remember, your equity (at least by our alternative definition) grows because of increasing property value and decreasing mortgage balance. As the mortgage paydown begins to accelerate, which it normally does over time, the equity growth may accelerate as well. If each year the cash flow grows a little and the equity grows a lot, the ROE will decline.

If the ROE declines, then it's time to ask yourself, "Is it the best use of my money to have it tied up as equity in this property?" That's not a rhetorical question—maybe it is the best use—but if not, perhaps you should consider refinancing to take out cash to reinvest. You might also sell outright and reinvest in a different, perhaps larger property.

Test Your Understanding

You purchase a property for $700,000 with a first mortgage of $500,000. Your first year's CFAT is $12,000. You forecast that the property will have an NOI of $82,225 and that the appropriate market capitalization rate will be 11.5%. The mortgage balance at the end of year 1 will be $489,500.

Calculate the ROE using each of the two methods above.

Answer

First method:
You purchase the property for $700,000 with a $500,000 mortgage, so your initial cash investment—your equity under this method—is $200,000. Now you can apply the formula:

Return on Equity = Cash Flow after Taxes / Initial Cash Investment
Return on Equity = 12,000 / 200,000
Return on Equity = 6%

Second method:
You must first calculate the estimated selling price by capitalizing the net operating income:

Present Value = Net Operating Income / Capitalization Rate
Present Value = 82,225 / 0.115
Present Value = 715,000

Next, apply the alternative ROE formula:

Return on Equity = Cash Flow after Taxes / (Resale Value less Mortgage
  Balance)
Return on Equity = 12,000 / (715,000 – 489,500)
Return on Equity = 12,000 / (225,500)
Return on Equity = 5.32%

32

Calculation 26: Loan-to-Value Ratio

What It Means

Loan-to-value ratio (LTV) is the ratio between the total amount of a property's mortgage financing and the property's appraised value or selling price, whichever is less. It is expressed as a percentage.

If the selling price is indeed less than the appraised value, the lender will base the LTV on the selling price. You will be tempted to argue that you negotiated a terrific deal, that you are buying below market, and that the lender should use the higher, appraised value in the LTV calculation. If you prevail, be sure to call a press conference because you will be the first investor ever to win this argument.

If you were to purchase a home as a personal residence, the maximum LTV (i.e., the most the bank would lend you) would typically be 80% for a conventional mortgage. To put this another way, you could borrow 80% of the value or purchase price. Private mortgage insurance and government programs such as FHA and VA are available to assist homebuyers, making it possible for you to purchase a home with an LTV approaching 100%. This author bought his first home many years ago with an FHA loan and a 1.5% down payment (98.5% LTV).

For investment property, however, you will often find that lenders expect your equity investment to be greater. Eighty percent is possible, but don't be surprised to see the LTV requirement at 70% or lower. There are at least two reasons why lenders want a lower LTV when financing investment property:

1. They do not want to have to take over the property in foreclosure and operate it while they try to sell it.
2. They don't want to lose money.

In regard to the first reason, the lender will usually be forced to take over the property if the borrower decides to walk away. This generally happens when the borrower runs into financial problems and can't make the payments. With a personal residence, it is usually the loss of personal income that is at fault. With an investment property, however, the problem could lie either in the owner's personal finances or in the building's failure to produce adequate cash flow.

One of the purposes of lending less than the full purchase price is to provide a disincentive for the borrower to abandon the property. In the case of a personal residence, the bank knows that if you default and go into foreclosure, you're going to have to clean out your sock drawer and move your family into a motel. A major life disruption is a strong disincentive to bail on your mortgage.

In the case of an investment property, the lender (having apparently read this book) knows that the property is all about the numbers, and in particular, the cash flow numbers. If your cash flow were to go up in smoke, you would need a good reason to prevent you from dropping the keys off at your nearest savings and loan branch. That reason is your equity stake in the property. The more of your own money you have tied up in this property, the less likely you are to give the property back to the bank.

The second reason the lender prefers a low LTV follows from the first. The lower the mortgage balance stands in relation to the property's value, the greater the likelihood that the lender will recover all it is owed and thus not lose any money in the event of a foreclosure. A corollary to this principle is that the ease with which you can obtain financing for a property is in direct proportion to the size of your own cash investment. The more you have at risk, the less the bank has at risk.

Rule of Thumb: What then of all the tapes and seminars you see hyping "no-money-down" real estate investing? Permit the author to indulge in a personal rant by suggesting that every time you hear about one of these tapes or courses, you take an amount equal to their cost and put it in a bank account; then use the money in that account as part of the down payment on your next property.

No-money-down violates the letter, the spirit, and the algebra of conventional investment. If you invest nothing, then you have no investment. It is also mathematically impossible to calculate the rate of return on nothing; hence, much of our discussion about measuring the quality of an investment opportunity would come to naught.

More practically, if you finance 100%, you may have some unpleasant realities to deal with. If you have nothing at risk, then the lender, or lenders, must absorb all the risk. Don't expect them then to give you a good deal on the interest rate—unless, of course, the seller is providing the financing and is making up for the good deal on that financing by inflating the price of the property.

Bad karma #2 has to do with cash flow. If your LTV is 100%, then obviously your mortgage amount is higher than it would be in a typical investment scenario, and so is your debt service. If the interest rate is also elevated because of the increased risk to the lender(s), that will give your debt service a second jolt upward. The elevated debt service decreases your cash flow, quite possibly causing it to be negative. Then you'll have to reach into your own pocket to make up the difference. Instead of coming up with the money for the down payment, you'll need to come up with money for the high-interest monthly mortgage payments. So much for "no cash, no problem."

How to Calculate

Loan-to-Value Ratio = Loan Amount / Lesser of Property's Appraised Value
   or Actual Selling Price

Example

1. You are purchasing an income property for $500,000. You will put down $150,000 and finance the rest. The bank's appraisal comes in at $500,000. What is the LTV?

   First, you have to calculate the loan amount:

Loan Amount = Purchase Price less Down Payment
Loan Amount = $500,000 less $150,000
Loan Amount = $350,000

   Then, you can apply the preceding formula. The selling price and the appraisal are the same, so you use $500,000 as the property's value.

Loan-to-Value Ratio = 350,000 / 500,000
Loan-to-Value Ratio = 70%

2. You are purchasing an income property for $550,000. You will put down $150,000 and finance the rest. The bank's appraisal comes in at $500,000. What is the LTV?

   First, calculate the amount of the loan:

Loan Amount = $550,000 less $150,000
Loan Amount = $400,000

   Now apply the formula. (Note that you use the appraised value, which is lower than the selling price.)

Loan-to-Value Ratio = 400,000 / 500,000
Loan-to-Value Ratio = 80%

3. You are purchasing an income property for $500,000. You will put down $150,000 and finance the rest. The bank's appraisal comes in at $550,000. What is the LTV?

First, calculate the amount of the loan:

Loan Amount = $500,000 less $150,000
Loan Amount = $350,000

Now apply the formula. (Note that this time, you use the selling price, which is lower than the appraised value; you always use whichever is lower.)

Loan-to-Value Ratio = 350,000 / 500,000
Loan-to-Value Ratio = 70%

Rule of Thumb: Many lenders look for an LTV on investment property of less than 80%. Be prepared to deal with a requirement of 70%, which is quite common.

Don't be surprised if the lender also requires an assignment of rents, allowing it to collect rent directly from your tenants if you fail to pay.

The lower the LTV, the better your chances are of negotiating favorable loan terms.

Test Your Understanding

You are purchasing a property for $400,000 and plan to put $120,000 down to satisfy your lender's requirement for a 70% LTV. However, the appraisal comes in at $375,000. You still want to go ahead with the deal. To what amount must you increase your down payment?

Answer

First, determine what the lender will use as the property value. It must be the lesser of the purchase price or the appraised value, so the lender will use $375,000.

Next, take the formula:

Loan-to-Value Ratio = Loan Amount / Property's Value

and transpose it so that you can solve for the loan amount:

Loan Amount = Property's Value × Loan-to-Value Ratio
Loan Amount = 375,000 × 0.70
Loan Amount = 262,500

Finally, subtract the loan amount from the actual purchase price to calculate your required down payment.

Down Payment = Purchase Price less Loan Amount
Down Payment = 400,000 less 262,500
Down Payment = 137,500

Instead of the $120,000 you were planning on, this lower appraisal will make it necessary for you to put down $137,500.

33

Calculation 27: Points

What It Means

Points are fees that you pay to the mortgage lender as a premium for making the loan. They represent a form of prepaid interest on the loan.

One point equals 1% of the mortgage loan amount.

With most lenders, you can negotiate an interest rate/points mix. The lender may offer a loan at a particular rate with no points, but also offer loans with progressively lower rates if you are willing to pay points. Questions such as, "Is it better to pay 6% with 2 points or 6.5% with no points?" invariably arise. The answer depends on the number of points, the interest rate reduction, and the length of time you are likely to keep this loan in place. A quick, although admittedly imprecise way, of answering that question is to ask another one: "How many years of saving interest dollars at the lower rate will it take to break even on what I spent to pay the points?"

In the preceding example, if you save 0.5% per year in interest, it would seemingly take you four years to recover the cost of paying 2 points (2.0%). Actually, it would take you a bit more than four years because (a) you have to pay for the points in full up front, meaning you do not have the use of the money to earn more money (it's that time value of money again); and (b) the mortgage is amortized, and so the number of dollars of interest you spend (or save due to the lower rate) decreases slightly with each payment.

If you agree to pay the points in this example, it is fair to say that it will take more than four years to break even on that decision; the benefit won't begin to accrue until after that time.

Another disappointing truth about loan points for investment property is that, unlike the points you might pay on your home mortgage, these cannot be deducted in full in the year you pay them. They must be amortized over the life of the loan. If you pay $2,500 in points to obtain a loan with a 25-year term, you can deduct $100 per year. Under current rules, if you pay off the loan because of a sale or refinance, you can then deduct the unamortized balance.

Some commercial loans require a "balloon" payment at the end of a certain number of years. The loan has a payment schedule as if it were a long-term loan, but it doesn't really run the full course. Instead, it requires a large payment—the balloon payment—to retire the loan earlier. For example, it may be set up with monthly payments as if it were a 360-month loan, but also require that the entire remaining balance be paid at the end of month 60. In this case, the points could be amortized over five years (60 months) because that is what you consider to be the term of the loan.

How to Calculate

1 Point (in dollars) = Mortgage Loan Amount / 100
Dollar Amount of Points Paid = Mortgage Loan Amount × No. Points / 100

Example

You are applying for a loan of $375,000 at 7% that requires you to pay 1.75 points. What is the dollar amount of the points?

Dollar Amount of Points Paid = Mortgage Loan Amount × No. Points / 100
Dollar Amount of Points Paid = 375,000 × 1.75 / 100
Dollar Amount of Points Paid = 6,562.50

If you hadn't noticed, the interest rate in the preceding example was irrelevant to the solution.

Rule of Thumb: Points generally are of greater benefit to the lender than to the borrower. Any advantage you might realize by trading points for a lower rate will happen only if you keep the mortgage in place beyond the break-even time described in the first section of this chapter—and that time may be several years. Keep in mind that during that time, you may decide to sell the property, or even more likely, to refinance it for a lower rate or to take out cash.

Unless you feel quite certain that you will not sell or refinance the property any time soon, you should keep loan points to the lowest possible amount.

Test Your Understanding

1. You are purchasing a property with a $400,000 mortgage at 7%. The lender charges 1.5 points. What is the cost of the points?

Answer

Dollar Amount of Points Paid = 400,000 × 1.5 / 100
Dollar Amount of Points Paid = 6,000

2. In the preceding example, you could secure the loan at 6.5% if you paid 3 points. How much would the points cost? About how long would it take for your interest saving to recover the cost of the additional points?

Answer

Dollar Amount of Points Paid = 400,000 × 3.0 / 100
Dollar Amount of Points Paid = 12,000

You are paying an additional 1.5 points (1.5% of the loan amount) to obtain the discounted rate. If the discount is 0.5% per year, it will take you about three years to recover the cost of the additional points. As discussed previously, if you were to take into account the time value of money, the time would be fractionally more than three years.

C H A P T E R

34

Calculation 28: Mortgage Payment/ Mortgage Constant

What It Means

You will typically purchase an investment property with the aid of one or more mortgage loans. You, the borrower, are called the mortgagor, and the lender is called the mortgagee. You give the lender a lien against the property, and the lender gives you a mortgage loan. The lender can be a bank, an insurance company, the property seller, or even a private third party. You can have more than one mortgage, called first mortgage, second, etc.

The parties can structure a mortgage loan in any of several ways. For example, you might pay interest only for a period of time, then the entire balance; interest only followed by amortizing principal and interest payments; amortizing payments for a time followed by an early payoff or "balloon"; or fixed principal payments plus interest. By far the most common is the loan that fully amortizes using a fixed periodic payment (combining interest and principal) over a specified time. Your home mortgage is probably just such a loan.

How to Calculate

Let's work with the typical loan, which is fully amortized through the use of monthly payments of principal and interest.

1. There is a mathematical formula, but for obvious reasons, it will not be your preferred method of calculating a payment:

   Payment = $(PV \times i) / (1 - [1 + i]\,\hat{}\, - n)$

   where PV is the amount of the loan, i is the interest rate per period, and n is the number of periods.
2. A second method is to use the table "Monthly Mortgage Payment per $1" at http://www.realdata.com/book, a snippet of which is displayed here:

Monthly Mortgage Payment per $1—Mortgage Constant

Years	6.000%	6.125%	6.250%	6.750%	6.875%	7.000%	7.125%
25	0.00644301	0.00651964	0.00659669	~ 0.00690912	0.00698825	0.00706779	0.00714773
26	0.00633677	0.00641422	0.00649211	~ 0.00680795	0.00688796	0.00696838	0.00704920
27	0.00623985	0.00631811	0.00639682	~ 0.00671601	0.00679687	0.00687815	0.00695984
28	0.00615124	0.00623030	0.00630980	~ 0.00663227	0.00671397	0.00679609	0.00687862
29	0.00607005	0.00614988	0.00623018	~ 0.00655585	0.00663836	0.00672130	0.00680466
30	0.00599551	0.00607611	0.00615717	~ 0.00648598	0.00656929	0.00665302	0.00673719

A bit of nomenclature that you will find useful in the chapters on loan balance and maximum loan amount: The factors shown in this table, each of which represents the monthly payment at a given rate and term, are called mortgage constants. You can have mortgage constants for any payment frequency, such as quarterly or annually. We can write the formula for the use of the chart like this:

Payment (monthly) = Present Value × Mortgage Constant (monthly)

3. A third method is to use Microsoft Excel to solve for the payment. You can open a blank Excel spreadsheet and use the "PMT" function in any cell:

=PMT(Periodic Rate, Number of Periods,-Present Value)

For example, to calculate the monthly payment for a $100,000 mortgage for 30 years (i.e., 360 months) at 12% per year (i.e., 1% per month), enter:

```
=PMT(0.01,360,-100000)
```

and when you press the "Enter" key, you see your monthly payment is $1,028.61.

4. Finally, as in Part I, Chapter 3, you can download the premade Excel template at http://www.realdata.com/book:

N	%I	Pmt	PV	
360	1.00%	1,028.61	100,000.00	calculate payment

Example

Using the preceding table of mortgage constants, what is the monthly payment required to amortize a $275,000 loan over 30 years at 6.875%?

If you look up the monthly mortgage constant for 30 years at 6.875% annually, you find it is 0.00656929. Apply the formula:

Payment (monthly) = Present Value × Mortgage Constant (monthly)
Payment (monthly) = 275000 × 0.00656929 = $1,806.55

> **Rule of Thumb:** The mortgage constant for a given rate and term is always higher than the periodic interest rate because it has to provide for reduction in principal as well as the payment of interest. The longer the term of the loan, the lower the mortgage constant (aka the payment) will be because you are stretching the principal repayment out over a longer period of time.

Test Your Understanding

1. You take a loan for $125,000 at 6% for 30 years. Solve for the payment using methods 2 through 4, described previously.

2. Your local bank's director of marketing has decided to make mortgage history by offering commercial loans at 6% for a term of 300 years. Assuming that you eat your veggies and live that long, what will your monthly payment be on a $100,000 loan? When will your loan really be paid off? Explain your answer.

Answer

1. First, use the chart and find the 6%, 30-year mortgage constant is 0.00599551. Apply the formula:

Payment (monthly) = 125000 × 0.00599551 = $749.44

Next, build your own Excel formula. Remember that 6% per year is 1/2% per month:

=PMT(0.005,360,-125000)

You'll see the result in the cell.

$749.44

Finally, use the template.

N	%I	Pmt	PV	
360	0.50%	749.44	125,000.00	calculate payment

2. Let's use the template, since our table of mortgage constants doesn't go out 300 years.

N	%I	Pmt	PV	
3600	0.50%	500.00	100,000.00	calculate payment

We get $500.00—that's a nice round number; so round, in fact, that it seems a little suspicious. What would your monthly payment be if you paid only interest and no principal? Multiply the periodic rate by the mortgage amount. Remember that you are expressing the rate as a decimal, not as a percentage, so move the decimal point two places to the left:

0.00500 × 100000 = 500.00

It certainly looks like the interest-only payment is the same as the amortizing payment. That's impossible, right?

If you were to expand the amortizing payment calculation out to 10 decimal places, you would see it really is just a bit more than $500.00, but nowhere near $500.01.

N	%I	Pmt	PV	
3600	0.5000%	500.0000079643	100,000.00	calculate payment

There is no way you can write a check for that amount, so the bank does the seemingly reasonable thing and rounds the payment to $500.00. Soon it also hires a new director of marketing because none of these 300-year loans will ever be amortized.

CHAPTER

35

Calculation 29: Principal Balance/ Balloon Payment

What It Means

When you have a mortgage that is amortized over a particular number of level payments, each of those payments reduces the outstanding balance of the loan. There are a number of reasons beyond mere curiosity why you might want to know the balance at a given point in the loan. You may be getting ready to sell or refinance the property, for example, and in either case, you'll have to pay off that balance.

Another occasion will occur when your loan calls for what is known as a "balloon payment." It is not uncommon for a commercial lender to structure a mortgage so that your monthly payment is based on a term of 15 years or more, but where the full balance comes due much earlier, perhaps in 5 to 10 years. Hence, the last payment you make "balloons" to include the entire loan balance at that time.

How to Calculate

1. The formula for the outstanding balance (more formally, the present value of an annuity) is the sort of intellectual exercise that may make you start smashing office furniture. For those who were planning to redecorate anyway, it is:

   PV of an annuity = $A \times (1 + i)^n - (Pmt / i) \times [(1 + i)^n - 1]$

   where A is the original amount of the loan and n is the number of payments made.

2. In the chapter on mortgage payments, you saw a chart called "Monthly Mortgage Payment per $1" and learned that the factors in that chart were called mortgage constants. If you find the reciprocal of the mortgage constant (i.e., if you divide the constant into 1.00), you'll have something called the *annuity factor*. If you take the annuity factor for the rate and the number of payments remaining and multiply it by the loan payment, you'll get the outstanding balance.

   We could make a table of annuity factors by dividing all the mortgage constants into 1.00, but we can just as easily use the constants themselves by rearranging the formula just a bit:

   PV of an annuity = Loan Payment / Mortgage Constant (for rate and remaining term)

   Keep in mind that if you use a monthly payment amount, you must use the monthly mortgage constant for the number of months remaining. If you use an annual payment, then you must use the annual constant for the number of years remaining.

3. As before, you can use Microsoft Excel to solve for the balance. Open a blank Excel spreadsheet and use the "PV" function in any cell:

   =PV(Periodic Rate, Number of Periods,-Periodic Payment)

   For example, to calculate the present value of a mortgage with a monthly payment of $1,028.61 and 300 payments remaining at 12% per year (i.e., 1% per month), enter:

=PV(0.01,300,-1028.61)

and when you press the "Enter" key, you see your balance is $97,662.97.

4. As in Part I, Chapter 3, you can download the premade Excel template (go to http://www.realdata.com/book) and use its second row:

N	%I	Pmt	PV	
360	1.00%	1,028.61	100,000.00	calculate payment
300	1.00%	1,028.61	97,662.97	calculate present value

5. One of the most useful utilities for anyone who owns real estate is software to produce an amortization schedule. This report shows how much of each payment goes to principal and to interest, as well as the balance that remains outstanding after each payment. A good schedule will also provide calendar-year summaries.

You can download a free Excel-based amortization schedule at http://www.realdata.com/book. A sample of its output is shown below. From the same website, you can download the RealData Real Estate Calculator (also free), which includes an amortization schedule. The calculator is a stand-alone Windows-based program that does not require Excel.

LOAN AMORTIZATION SCHEDULE
© Copyright 1982–2015, RealData®, Inc.

Data Input:

Beginning Balance:	100,000.00	Ann. Int. Rate:	12.000%
Term, Months:	360	First Pmt Month:	1
Calculated Pmt:	$1,028.61	First Pmt Year:	2020

	INTEREST	PRINCIPAL	BALANCE
January	1,000.00	28.61	99,971.39
February	999.71	28.90	99,942.49
March	999.42	29.19	99,913.30
April	999.13	29.48	99,883.82
May	998.84	29.77	99,854.05
June	998.54	30.07	99,823.98
July	998.24	30.37	99,793.61

August	997.94	30.67	99,762.94
September	997.63	30.98	99,731.96
October	997.32	31.29	99,700.67
November	997.01	31.60	99,669.07
December	996.69	31.92	99,637.15
Total 2020	11,980.47	362.85	

Example

Using the table of mortgage constants shown in the previous chapter, what is the unpaid balance on a mortgage that has a 6.25% annual rate and 336 monthly payments of $1,000 remaining? Use the template in #4 above to confirm the answer.

First, look up the monthly mortgage constant for 28 years (the same as 336 months) at 6.25% annually. You should find that it is 0.0063098. Apply the formula:

PV of an annuity = Loan Payment / Mortgage Constant (for rate and remaining term)

PV of an annuity = 1,000 / 0.0063098 = 158,483.63

With the template:

N	%I	Pmt	PV	
300	0.67%	771.82	100,000.00	calculate payment
336	0.52%	1,000.00	158,483.63	calculate present value

Rule of Thumb: You may notice that, when you use the table or formulas to calculate the remaining loan balance, you often get a result that is different by a few cents from what you find when you use an amortization schedule. The tables and formulas allow calculations to be carried out many decimal places, while the amortization rounds each step according to dollars and cents. While the latter method is less precise, it is probably also closer to what happens in real life, because the payments we make, in fact, go only to the second decimal place.

> You should create and print out an amortization schedule for every loan.
> It will keep you apprised of your outstanding balance and alert you to
> any error your lender may make when reporting your interest paid for
> tax purposes.

Test Your Understanding

1. Write an Excel formula to calculate the outstanding balance (present value) of a loan with 226 payments of $2,254 remaining. The annual interest rate on this loan is 9%.
2. Examine the sample page from the amortization schedule, #5 above. If you want to pay this loan off on June 15, how big a check will the bank be looking for? (Assume, of course, that you're not in arrears.)

Answer

1. The general format is:

   =PV(Periodic Rate, Number of Periods,-Periodic Payment)

   Fill in the variables, remembering to convert the annual interest rate to a monthly rate:

   =PV(0.0075,226,-2254)

   You'll see the result in the cell.

   $245,005.56

2. Looking at the table, it's clear that you owe $99,854.05 at the end of May. That is your principal balance. However, your lender expects to get paid for the 15 days in June when you will still be using the bank's money. Looking at the table again, you can see that the bank would expect to earn interest of $998.54 for the entire month of June. Since you'll be using the money for exactly one-half of the month, you'll owe exactly one-half of the interest, or $499.27.

The bank will give you a "payoff" figure of $100,353.32, which represents the $99,854.05 outstanding balance plus $499.27 of interest that accrues for 15 days in June.

> **Rule of Thumb:** We've made this example uncomplicated by taking exactly one-half month so that we could simply divide the total monthly interest in half. To handle a situation where the closing occurs at some nonhalfway point, the customary procedure is to calculate the interest per diem and multiply it by the number of days. In this case, the interest for the full 30 days of June is $998.54, so the per diem amount is 1/30 of that total, or 33.28466. If your closing were delayed and you couldn't pay off the loan until the 16th, your interest for June would be 16 × 33.28466, or $532.55.

36

Calculation 30: Principal and Interest per Period

What It Means

In an amortized mortgage with level payments, a portion of each payment represents interest, and the balance is applied to the reduction of principal. How do you figure the interest/principal breakdown for a given payment?

In the chapter "Principal Balance/Balloon Payment," you saw a page from an amortization schedule that helps make this clear. In the particular loan shown there, the annual interest rate is 12%. You can calculate the monthly payment amount by using any of the techniques in the "Mortgage Payment/Mortgage Constant" chapter or by simply letting the amortization schedule software do it for you. At 12% interest and over a term of 360 months, the monthly payment required to amortize the loan is $1,028.61. The following schedule shows the progression of interest and principal over one year.

What are the mechanics of this progression? We've chosen an interest rate of 12% annually to make the schedule easy to follow. You make payments monthly; that means you are paying 1% per month on the outstanding balance. You must allocate your payment first to cover the interest, and then apply whatever is left over to reduce the principal. You borrowed $100,000, so you have use of that amount for one month at 1% per month, which costs $1,000 in interest. Because your payment is $1,028.61, there is $28.61 left to reduce the principal.

LOAN AMORTIZATION SCHEDULE
© Copyright 1982–2015, RealData®, Inc.

Data Input:

Beginning Balance:	100,000.00	Ann. Int. Rate:	12.000%
Term, Months:	360	First Pmt Month:	1
Calculated Pmt:	$1,028.61	First Pmt Year:	2020

	INTEREST	PRINCIPAL	BALANCE
January	1,000.00	28.61	99,971.39
February	999.71	28.90	99,942.49
March	999.42	29.19	99,913.30
April	999.13	29.48	99,883.82
May	998.84	29.77	99,854.05
June	998.54	30.07	99,823.98
July	998.24	30.37	99,793.61
August	997.94	30.67	99,762.94
September	997.63	30.98	99,731.96
October	997.32	31.29	99,700.67
November	997.01	31.60	99,669.07
December	996.69	31.92	99,637.15
Total 2020	11,980.47	362.85	

After the January payment, you have an outstanding balance of $99,971.39. You have the use of that amount of the lender's money for the second month, so that's the sum on which you must pay interest. One percent of 99,971.39 is 999.71. Again, your payment takes care of the interest first, which leaves 28.90 to apply to the principal. This process continues each month until all the principal is paid.

How to Calculate

Interest portion of a payment = Outstanding Principal Balance × Periodic Rate

Principal portion of a payment = Payment amount less Interest portion

Example

You have a mortgage with an annual interest rate of 6%. After you make your June payment of $2,700, a balance of exactly $400,000 remains on the loan. What is the interest and principal breakdown of your July payment?

If your annual interest rate is 6% (0.06), then your monthly rate is 1/12 of that, or 0.005. Apply the formula for the interest portion:

Interest portion of a payment = Outstanding Principal Balance × Periodic Rate
Interest portion of a payment = 400,000 × 0.005 = 2,000

Now that you know the interest portion is $2,000, it is easy to calculate the principal:

Principal portion of a payment = Payment amount less Interest portion
Principal portion of a payment = 2,700 less 2,000 = 700

Rule of Thumb: In a typical mortgage, you pay interest in arrears (i.e., after you have used the money). The preceding amortization schedule shows your first payment due in January, which means you had first use of the money in December.

If you exercise regularly and never sell or refinance the property, you will eventually reach the last payment on your mortgage. When you do, you will probably find that the amount is different from all the prior payments. This difference is caused by the cumulative effect of rounding errors. Look at the March payment in the preceding schedule. The interest there is $999.42, based on a prior balance of $99,942.49. If the prior balance had been just a penny more, you would have rounded the interest portion up to $999.43, leaving one cent less to apply to principal. A penny isn't much, but the cumulative effect of rounding can add up to several dollars by the time you reach the end of the line.

Test Your Understanding

Why are amortizing mortgage payments more heavily weighted toward interest early in the life of the loan but gradually shift toward principal repayment as the loan progresses (as the loan becomes "seasoned," to use the parlance of commercial lenders)?

Answer

The interest component of your payment is highest at the very beginning of the loan because your utilization of the lender's funds is highest at that point. During the first month, you're using the full face amount of the loan, so you must pay the highest fee (i.e., interest). With each installment, you are also repaying some of the principal, so the amount of the lender's money you are using goes down each month, and so does your interest charge. The payment is a fixed amount; as the interest component declines (because you are paying for the use of less and less of the lender's money), the principal component increases.

37

Calculation 31: Maximum Loan Amount

What It Means

You know that when you apply for a home mortgage, you typically need to pass muster according to certain underwriting ratios. Most lenders require that your housing costs and your total debt payments not exceed specific percentages of your income.

With commercial mortgages, your personal credit is not irrelevant (being a deadbeat is seldom an advantage when it comes to borrowing money), but you will find that the lender is particularly interested in the ability of the property to produce income.

Even if you are a great credit risk, the amount of financing you are likely to obtain against a piece of income property will be limited by the interaction of three factors:

1. Net operating income (NOI)
2. Lender's minimum debt coverage ratio (DCR)
3. Loan terms (as expressed by the annual mortgage constant)

We discussed these factors in Chapters 3 through 5 of Part I; each also has a chapter of its own in Part II. If you're not yet familiar with these terms, you should review that material first.

How to Calculate

Maximum Loan Amount = Net Operating Income / Minimum Debt
Coverage Ratio / Mortgage Constant (annual)

In this formula, the NOI represents the property's ability to produce income before financing; the mortgage constant accounts for the effects of financing; and the DCR expresses the amount of breathing room that must be maintained between the NOI and the debt service.

A table of monthly mortgage constants is available at http://www .realdata.com/book. For the purposes of the examples in this chapter, you can use the excerpt from that table that you see below. Because the table provides monthly constants and you need the annual factors, you must multiply the constant by 12. The revised formula now reads:

Maximum Loan Amount = Net Operating Income / Minimum Debt
Coverage Ratio / (Monthly Mortgage Constant × 12)

Monthly Mortgage Payment per $1

Rate	15 years	16 years	17 years	18 years	19 years	20 years
7.0000	0.00898828	0.00867208	0.00839661	0.00815502	0.00794192	0.00775299
7.1250	0.00905831	0.00874318	0.00846876	0.00822821	0.00801613	0.00782820
7.2500	0.00912863	0.00881458	0.00854122	0.00830172	0.00809068	0.00790376
7.3750	0.00919923	0.00888628	0.00681400	0.00837556	0.00816556	0.00797967
7.5000	0.00927012	0.00895828	0.00868709	0.00844973	0.00824079	0.00805593
7.6250	0.00934130	0.00903058	0.00876050	0.00852423	0.00831635	0.00813254
7.7500	0.00941276	0.00910317	0.00883421	0.00859904	0.00839224	0.00820949
7.8750	0.00948450	0.00917606	0.00890824	0.00867417	0.00846846	0.00828677
8.0000	0.00955652	0.00924925	0.00898257	0.00874963	0.00854501	0.00836440
8.1250	0.00962882	0.00932273	0.00905720	0.00882539	0.00862189	0.00844236
8.2500	0.00970140	0.00939650	0.00913214	0.00890148	0.00869909	0.00852066
8.3750	0.00977246	0.00947056	0.00920738	0.00897787	0.00877661	0.00859928
8.5000	0.00984740	0.00954491	0.00928292	0.00905457	0.00885446	0.00867823

Example

You want to refinance a property that has an NOI of $120,000. Your lender offers a loan at 8% for 20 years and requires a DCR no less than 1.20. Under these terms, what is the maximum loan your property would support? Round the answer to the nearest $5,000.

Maximum Loan Amount = Net Operating Income / Minimum Debt
   Coverage Ratio / (Monthly Mortgage Constant × 12)
Maximum Loan Amount = 120,000 / 1.2 / (0.00836440 × 12)
Maximum Loan Amount = 996,286 (round to 995,000)

Rule of Thumb: You can achieve a higher maximum loan amount with a longer loan term or a lower interest rate because either change will result in a lower mortgage constant (i.e., debt service). Your maximum loan will also be higher if your lender requires a lower DCR. Keep in mind that most lenders will be reluctant to go below 1.20.

Test Your Understanding

You're seeking financing for a property with an NOI of $100,000. One lender requires a DCR of 1.3 at 7.875% for 20 years. A second lender requires a DCR of 1.2 at 7.625% for 15 years. Which lender is likely to give you the largest loan? Would the outcome change if both lenders offered loans for 20 years?

Answer

First lender at 20 years, 7.875%, 1.3 DCR:

Maximum Loan Amount = Net Operating Income / Minimum Debt
   Coverage Ratio / (Monthly Mortgage Constant × 12)
Maximum Loan Amount = 100,000 / 1.3 / (0.00828677 × 12)
Maximum Loan Amount = 773,553 (round to 775,000)

Second lender at 15 years, 7.625%, 1.2 DCR:

Maximum Loan Amount = 100,000 / 1.2 / (0.00934130 × 12)
Maximum Loan Amount = 743,413 (round to 740,000)

Second lender at 20 years, 7.625%, 1.2 DCR:

Maximum Loan Amount = 100,000 / 1.2 / (0.00813254 × 12)
Maximum Loan Amount = 853,909 (round to 855,000)

In the question as stated originally, the first lender presented a more restrictive DCR and a higher interest rate. However, it also permitted a longer loan term, and that longer term reduced the debt service enough to justify a greater maximum loan. When the second lender matched the 20-year term, its lower rate and lower DCR requirement clearly gave it the advantage.

38

Calculation 32: Assessed Value, Property Taxes, and Value Indicated by Assessment

What It Means

In most areas of the country, real property is taxed using a calculation that has four components:

- **Appraised value.** The value of the property as set by the assessor. Generally, all properties in a town, city, or county are appraised at a particular point in time, and those appraisals represent the market value at that time. Properties that are newly constructed or improved are usually assessed when construction is completed. Revaluation (or reassessment, as it is sometimes called) may not occur again for several years, so as time passes, these values may become less indicative of current market value.

- **Assessment ratio.** The percentage of the appraised value used for tax purposes. The state or the taxing district usually prescribes that the property tax is to be based on a percentage of the appraised value. Some states use a variety of percentages; for example, one percentage for residential, another for commercial, and perhaps a third for farm land.
- **Assessed value.** The amount on which the property will be taxed, determined by multiplying the appraised value by the assessment ratio.
- **Tax rate.** The rate applied to the assessed value to determine the actual number of dollars of property tax. Often this is called the "mill rate" (sometimes written "mil rate") because it is expressed as the tax rate per thousand dollars of assessed value.

How to Calculate

Two useful calculations can be performed here. One is the amount of property tax that you must pay. As a rule, the information you will find on the assessor's record for your property is the assessed value. You apply the current tax rate to determine the annual taxes:

Property Taxes = Assessed Value × Tax Rate

The other calculation you might want to make involves working backward from the assessed value to determine the appraised value:

Appraised Value = Assessed Value / Assessment Ratio

If local properties recently underwent revaluation, then it's reasonable to believe that the appraised valuations represent the market values at that time. There are a number of situations where your knowledge of the appraised value can be useful. It can help you justify an asking price or offer to buy. It can also prove useful if you're trying to refinance a property or establish credit for any purpose, since it provides an objective estimate of value that doesn't cost you anything (or at least it doesn't cost you anything extra beyond your taxes).

Example

Your property has an assessed value of $234,500. Your local mill rate is 42.50. What are your property taxes?

Remember that "mill rate" means tax rate per $1,000 of assessed value. You have 234.5 thousand, so you multiply that number times the rate to calculate the annual taxes:

Property Taxes = Assessed Value × Tax Rate
Property Taxes = 234.5 × 42.50
Property Taxes = 9,966.25

Rule of Thumb: If you receive a new property assessment, use it to calculate the appraised value so that you can begin to make a judgment about whether your property has been assessed fairly and whether or not you should appeal the assessment. Keep the following in mind:

1. It's not good enough to be satisfied that the assessment suggests a reasonable property value. It's more important that your valuation is in line with other comparable properties. If your property is commercial or a larger residential income property, determine the cap rate that must have been used to come up with this appraised value. Is that cap rate reasonable for your market? If not, you have the basis for a clear, unemotional, numbers-based appeal. This writer encountered just such a situation and won a substantial assessment reduction by showing that the cap rate used was too low, producing a value that was too high. The independent company that had performed the appraisals for the town agreed immediately that the assessment was in error. Someone had used an erroneous cap rate in the calculation.

2. If your property is a smaller residential building (or even your personal residence), the assessor or appraiser will probably have used comparable sales rather than income capitalization to establish value. Once again, the issue is not really whether the value seems realistic, but whether it is in line with other similar properties. In other words, even if you think your property really is worth $500,000, if similar properties similarly located were valued at $475,000, then yours should be too. Otherwise you are bearing a disproportionate share of the municipal tax burden in relation to the market value of the property you own.

Test Your Understanding

Your new tax bill shows an assessed value of $350,000. The local assessment ratio is 70%.

1. What is the appraised value of your property?
2. Your property's net operating income is $57,500. What cap rate did the appraiser use in estimating the value of this property?

Answer

1. Appraised Value = Assessed Value / Assessment Ratio
   Appraised Value = 350,000 / 0.70
   Appraised Value = 500,000

2. Capitalization Rate = Net Operating Income / Present Value
   Capitalization Rate = 57,500 / 500,000
   Capitalization Rate = 0.115 = 11.5%

39

Calculation 33: Adjusted Basis

What It Means

When you sell an income-property investment, the taxable profit that you realize is called the gain on sale (see Part II, Calculation 35), or simply gain. In order to calculate the gain, you need to know the selling price of the property as well as its *adjusted basis*. Under the current tax code, the adjusted basis is the original cost of an asset such as real estate, plus capital improvements and costs of sale, less accumulated depreciation.

In order to determine the gain on sale, you first calculate the adjusted basis and then find the difference between that amount and the selling price.

How to Calculate

The formula for adjusted basis reads as follows:

Original Basis (Purchase Price)
plus Capital Additions
plus Costs of Sale
less Cumulative Depreciation, Real Estate

less Cumulative Depreciation, Capital Additions

= Adjusted Basis

Example

You purchase a property for $200,000. The next year, you make $50,000 in capital additions. By the time you sell the property, you have taken $19,000 in depreciation on the original property and $5,100 on the additions. You sell the property, paying $22,000 as costs of sale. What is your adjusted basis?

The following is a form you can use for adjusted basis calculations:

Adjusted Basis	
Date:	
Prepared by:	
ORIGINAL BASIS, Purchase Price of Real Estate	
Plus Cumulative Capital Additions	
Plus Costs of Sale	
Less Cumulative Depreciation, Real Estate	
Less Cumulative Depreciation, Capital Improvements	
ADJUSTED BASIS AT SALE	

Now fill in the amounts, and you'll find that your adjusted basis for this property is $247,900:

ORIGINAL BASIS, Purchase Price of Real Estate	200,000
plus Cumulative Capital Additions	50,000
plus Costs of Sale	22,000
less Cumulative Depreciation, Real Estate	19,000
less Cumulative Depreciation, Capital Improvements	5,100
ADJUSTED BASIS AT SALE	247,900

Test Your Understanding

You purchase a property for $250,000. At the end of the first year, you make a $35,000 capital addition. At the end of the second year, you make a $30,000 addition. After five years, you sell the property for $475,000. At the time of sale, you have accumulated $25,000 depreciation on the original property, $3,500 on the first addition, and $3,000 on the second addition. You expect to pay selling costs of 6%.

1. What is your adjusted basis at the time of sale?
2. What is your gain on sale?

Answer

1. You need to start with a few preliminary calculations. You have two capital additions; add those together for a total of 65,000. Similarly, you must combine their cumulative depreciation, which totals 6,500. Finally, you need to calculate the costs of sale—6% of 475,000, or 28,500. Now you're ready to fill in the form:

ORIGINAL BASIS, Purchase Price of Real Estate	250,000
plus Cumulative Capital Additions	65,000
plus Costs of Sale	28,500
less Cumulative Depreciation, Real Estate	25,000
less Cumulative Depreciation, Capital Improvements	6,500
ADJUSTED BASIS AT SALE	312,000

   Your property's adjusted basis is $312,000.

2. To find the gain on sale, you calculate the difference between the selling price and the adjusted basis:

Selling Price	475,000
less Adjusted Basis	312,000
= Gain on Sale	163,000

   Your gain on sale is $163,000.

40

Calculation 34: Depreciation

What It Means

Depreciation (also called *cost recovery*) is the amount of the tax deduction that a property owner may take each year until he or she has written off the entire depreciable asset. With real estate, you treat the physical structures (called improvements) as your depreciable assets, but not the land. Therefore, there is no depreciation allowance for the value of the land.

The exact amount of your depreciation deduction each year is determined by the asset's *useful life* as specified in the tax code. The useful life for tax purposes is not necessarily the same as the actual physical life expectancy of a particular asset. As of this writing, the useful life for residential property is 27.5 years, and for nonresidential, it is 39 years.

You begin depreciating real property according to the time you place it in service. If you're buying an existing income property, that time is usually when you take title. If you make additions or capital improvements to the property, you depreciate these according to the same useful life and begin doing so at the time you place the additions or improvements in service.

The current tax code also provides for what is called the half-month convention. In whatever month you place an asset in service and whatever month you dispose of it, you're allowed to take only one-half of the depreciation normally allowed. So, if you buy a property in January and continue to own it throughout the year, you can take only 11.5 months of depreciation for that first year.

How to Calculate

1. Determine the depreciable basis by separating the value of the improvements from the value of the land.
2. Determine the useful life according to the current tax code.
3. Apply the formula:

Depreciation Allowance (annual) = Depreciable Basis / Useful Life

In the month you place the property in service or dispose of the property, prorate according to the months owned, and reduce the total by one-half month for the month placed in service and one-half month for the month disposed.

Example

You purchase a commercial property in January under the tax rules described above. The purchase price is $500,000, of which you attribute $390,000 to the building and $110,000 to the land. Assuming you do not sell the property, what is your depreciation allowance for the first full year?

The depreciable basis is specified in the example as $390,000, and the useful life is 39 years because commercial property is nonresidential.

Depreciation Allowance (annual) = Depreciable Basis / Useful Life
Depreciation Allowance (annual) = 390,000 / 39 = 10,000

Because the property is placed in service this year, you must apply the half-month convention and reduce this amount by the equivalent of one-half month's depreciation. If 12 months of depreciation equals $10,000, then one month equals 1/12, or $833.33, and one-half month equals $416.67. (You can save a step by dividing the annual deprecia-tion by 24 to get the half-month amount.)

First-year depreciation allowed = 10,000 less 416.67 = 9,583.33

Rule of Thumb: When you purchase an existing property, a good (and defensible) method of separating the value of the buildings from the value of the land is to examine the tax assessments. Their actual dollar amounts may be far less than the purchase price because many states assess according to a percentage of value and because the assessments may have been determined a year or more in the past; but the proportion between the assessed value of the building and the assessed value of the land should remain meaningful.

Test Your Understanding

In April, you purchase a residential income property under the tax rules described above for $687,500. You examine the local tax records and find that the building has an assessed value of $400,000 and the land has an assessed value of $100,000. You sell the property during the third year of your ownership, in November. What is your depreciation allowance for each of the three calendar years?

Answer

1. First, you must determine the depreciable basis. According to the tax assessor, the building is or was recently worth $400,000 and the land $100,000. Hence, the building represents 80% of the value of the entire parcel, and you can reasonably conclude that its depreciable basis is 80% of the purchase price.

   Depreciable Basis = 0.80 × 687,500 = 550,000

2. Second, choose the appropriate useful life; according to the tax code du jour, that life is 27.5 years because the property is residential.

3. Next, calculate the standard annual allowance for depreciation.

Depreciation Allowance (annual) = Depreciable Basis / Useful Life
Depreciation Allowance (annual) = 550,000 / 27.5 = 20,000

4. You purchased the property in April, so you owned it for nine months during the first year. Because of the half-month convention, you can take only one-half month of depreciation in April, so you're entitled to 8.5 months. Find the monthly depreciation and multiply by 8.5 to determine your depreciation allowance for the first year.

First-year depreciation = (20,000 / 12) × 8.5 = 14,166.67

5. You own the property for all of the second year, and you did not place it in service or dispose of it during that year, so you're entitled to the full annual amount.

Second-year depreciation = 20,000

6. You sell the property in November of the third year. Once again, you must apply the half-month convention because you are entitled to take only a half-month of depreciation in the month you dispose of the property. Find the monthly depreciation and multiply by 10.5 to determine your depreciation allowance for the first year.

Third-year depreciation = (20,000 / 12) × 10.5 = 17,500

41

Calculation 35: Gain on Sale

What It Means

The *gain on sale* (or simply *gain*) is the taxable profit that you make when you sell an income-property investment. Under current rules, if you have held the property for more than 12 months, then the gain is a capital gain, which means that at least some of it will be taxed at a rate that is lower than what you pay on ordinary income.

How to Calculate

It would be nice to tell you that the gain on sale is merely the difference between what you paid for a property and the price for which you eventually sell it. Nice, but not accurate. It is actually the difference between the property's adjusted basis and its selling price.

To keep focused here on the concept of gain, we have discussed the calculation of adjusted basis in a separate chapter (Part II, Calculation 33), which you should review if you haven't already. For now, think of it in these simplified terms: In general, the adjusted basis represents your original purchase price less the cumulative amount of depreciation taken. Therefore, your taxable profit (gain) is measured not against what you originally paid for the property, but against what you paid minus all the depreciation to date. The more depreciation you've taken by the time you sell, the lower your adjusted basis will be; the lower the adjusted basis, the greater the difference between it and the selling price—and the greater your taxable gain on sale.

The formula reads as follows:

```
Selling Price
less Adjusted Basis
= Gain on Sale
```

Example

You estimate that you will sell your property for $500,000. You purchased it five years ago for $300,000. By the time you sell, you have taken $28,300 in depreciation, and this depreciation is the only "adjustment" in your adjusted basis. What is your gain on sale?

If the depreciation is the only item that needs to be accounted for in your adjusted basis, then that adjusted basis is the original purchase price of 300,000 less the 28,300 cumulative depreciation, or 271,700.

Selling Price	500,000
less Adjusted Basis	271,700
= Gain on Sale	228,300

Rule of Thumb: If you have an opportunity to turn a quick profit by reselling an income property, don't make the mistake of being too quick. Under the current tax code, if you hold for 12 months and then sell, you qualify for the lower long-term capital gain tax rate. Rates and rules change, so it's worth asking your accountant before you schedule a closing—but the savings could easily be in the thousands of dollars if the gain qualifies as long term.

Test Your Understanding

You plan to sell your property five years from now. You project that it will have an annual net operating income of $38,000 at that time.

Investors in your market currently expect a cap rate of 11%, and you anticipate that same rate to prevail when you sell. The adjusted basis on your property when you sell will be $198,000.

What do you estimate will be your gain on sale?

Answer

You first have to estimate what the property will be worth when you sell. Use the formula from our chapter on capitalization rates:

Present Value = Net Operating Income / Capitalization Rate
Present Value = 38,000 / 0.11
Present Value = 345,455 (round to 345,000)

Now apply the formula for gain on sale:

Selling Price	345,000
less Adjusted Basis	198,000
= Gain on Sale	147,000

You estimate a gain on sale of $147,000.

42

Calculation 36: Land Measurements

What It Means

Anyone who gets involved in real estate, whether as an investor or just a homeowner, needs to understand the basics of land measurement. You will almost always describe a parcel's size in terms of its area. If the parcel is a perfect rectangle, you calculate the area by multiplying length times width. If the land is in the form of anything but a perfect rectangle, you might need to get into some serious geometry in order to come up with an accurate measurement. That's a job better left to a professional. Unless you are trying to subdivide a larger piece, it is also a job that probably has been completed already by the local tax assessor; you should be able to find out the size of any existing lot by checking the assessor's records.

Measuring the land is not really a job for you as an investor, but you should understand how those measurements are expressed and how to convert among the ways of describing lot size.

In the United States, you typically describe land in terms of acres or square feet. One acre equals 43,560 square feet. In countries that use the metric system, you usually describe land in terms of hectares. One hectare is a little less than 2.5 acres.

Investors often talk about commercial land in terms of square feet in the same way they talk about commercial buildings. The square foot serves as a unit of comparison. It is not uncommon to hear someone say that she purchased a piece of land for $3 per square foot or that she leased the land to a developer for $1 per square foot.

The square footage of the land can also be important because local zoning laws may prescribe the maximum building footprint or the maximum gross building area in relation to the number of square feet of land.

Occasionally, land is described in terms of its "front feet," that is, the number of feet of road frontage. A municipality may describe a piece of land this way when figuring out how to charge you for your share of the installation of a sewer line in front of your property. If your land has 100 feet of road frontage, then the city or town will be inclined to charge you for 100 feet of excavation and pipe, regardless of how deep the lot is. Another time that you may hear a property's size described in terms of front footage is when the land is suitable for retail use. The more exposure the property has to passing traffic, the more valuable it is likely to be. Even though two parcels might lie very close to each other, exhibit substantial similarity in most respects, and contain the same total area, the piece with the greatest number of front feet—and hence the greatest public exposure—would usually command the higher price.

How to Calculate

You should know how to convert between acres and square feet because you'll hear one or the other of these terms used to describe the land portion of every property you encounter.

We've also listed a number of other useful conversion factors. You won't use these nearly as often, but now you'll know where to find them when you need them. Keep in mind that some of these factors have been rounded:

Acres to Square Feet—multiply by	43,560
Square Feet to Acres—multiply by	0.000023 (or divide by 43,560)
Acres to Hectares—multiply by	0.4046856

Hectares to Acres—multiply by	2.471054
Acres to Square Meters—multiply by	4046.86
Square Meters to Acres—multiply by	0.000247
Acres to Square Miles—multiply by	0.0015625
Square Miles to Acres—multiply by	640
Square Meters to Square Feet—multiply by	10.76391
Square Feet to Square Meters—multiply by	0.092903
Meters to Feet—multiply by	3.2808399
Feet to Meters—multiply by	0.3048

Example

A building offered for sale sits on 0.24 acre. How many square feet of land does that equal? The adjacent property has 30,000 square feet of land. How many acres does that equal?

First property:

Square Feet = Acres × 43,560
Square Feet = 0.24 × 43,560
Square Feet = 10,454

Second property:

Acres = Square Feet × 0.000023
Acres = 30,000 × 0.000023
Acres = 0.69

Rule of Thumb: It can be very helpful to get a mental picture of just how big an acre is. A piece of land that is 200' by 200' contains 40,000 square feet, just a bit under the 43,560 that make up an acre. So also does a parcel that is 100' by 400'. When you're looking at a piece of land or at the map of a property and you don't know the acreage, think in terms of how many 200' by 200' or 100' by 400' rectangles might fit on that property in order to make a rough estimate of size.

Test Your Understanding

You own a piece of commercial land in the shape shown here:

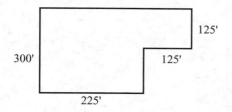

1. What is the square footage of this parcel?
2. What is its area in acres?
3. A foreign investor asks you what the area of this parcel is in hectares. What is your answer?

Answer

Look at the parcel as being made of two attached rectangles:

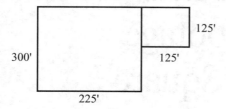

1. The area in square feet is the sum of the areas of the two rectangles:

   225 × 300 = 67,500
   125 × 125 = 15,625
   Total = 83,125 square feet

2. Acres = Square Feet × 0.000023
   Acres = 83,125 × 0.000023
   Acres = 1.92

3. Hectares = Acres × 0.4046856
   Hectares = 1.92 × 0.4046856
   Hectares = 0.78

43

Calculation 37: Building Measurements—Gross Building Area, Usable Square Footage, Rentable Square Footage, Loss Ratio, Net Rentable Area

What It Means

You typically rent out commercial space by the square foot, and for this reason, the measurement of commercial space is important. One would think that a square foot is a square foot and that would be all there is to it. But no, there are different kinds of square-foot measurements in commercial leasing, and you should know what each means. Because these various measurements are closely interrelated, we'll consider them together in this one chapter.

The first of these measurements, *gross building area* (GBA), is perhaps the most straightforward. GBA represents a building's total floor area, as measured from the outer surface of exterior walls and windows, and includes elevator shafts, utility rooms, and basement space.

Usable square footage (USF) is the actual space contained within a tenant's (or all tenants') premises. In the terminology of commercial leasing, it is the space contained within the tenant's "demising walls." The demising walls separate a tenant's space from that of other tenants and from public corridors. In the plainest terms, usable square footage is the actual physical space that the tenant occupies, even if not every square foot is truly usable.

Rentable square footage (RSF) is the number of square feet on which the tenant's rent is based. This is where geometry usually leaves off and creativity begins. A number of organizations in the commercial real estate industry have attempted to establish standards for the computation of RSF, but it remains a fuzzy notion. Ultimately, the RSF is whatever number the landlord and tenant agree on for purposes of their lease. If a commercial tenant occupies a space of 1,900 USF and agrees to a lease that defines the space as 2,000 RSF, then the rent will be based on the 2,000 RSF.

Why would a landlord consider it necessary to base the tenant's rent on more than the tenant's USF? Because, in order to provide the usable area, the commercial building owner must also provide so-called common area that does not generate revenue: lobby, corridors, restrooms, utility rooms, elevator shafts, etc. The *loss ratio* is the percentage of the GBA that is not USF. In other words, it is the percentage of the building that is common area.

The owner will typically take a percentage of the square footage that makes up the common area and add that to the USF to make what is called the *net rentable area* (NRA).

These are a lot of new terms for one chapter, seemingly designed to camouflage some fairly straightforward ideas. The short version of commercial space measurement might read like this:

A commercial building has an overall size, called the GBA. Tenants are able to occupy and use most of that space—the USF—but there remain common areas such as lobbies and corridors that cannot be rented. The percentage of the building that cannot be rented is called the "loss percentage." Typically, the owner takes a portion of that loss and tacks it onto the usable space to make the NRA. Effectively, the landlord says to the tenant, "I'm going to base your rent on the space you actually use, plus a portion of the space that is available in common to everyone, and we're going to call that combination the rentable square footage."

How to Calculate

Gross Building Area = Total area of all floors, including basement
Usable Square Footage = Actual space occupied by a tenant;
   for an entire building, Gross Building Area less Common Area
Rentable Square Feet = Defined by lease, but often USF + an allocated
   portion of Common Area
Loss Ratio = Common Area / Gross Building Area

Example

A commercial building contains 24,000 total square feet. Common area is 4,800 square feet. What is the GBA? What is the USF? What is the loss ratio?

By definition, the GBA is the total square footage, given as 24,000.

Usable Square Footage = Gross Building Area less Common Area
Usable Square Footage = 24,000 − 4,800
Usable Square Footage = 19,200
Loss Ratio = Common Area / Gross Building Area
Loss Ratio = 4,800 / 24,000 = 20%

Rule of Thumb: How much higher is RSF than USF? The difference will obviously depend on the building's proportions, but 15 to 20% is not uncommon.

> When leasing commercial space, it is useful to offer it in terms of dollars per square foot because prospective tenants feel comfortable using a common denominator for comparison. When negotiating real lease terms, however, you may want to translate the dollars per square foot into actual dollar amounts of rent to head off measurement disputes.

Test Your Understanding

A commercial building has nine floors plus a basement. The building dimensions are 60' × 80'. Common area is 8,640 square feet.

1. What is the GBA? What is the USF? What is the loss ratio?
2. A tenant occupies 4,000 square feet. The tenant's RSF will be based on USF plus 7% of the common area. What is the tenant's RSF?
3. The tenant will pay $20 per RSF per year. What is the tenant's annual rent?

Answer

The building has 10 levels, each 60' × 80'.

1. Gross Building Area = 60 × 80 × 10
   Gross Building Area = 48,000 square feet
   Usable Square Footage = Gross Building Area less Common Area
   Usable Square Footage = 48,000 − 8,640
   Usable Square Footage = 39,360
   Loss Ratio = Common Area / Gross Building Area
   Loss Ratio = 8,640 / 48,000
   Loss Ratio = 18%
2. Tenant allocation of Common Area = 7% of 8,640
   Tenant allocation of Common Area = 605 square feet (rounded)
   Rentable Square Feet = USF + allocated portion of Common Area
   Rentable Square Feet = 4,000 + 605
   Rentable Square Feet = 4,605

3. Tenant's annual rent = rate per RSF × RSF
   Tenant's annual rent = 20 × 4,605
   Tenant's rent = 92,100

Appendix

On the following pages you will find excerpts from two tables that we have used in the text.

The first, "Annual Present Value Factors," is discussed in Part II, Calculation 16 ("Discounted Cash Flow") and Calculation 17 ("Net Present Value"). The second table, "Monthly Mortgage Payment per $1—Mortgage Constant," is covered in Part II, Calculation 28 ("Mortgage Payment/Mortgage Constant") and Calculation 29 ("Principal Balance/Balloon Payment"). You will also see this table used in Part 1, Chapter 3, "How the 'Time Value of Money' Should Influence Your Real Estate Investing Decisions."

Lengthy tables filled with tiny numbers can be daunting; even worse, they may remind you of the instruction booklet for your tax return. We've included only a few pages from each table here, just enough to make it possible for you to follow the examples in the text.

You can download longer versions of these tables, as well as a number of other useful tools, from RealData's website. Just go to http://www.realdata.com/book. There you will find a page with links to a free real estate calculator program, several Microsoft Excel templates shown in this book, and a number of other useful tools.

Annual Present Value Factors

Years	3.000%	3.125%	3.250%	3.375%	3.500%	3.625%	3.750%	3.875%	4.000%	4.125%	4.250%
1	0.970874	0.969697	0.968523	0.967352	0.966184	0.965018	0.963855	0.962696	0.961538	0.960384	0.959233
2	0.942596	0.940312	0.938037	0.935770	0.933511	0.931260	0.929017	0.926783	0.924556	0.922338	0.920127
3	0.915142	0.911818	0.908510	0.905219	0.901943	0.898683	0.895438	0.892210	0.888996	0.885799	0.882616
4	0.888487	0.884187	0.879913	0.875665	0.871442	0.867245	0.863073	0.858926	0.854804	0.850707	0.846634
5	0.862609	0.857394	0.852216	0.847076	0.841973	0.836907	0.831878	0.826884	0.821927	0.817005	0.812119
6	0.837484	0.831412	0.825391	0.819421	0.813501	0.807631	0.801810	0.796038	0.790315	0.784639	0.779011
7	0.813092	0.806218	0.799410	0.792668	0.785991	0.779378	0.772829	0.766342	0.759918	0.753555	0.747253
8	0.789409	0.781787	0.774247	0.766789	0.759412	0.752114	0.744895	0.737754	0.730690	0.723702	0.716789
9	0.766417	0.758098	0.749876	0.741755	0.733731	0.725804	0.717971	0.710233	0.702587	0.695032	0.687568
10	0.744094	0.735124	0.726272	0.717538	0.708919	0.700414	0.692020	0.683738	0.675564	0.667498	0.659537
11	0.722421	0.712847	0.703411	0.694112	0.684946	0.675912	0.667008	0.658231	0.649581	0.641054	0.632650
12	0.701380	0.691246	0.681270	0.671450	0.661783	0.652267	0.642899	0.633676	0.624597	0.615658	0.606858
13	0.680951	0.670299	0.659826	0.649528	0.639404	0.629450	0.619662	0.610037	0.600574	0.591269	0.582118
14	0.661118	0.649987	0.639056	0.628323	0.617782	0.607430	0.597264	0.587280	0.577475	0.567845	0.558387
15	0.641862	0.630290	0.618941	0.607809	0.596891	0.586181	0.575676	0.565372	0.555265	0.545349	0.535623
16	0.623167	0.611191	0.599458	0.587965	0.576706	0.565675	0.554869	0.544281	0.533908	0.523745	0.513787
17	0.605016	0.592670	0.580589	0.568769	0.557204	0.545887	0.534813	0.523977	0.513373	0.502996	0.492841
18	0.587395	0.574710	0.562314	0.550200	0.538361	0.526791	0.515483	0.504430	0.493628	0.483070	0.472749
19	0.570286	0.557294	0.544614	0.532237	0.520156	0.508363	0.496851	0.485613	0.474642	0.463932	0.453477
20	0.553676	0.540407	0.527471	0.514860	0.502566	0.490579	0.478892	0.467497	0.456387	0.445553	0.434989
21	0.537549	0.524031	0.510868	0.498051	0.485571	0.473418	0.461583	0.450058	0.438834	0.427902	0.417256
22	0.521893	0.508151	0.494787	0.481791	0.469151	0.456857	0.444899	0.433269	0.421955	0.410951	0.400246
23	0.506692	0.492753	0.479213	0.466061	0.453286	0.440875	0.428819	0.417106	0.405726	0.394671	0.383929
24	0.491934	0.477821	0.464129	0.450845	0.437957	0.425452	0.413319	0.401546	0.390121	0.379035	0.368277
25	0.477606	0.463341	0.449519	0.436126	0.423147	0.410569	0.398380	0.386566	0.375117	0.364019	0.353263
26	0.463695	0.449301	0.435370	0.421887	0.408838	0.396207	0.383981	0.372146	0.360689	0.349599	0.338862
27	0.450189	0.435685	0.421666	0.408113	0.395012	0.382347	0.370102	0.358263	0.346817	0.335749	0.325047
28	0.437077	0.422483	0.408393	0.394789	0.381654	0.368971	0.356725	0.344898	0.333477	0.322448	0.311796
29	0.424346	0.409680	0.395538	0.381900	0.368748	0.356064	0.343831	0.332032	0.320651	0.309674	0.299085
30	0.411987	0.397266	0.383088	0.369432	0.356278	0.343608	0.331403	0.319646	0.308319	0.297406	0.286892

Annual Present Value Factors

Years	4.375%	4.500%	4.625%	4.750%	4.875%	5.000%	5.125%	5.250%	5.375%	5.500%	5.625%
1	0.958084	0.956938	0.955795	0.954654	0.953516	0.952381	0.951249	0.950119	0.948992	0.947867	0.946746
2	0.917925	0.915730	0.913543	0.911364	0.909193	0.907029	0.904874	0.902726	0.900585	0.898452	0.896327
3	0.879449	0.876297	0.873160	0.870037	0.866930	0.863838	0.860760	0.857697	0.854648	0.851614	0.848594
4	0.842586	0.838561	0.834561	0.830585	0.826632	0.822702	0.818796	0.814914	0.811054	0.807217	0.803402
5	0.807268	0.802451	0.797669	0.792921	0.788207	0.783526	0.778879	0.774265	0.769683	0.765134	0.760618
6	0.773430	0.767896	0.762408	0.756965	0.751568	0.746215	0.740907	0.735643	0.730423	0.725246	0.720111
7	0.741011	0.734828	0.728705	0.722640	0.716632	0.710681	0.704787	0.698949	0.693165	0.687437	0.681762
8	0.709951	0.703185	0.696492	0.689871	0.683320	0.676839	0.670428	0.664084	0.657808	0.651599	0.645455
9	0.680192	0.672904	0.665703	0.658588	0.651557	0.644609	0.637743	0.630959	0.624255	0.617629	0.611082
10	0.651681	0.643928	0.636276	0.628723	0.621270	0.613913	0.606652	0.599486	0.592412	0.585431	0.578539
11	0.624365	0.616199	0.608149	0.600213	0.592391	0.584679	0.577077	0.569583	0.562194	0.554911	0.547729
12	0.598194	0.589664	0.581265	0.572996	0.564854	0.556837	0.548944	0.541171	0.533518	0.525982	0.518560
13	0.573120	0.564272	0.555570	0.547013	0.538598	0.530321	0.522182	0.514177	0.506304	0.498561	0.490945
14	0.549097	0.539973	0.531011	0.522208	0.513561	0.505068	0.496725	0.488529	0.480478	0.472569	0.464800
15	0.526081	0.516720	0.507537	0.498528	0.489689	0.481017	0.472509	0.464161	0.455970	0.447933	0.440047
16	0.504030	0.494469	0.485101	0.475922	0.466926	0.458112	0.449473	0.441008	0.432712	0.424581	0.416613
17	0.482903	0.473176	0.463657	0.454341	0.445222	0.436297	0.427561	0.419010	0.410640	0.402447	0.394426
18	0.462661	0.452800	0.443161	0.433738	0.424526	0.415521	0.406717	0.398109	0.389694	0.381466	0.373421
19	0.443268	0.433302	0.423571	0.414070	0.404793	0.395734	0.386889	0.378251	0.369816	0.361579	0.353535
20	0.424688	0.414643	0.404847	0.395293	0.385976	0.376889	0.368027	0.359383	0.350952	0.342729	0.334708
21	0.406887	0.396787	0.386950	0.377368	0.368035	0.358942	0.350085	0.341457	0.333051	0.324862	0.316883
22	0.389832	0.379701	0.369845	0.360256	0.350927	0.341850	0.333018	0.324425	0.316063	0.307926	0.300008
23	0.373492	0.363350	0.353496	0.343920	0.334614	0.325571	0.316783	0.308242	0.299941	0.291873	0.284031
24	0.357836	0.347703	0.337869	0.328324	0.319060	0.310068	0.301339	0.292866	0.284641	0.276657	0.268905
25	0.342837	0.332731	0.322934	0.313436	0.304229	0.295303	0.286649	0.278258	0.270122	0.262234	0.254584
26	0.328467	0.318402	0.308658	0.299223	0.290087	0.281241	0.272674	0.264378	0.256344	0.248563	0.241027
27	0.314699	0.304691	0.295014	0.285655	0.276603	0.267848	0.259381	0.251190	0.243268	0.235605	0.228191
28	0.301508	0.291571	0.281973	0.272701	0.263745	0.255094	0.246736	0.238661	0.230859	0.223322	0.216039
29	0.288870	0.279015	0.269508	0.260335	0.251485	0.242946	0.234707	0.226756	0.219084	0.211679	0.204534
30	0.276761	0.267000	0.257594	0.248530	0.239795	0.231377	0.223265	0.215445	0.207909	0.200644	0.193641

Annual Present Value Factors

Years	5.750%	5.875%	6.000%	6.125%	6.250%	6.375%	6.500%	6.625%	6.750%	6.875%	7.000%
1	0.945526	0.944510	0.943396	0.942285	0.941176	0.940071	0.938967	0.937866	0.936768	0.935673	0.934579
2	0.894209	0.892099	0.889996	0.887901	0.885813	0.883733	0.881659	0.879593	0.877535	0.875483	0.873439
3	0.845588	0.842597	0.839619	0.836656	0.833706	0.830771	0.827849	0.824941	0.822046	0.819165	0.816298
4	0.799611	0.795841	0.792094	0.788368	0.784665	0.780983	0.777323	0.773684	0.770067	0.766471	0.762895
5	0.756133	0.751680	0.747258	0.742868	0.738508	0.734179	0.729881	0.725613	0.721374	0.717165	0.712986
6	0.715019	0.709969	0.704961	0.699993	0.695067	0.690180	0.685334	0.680528	0.675760	0.671032	0.666342
7	0.676141	0.670573	0.665057	0.659593	0.654180	0.648818	0.643506	0.638244	0.633031	0.627866	0.622750
8	0.639377	0.633363	0.627412	0.621525	0.615699	0.609935	0.604231	0.598588	0.593003	0.587477	0.582009
9	0.604612	0.598218	0.591898	0.585653	0.579481	0.573382	0.567353	0.561395	0.555506	0.549686	0.543934
10	0.571737	0.565023	0.558395	0.551852	0.545394	0.539019	0.532726	0.526514	0.520381	0.514326	0.508349
11	0.540650	0.533669	0.526788	0.520002	0.513312	0.506716	0.500212	0.493799	0.487476	0.481241	0.475093
12	0.511253	0.504056	0.496969	0.489990	0.483117	0.476349	0.469683	0.463118	0.456652	0.450284	0.444012
13	0.483454	0.476086	0.468839	0.461711	0.454699	0.447802	0.441017	0.434343	0.427777	0.421318	0.414964
14	0.457167	0.449668	0.442301	0.435063	0.427952	0.420965	0.414100	0.407355	0.400728	0.394216	0.387817
15	0.432309	0.424716	0.417265	0.409953	0.402778	0.395737	0.388827	0.382045	0.375389	0.368857	0.362446
16	0.408803	0.401149	0.393646	0.386293	0.379085	0.372020	0.365095	0.358307	0.351653	0.345129	0.338735
17	0.386575	0.378889	0.371364	0.363998	0.356786	0.349725	0.342813	0.336044	0.329417	0.322928	0.316574
18	0.365555	0.357864	0.350344	0.342990	0.335799	0.328767	0.321890	0.315164	0.308587	0.302155	0.295864
19	0.345679	0.338006	0.330513	0.323194	0.316046	0.309064	0.302244	0.295582	0.289075	0.282718	0.276508
20	0.326883	0.319250	0.311805	0.304541	0.297455	0.290542	0.283797	0.277217	0.270796	0.264532	0.258419
21	0.309109	0.301535	0.294155	0.286965	0.279958	0.273130	0.266476	0.259992	0.253673	0.247515	0.241513
22	0.292302	0.284803	0.277505	0.270402	0.263490	0.256761	0.250212	0.243838	0.237633	0.231593	0.225713
23	0.276408	0.268999	0.261797	0.254796	0.247990	0.241374	0.234941	0.228687	0.222607	0.216695	0.210947
24	0.261379	0.254073	0.246979	0.240091	0.233402	0.226908	0.220602	0.214478	0.208531	0.202756	0.197147
25	0.247167	0.239974	0.232999	0.226234	0.219673	0.213310	0.207138	0.201152	0.195345	0.189713	0.184249
26	0.233728	0.226658	0.219810	0.213177	0.206751	0.200526	0.194496	0.188653	0.182993	0.177509	0.172195
27	0.221019	0.214081	0.207368	0.200873	0.194589	0.188509	0.182625	0.176932	0.171422	0.166090	0.160930
28	0.209002	0.202201	0.195630	0.189280	0.183143	0.177212	0.171479	0.165938	0.160583	0.155406	0.150402
29	0.197637	0.190981	0.184557	0.178356	0.172370	0.166591	0.161013	0.155628	0.150429	0.145409	0.140563
30	0.186891	0.180384	0.174110	0.168062	0.162230	0.156608	0.151186	0.145958	0.140917	0.136056	0.131367

Annual Present Value Factors

Years	7.125%	7.250%	7.375%	7.500%	7.625%	7.750%	7.875%	8.000%	8.125%	8.250%	8.375%
1	0.933489	0.932401	0.931315	0.930233	0.929152	0.928074	0.926999	0.925926	0.924855	0.923788	0.922722
2	0.871402	0.869371	0.867349	0.865333	0.863324	0.861322	0.859327	0.857339	0.855358	0.853345	0.851416
3	0.813444	0.810603	0.807775	0.804961	0.802159	0.799371	0.796595	0.793832	0.791082	0.788345	0.785620
4	0.759341	0.755807	0.752293	0.748801	0.745328	0.741875	0.738443	0.735030	0.731637	0.728263	0.724909
5	0.708836	0.704715	0.700623	0.696559	0.692523	0.688515	0.684535	0.680583	0.676658	0.672760	0.668890
6	0.661691	0.657077	0.652501	0.647962	0.643459	0.638993	0.634564	0.630170	0.625811	0.621488	0.617199
7	0.617681	0.612659	0.607684	0.602755	0.597871	0.593033	0.588240	0.583490	0.578785	0.574123	0.569503
8	0.576598	0.571244	0.565945	0.560702	0.555514	0.550379	0.545298	0.540269	0.535292	0.530367	0.525493
9	0.538248	0.532628	0.527074	0.521583	0.516157	0.510792	0.505490	0.500249	0.495068	0.489947	0.484884
10	0.502449	0.496623	0.490872	0.485194	0.479588	0.474053	0.468589	0.463193	0.457866	0.452607	0.447413
11	0.469030	0.463052	0.457757	0.451343	0.445610	0.439957	0.434381	0.428883	0.423460	0.418112	0.412838
12	0.437835	0.431750	0.425757	0.419854	0.414040	0.408312	0.402671	0.397114	0.391640	0.386247	0.380935
13	0.408714	0.402564	0.396514	0.390562	0.384706	0.378944	0.373276	0.367698	0.362210	0.356810	0.351497
14	0.381530	0.375351	0.369280	0.363313	0.357450	0.351688	0.346026	0.340461	0.334992	0.329617	0.324334
15	0.356154	0.349978	0.343916	0.337966	0.332126	0.326393	0.320766	0.315242	0.309819	0.304496	0.299270
16	0.332466	0.326320	0.320294	0.314387	0.308595	0.302917	0.297349	0.291890	0.286538	0.281289	0.276143
17	0.310353	0.304261	0.298295	0.292453	0.286732	0.281129	0.275643	0.270269	0.265006	0.259852	0.254803
18	0.289711	0.283693	0.277807	0.272049	0.266418	0.260909	0.255520	0.250249	0.245092	0.240048	0.235113
19	0.270442	0.264516	0.258726	0.253069	0.247543	0.242143	0.236867	0.231712	0.226675	0.221753	0.216944
20	0.252455	0.246635	0.240955	0.235413	0.230005	0.224727	0.219575	0.214548	0.209642	0.204853	0.200179
21	0.235664	0.229962	0.224405	0.218989	0.213709	0.208563	0.203546	0.198656	0.193888	0.189240	0.184709
22	0.219989	0.214417	0.208992	0.203711	0.198569	0.193562	0.188687	0.183941	0.179319	0.174818	0.170435
23	0.205358	0.199923	0.194638	0.189498	0.184500	0.179640	0.174913	0.170315	0.165844	0.161495	0.157264
24	0.191699	0.186408	0.181269	0.176277	0.171429	0.166719	0.162144	0.157699	0.153382	0.149187	0.145111
25	0.178949	0.173807	0.168819	0.163979	0.159284	0.154728	0.150307	0.146018	0.141856	0.137817	0.133897
26	0.167047	0.162058	0.157223	0.152539	0.147999	0.143599	0.139335	0.135202	0.131196	0.127314	0.123550
27	0.155936	0.151103	0.146425	0.141896	0.137513	0.133270	0.129163	0.125187	0.121337	0.117611	0.114002
28	0.145565	0.140889	0.136368	0.131997	0.127771	0.123685	0.119734	0.115914	0.112220	0.108647	0.105193
29	0.135883	0.131365	0.127001	0.122788	0.118718	0.114789	0.110993	0.107328	0.103787	0.100367	0.097063
30	0.126845	0.122484	0.118278	0.114221	0.110308	0.106532	0.102891	0.099377	0.095988	0.092718	0.089563

Monthly Mortgage Payment per $1—Mortgage Constant

Years	3.250%	3.375%	3.500%	3.625%	3.750%	3.875%	4.000%	4.125%	4.250%	4.375%
1	0.08480762	0.08486461	0.08492163	0.08497867	0.08503572	0.08509280	0.08514990	0.08520703	0.08526417	0.08532134
2	0.04309188	0.04314728	0.04320272	0.04325821	0.04331374	0.04336931	0.04342492	0.04348058	0.04353628	0.04359202
3	0.02919152	0.02924677	0.02930208	0.02935744	0.02941290	0.02946841	0.02952399	0.02957962	0.02963533	0.02969109
4	0.02224499	0.02230045	0.02235600	0.02241164	0.02246736	0.02252316	0.02257905	0.02263503	0.02269110	0.02274725
5	0.01808000	0.01813582	0.01819174	0.01824778	0.01830392	0.01836017	0.01841652	0.01847299	0.01852956	0.01858623
6	0.01530578	0.01536202	0.01541840	0.01547490	0.01553153	0.01558829	0.01564518	0.01570220	0.01575935	0.01581663
7	0.01332627	0.01338299	0.01343985	0.01349686	0.01355403	0.01361134	0.01366881	0.01372642	0.01378418	0.01384210
8	0.01184347	0.01190067	0.01195805	0.01201560	0.01207332	0.01213121	0.01218928	0.01224751	0.01230591	0.01236449
9	0.01069179	0.01074951	0.01080741	0.01086551	0.01092381	0.01098229	0.01104097	0.01109984	0.01115890	0.01121815
10	0.00977190	0.00983014	0.00988859	0.00994725	0.01000612	0.01006521	0.01012451	0.01018403	0.01024375	0.01030369
11	0.00902058	0.00907935	0.00913834	0.00919758	0.00925704	0.00931674	0.00937667	0.00943684	0.00949723	0.00955786
12	0.00839569	0.00845499	0.00851454	0.00857434	0.00863440	0.00869472	0.00875528	0.00881610	0.00887718	0.00893850
13	0.00786805	0.00792788	0.00798798	0.00804837	0.00810902	0.00816996	0.00823116	0.00829264	0.00835439	0.00841641
14	0.00741681	0.00747718	0.00753784	0.00759880	0.00766006	0.00772161	0.00778346	0.00784559	0.00790802	0.00797075
15	0.00702669	0.00708760	0.00714883	0.00721037	0.00727222	0.00733440	0.00739688	0.00745968	0.00752278	0.00758620
16	0.00668623	0.00674768	0.00680947	0.00687159	0.00693405	0.00699684	0.00705996	0.00712342	0.00718720	0.00725132
17	0.00638666	0.00644866	0.00651100	0.00657371	0.00663676	0.00670017	0.00676393	0.00682805	0.00689251	0.00695732
18	0.00612117	0.00618371	0.00624661	0.00630990	0.00637355	0.00643758	0.00650198	0.00656674	0.00663188	0.00669738
19	0.00588437	0.00594745	0.00601091	0.00607478	0.00613903	0.00620367	0.00626870	0.00633412	0.00639993	0.00646612
20	0.00567196	0.00573557	0.00579960	0.00586404	0.00592888	0.00599414	0.00605980	0.00612587	0.00619234	0.00625922
21	0.00548044	0.00554459	0.00560918	0.00567419	0.00573963	0.00580550	0.00587179	0.00593851	0.00600564	0.00607320
22	0.00530697	0.00537166	0.00543680	0.00550238	0.00556842	0.00563489	0.00570181	0.00576917	0.00583696	0.00590520
23	0.00514919	0.00521442	0.00528011	0.00534626	0.00541288	0.00547996	0.00554750	0.00561550	0.00568395	0.00575286
24	0.00500514	0.00507089	0.00513714	0.00520386	0.00527106	0.00533875	0.00540691	0.00547554	0.00554464	0.00561421
25	0.00487316	0.00493945	0.00500624	0.00507352	0.00514131	0.00520959	0.00527837	0.00534763	0.00541738	0.00548761
26	0.00475186	0.00481868	0.00488601	0.00495386	0.00502223	0.00509111	0.00516049	0.00523038	0.00530077	0.00537166
27	0.00464006	0.00470740	0.00477527	0.00484368	0.00491262	0.00498209	0.00505208	0.00512259	0.00519362	0.00526516
28	0.00453672	0.00460458	0.00467300	0.00474196	0.00481148	0.00488153	0.00495212	0.00502325	0.00509491	0.00516709
29	0.00444098	0.00450936	0.00457831	0.00464783	0.00471791	0.00478854	0.00485973	0.00493147	0.00500376	0.00507658
30	0.00435206	0.00442096	0.00449045	0.00456051	0.00463116	0.00470237	0.00477415	0.00484650	0.00491940	0.00499285

Monthly Mortgage Payment per $1—Mortgage Constant

Years	4.500%	4.625%	4.750%	4.875%	5.000%	5.125%	5.250%	5.375%	5.500%	5.625%
1	0.08537852	0.08543573	0.08549296	0.08555021	0.08560748	0.08566478	0.08572209	0.08577943	0.08583678	0.08589416
2	0.04364781	0.04370364	0.04375951	0.04381543	0.04387139	0.04392739	0.04398344	0.04403953	0.04409566	0.04415183
3	0.02974692	0.02980282	0.02985878	0.02991481	0.02997090	0.03002705	0.03008327	0.03013955	0.03019590	0.03025231
4	0.02280349	0.02285981	0.02291622	0.02297271	0.02302929	0.02308596	0.02314271	0.02319955	0.02325648	0.02331349
5	0.01864302	0.01869991	0.01875691	0.01881402	0.01887123	0.01892856	0.01898598	0.01904352	0.01910116	0.01915891
6	0.01587403	0.01593156	0.01598922	0.01604701	0.01610493	0.01616298	0.01622115	0.01627946	0.01633789	0.01639645
7	0.01390016	0.01395837	0.01401674	0.01407525	0.01413391	0.01419272	0.01425168	0.01431079	0.01437004	0.01442945
8	0.01242323	0.01248215	0.01254124	0.01260049	0.01265992	0.01271952	0.01277928	0.01283922	0.01289932	0.01295960
9	0.01127759	0.01133723	0.01139705	0.01145707	0.01151727	0.01157767	0.01163826	0.01169903	0.01176000	0.01182115
10	0.01036384	0.01042420	0.01048477	0.01054556	0.01060655	0.01066776	0.01072917	0.01079079	0.01085263	0.01091467
11	0.00961873	0.00967982	0.00974115	0.00980270	0.00986449	0.00992651	0.00998875	0.01005123	0.01011393	0.01017687
12	0.00900008	0.00906191	0.00912399	0.00918632	0.00924890	0.00931174	0.00937482	0.00943814	0.00950172	0.00956555
13	0.00847871	0.00854128	0.00860411	0.00866722	0.00873060	0.00879424	0.00885816	0.00892234	0.00898679	0.00905150
14	0.00803376	0.00809706	0.00816065	0.00822454	0.00828871	0.00835317	0.00841791	0.00848294	0.00854826	0.00861386
15	0.00764993	0.00771397	0.00777832	0.00784297	0.00790794	0.00797320	0.00803878	0.00810465	0.00817083	0.00823732
16	0.00731576	0.00738053	0.00744563	0.00751106	0.00757681	0.00764288	0.00770928	0.00777600	0.00784304	0.00791040
17	0.00702247	0.00708798	0.00715383	0.00722002	0.00728655	0.00735343	0.00742064	0.00748820	0.00755609	0.00762432
18	0.00676325	0.00682948	0.00689607	0.00696302	0.00703034	0.00709801	0.00716604	0.00723443	0.00730316	0.00737225
19	0.00653269	0.00659964	0.00666698	0.00673469	0.00680278	0.00687124	0.00694008	0.00700928	0.00707886	0.00714881
20	0.00632649	0.00639417	0.00646224	0.00653070	0.00659956	0.00666881	0.00673844	0.00680847	0.00687887	0.00694966
21	0.00614117	0.00620956	0.00627836	0.00634757	0.00641719	0.00648721	0.00655764	0.00662847	0.00669970	0.00677133
22	0.00597386	0.00604296	0.00611248	0.00618243	0.00625281	0.00632360	0.00639482	0.00646645	0.00653849	0.00661095
23	0.00582221	0.00589201	0.00596225	0.00603294	0.00610406	0.00617562	0.00624761	0.00632003	0.00639288	0.00646615
24	0.00568425	0.00575475	0.00582570	0.00589711	0.00596898	0.00604129	0.00611405	0.00618725	0.00626089	0.00633497
25	0.00555832	0.00562951	0.00570117	0.00577330	0.00584590	0.00591896	0.00599248	0.00606645	0.00614087	0.00621575
26	0.00544304	0.00551491	0.00558727	0.00566011	0.00573344	0.00580723	0.00588150	0.00595623	0.00603143	0.00610709
27	0.00533720	0.00540976	0.00548281	0.00555635	0.00563039	0.00570491	0.00577992	0.00585541	0.00593137	0.00600780
28	0.00523980	0.00531302	0.00538675	0.00546099	0.00553574	0.00561098	0.00568672	0.00576295	0.00583966	0.00591685
29	0.00514993	0.00522382	0.00529823	0.00537316	0.00544860	0.00552456	0.00560101	0.00567797	0.00575542	0.00583336
30	0.00506685	0.00514140	0.00521647	0.00529208	0.00536822	0.00544487	0.00552204	0.00559971	0.00567789	0.00575656

Monthly Mortgage Payment per $1—Mortgage Constant

Years	5.750%	5.875%	6.000%	6.125%	6.250%	6.375%	6.500%	6.625%	6.750%	6.875%
1	0.08595156	0.08600899	0.08606643	0.08612389	0.08618138	0.08623889	0.08629642	0.08635397	0.08641154	0.08646913
2	0.04420805	0.04426431	0.04432061	0.04437696	0.04443334	0.04448978	0.04454625	0.04460277	0.04465933	0.04471593
3	0.03030879	0.03036533	0.03042194	0.03047696	0.03053534	0.03059214	0.03064900	0.03070593	0.03076292	0.03081998
4	0.02337058	0.02342776	0.02348503	0.02354238	0.02359982	0.02365734	0.02371495	0.02377265	0.02383043	0.02388829
5	0.01921677	0.01927473	0.01933280	0.01939098	0.01944926	0.01950765	0.01956615	0.01962475	0.01968346	0.01974228
6	0.01645513	0.01651395	0.01657289	0.01663196	0.01669115	0.01675048	0.01680993	0.01686951	0.01692921	0.01698905
7	0.01448900	0.01454870	0.01460855	0.01466855	0.01472870	0.01478899	0.01484944	0.01491003	0.01497076	0.01503165
8	0.01302004	0.01308065	0.01314143	0.01320238	0.01326350	0.01332478	0.01338623	0.01344785	0.01350964	0.01357160
9	0.01188250	0.01194403	0.01200575	0.01206766	0.01212976	0.01219204	0.01225452	0.01231718	0.01238002	0.01244306
10	0.01097692	0.01103938	0.01110205	0.01116493	0.01122801	0.01129130	0.01135480	0.01141850	0.01148241	0.01154653
11	0.01024003	0.01030342	0.01036703	0.01043088	0.01049495	0.01055925	0.01062377	0.01068851	0.01075349	0.01081868
12	0.00962962	0.00969394	0.00975850	0.00982331	0.00988837	0.00995367	0.01001921	0.01008500	0.01015103	0.01021730
13	0.00911648	0.00918172	0.00924723	0.00931301	0.00937904	0.00944534	0.00951190	0.00957872	0.00964580	0.00971314
14	0.00867974	0.00874591	0.00881236	0.00887909	0.00894610	0.00901339	0.00908096	0.00914881	0.00921693	0.00928533
15	0.00830410	0.00837118	0.00843857	0.00850625	0.00857423	0.00864250	0.00871107	0.00877994	0.00884909	0.00891854
16	0.00797807	0.00804607	0.00811438	0.00818300	0.00825194	0.00832119	0.00839075	0.00846062	0.00853080	0.00860129
17	0.00769288	0.00776178	0.00783101	0.00790057	0.00797045	0.00804067	0.00811121	0.00818208	0.00825327	0.00832478
18	0.00744170	0.00751149	0.00758162	0.00765211	0.00772293	0.00779410	0.00786561	0.00793746	0.00800965	0.00808217
19	0.00721912	0.00728979	0.00736083	0.00743223	0.00750398	0.00757609	0.00764856	0.00772138	0.00779455	0.00786806
20	0.00702084	0.00709238	0.00716431	0.00723661	0.00730928	0.00738232	0.00745573	0.00752950	0.00760364	0.00767814
21	0.00684335	0.00691577	0.00698857	0.00706176	0.00713534	0.00720929	0.00728363	0.00735834	0.00743343	0.00750889
22	0.00668381	0.00675707	0.00683074	0.00690481	0.00697928	0.00705414	0.00712939	0.00720503	0.00728105	0.00735746
23	0.00653984	0.00661395	0.00668847	0.00676341	0.00683875	0.00691450	0.00699065	0.00706719	0.00714414	0.00722147
24	0.00640948	0.00648442	0.00655978	0.00663557	0.00671177	0.00678839	0.00686543	0.00694287	0.00702071	0.00709895
25	0.00629106	0.00636682	0.00644301	0.00651964	0.00659669	0.00667417	0.00675207	0.00683039	0.00690912	0.00698825
26	0.00618320	0.00625976	0.00633677	0.00641422	0.00649211	0.00657043	0.00664918	0.00672835	0.00680795	0.00688796
27	0.00608469	0.00616204	0.00623985	0.00631811	0.00639682	0.00647597	0.00655555	0.00663556	0.00671601	0.00679687
28	0.00599451	0.00607264	0.00615124	0.00623030	0.00630980	0.00638976	0.00647016	0.00655100	0.00663227	0.00671397
29	0.00591178	0.00599068	0.00607005	0.00614988	0.00623018	0.00631093	0.00639213	0.00647377	0.00655585	0.00663836
30	0.00583573	0.00591538	0.00599551	0.00607611	0.00615717	0.00623870	0.00632068	0.00640311	0.00648598	0.00656929

Monthly Mortgage Payment per $1—Mortgage Constant

Years	7.000%	7.125%	7.250%	7.375%	7.500%	7.625%	7.750%	7.875%	8.000%	8.125%
1	0.08652675	0.08658438	0.08664204	0.08669972	0.08675742	0.08681514	0.08687288	0.08693064	0.08698843	0.08704624
2	0.04477258	0.04482927	0.04488600	0.04494277	0.04499959	0.04505645	0.04511336	0.04517030	0.04522729	0.04528432
3	0.03087710	0.03093428	0.03099153	0.03104884	0.03110622	0.03116366	0.03122116	0.03127873	0.03133637	0.03139406
4	0.02394624	0.02400428	0.02406240	0.02412061	0.02417890	0.02423728	0.02429574	0.02435429	0.02441292	0.02447164
5	0.01980120	0.01986023	0.01991936	0.01997860	0.02003795	0.02009740	0.02015696	0.02021662	0.02027639	0.02033627
6	0.01704901	0.01710909	0.01716931	0.01722965	0.01729011	0.01735071	0.01741142	0.01747227	0.01753324	0.01759434
7	0.01509268	0.01515386	0.01521518	0.01527666	0.01533828	0.01540004	0.01546195	0.01552401	0.01558621	0.01564856
8	0.01363372	0.01369601	0.01375846	0.01382108	0.01388387	0.01394682	0.01400994	0.01407323	0.01413668	0.01420029
9	0.01250628	0.01256968	0.01263328	0.01269705	0.01276102	0.01282516	0.01288950	0.01295401	0.01301871	0.01308360
10	0.01161085	0.01167537	0.01174010	0.01180504	0.01187018	0.01193552	0.01200106	0.01206681	0.01213276	0.01219891
11	0.01088410	0.01094974	0.01101561	0.01108170	0.01114801	0.01121454	0.01128129	0.01134826	0.01141545	0.01148286
12	0.01028381	0.01035056	0.01041756	0.01048479	0.01055226	0.01061997	0.01068792	0.01075611	0.01082453	0.01089318
13	0.00978074	0.00984860	0.00991671	0.00998508	0.01005370	0.01012258	0.01019172	0.01026110	0.01033074	0.01040063
14	0.00935401	0.00942295	0.00949218	0.00956167	0.00963143	0.00970147	0.00977177	0.00984234	0.00991318	0.00998429
15	0.00898828	0.00905831	0.00912863	0.00919923	0.00927012	0.00934130	0.00941276	0.00948450	0.00955652	0.00962882
16	0.00867208	0.00874318	0.00881458	0.00888628	0.00895828	0.00903058	0.00910317	0.00917606	0.00924925	0.00932273
17	0.00839661	0.00846876	0.00854122	0.00861400	0.00868709	0.00876050	0.00883421	0.00890824	0.00898257	0.00905720
18	0.00815502	0.00822821	0.00830172	0.00837556	0.00844973	0.00852423	0.00859904	0.00867417	0.00874963	0.00882539
19	0.00794192	0.00801613	0.00809068	0.00816556	0.00824079	0.00831635	0.00839224	0.00846846	0.00854501	0.00862189
20	0.00775299	0.00782820	0.00790376	0.00797967	0.00805593	0.00813254	0.00820949	0.00828677	0.00836440	0.00844236
21	0.00758472	0.00766091	0.00773747	0.00781439	0.00789166	0.00796929	0.00804727	0.00812560	0.00820428	0.00828330
22	0.00743424	0.00751140	0.00758893	0.00766684	0.00774510	0.00782374	0.00790273	0.00798208	0.00806178	0.00814183
23	0.00729919	0.00737730	0.00745579	0.00753465	0.00761389	0.00769350	0.00777348	0.00785382	0.00793453	0.00801558
24	0.00717760	0.00725663	0.00733605	0.00741586	0.00749605	0.00757662	0.00765756	0.00773887	0.00782054	0.00790258
25	0.00706779	0.00714773	0.00722807	0.00730880	0.00738991	0.00747141	0.00755329	0.00763554	0.00771816	0.00780115
26	0.00696838	0.00704920	0.00713043	0.00721206	0.00729407	0.00737648	0.00745927	0.00754244	0.00762598	0.00770989
27	0.00687815	0.00695984	0.00704194	0.00712444	0.00720734	0.00729063	0.00737430	0.00745836	0.00754280	0.00762761
28	0.00679609	0.00687862	0.00696157	0.00704492	0.00712868	0.00721282	0.00729736	0.00738229	0.00746759	0.00755326
29	0.00672130	0.00680466	0.00688843	0.00697262	0.00705720	0.00714218	0.00722756	0.00731332	0.00739946	0.00748597
30	0.00665302	0.00673719	0.00682176	0.00690675	0.00699215	0.00707794	0.00716412	0.00725069	0.00733765	0.00742497

Index

About the Author

Frank Gallinelli is the founder and president of RealData, Inc., a real estate software firm that has offered analysis and presentation tools for income-property investors and developers since 1982. A graduate of Yale University, he serves as Adjunct Assistant Professor of Real Estate Development at Columbia University.